MOBILE TECHNOLOGIES IN CHILDREN'S LANGUAGE AND LITERACY

MOBILE TECHNOLOGIES IN CHILDREN'S LANGUAGE AND LITERACY: INNOVATIVE PEDAGOGY IN PRESCHOOL AND PRIMARY EDUCATION

EDITED BY

GRACE OAKLEY
The University of Western Australia, Australia

United Kingdom – North America – Japan – India – Malaysia – China

Emerald Publishing Limited
Howard House, Wagon Lane, Bingley BD16 1WA, UK

First edition 2019

Copyright © 2019 Emerald Publishing Limited

Reprints and permissions service
Contact: permissions@emeraldinsight.com

No part of this book may be reproduced, stored in a retrieval system, transmitted in any form or by any means electronic, mechanical, photocopying, recording or otherwise without either the prior written permission of the publisher or a licence permitting restricted copying issued in the UK by The Copyright Licensing Agency and in the USA by The Copyright Clearance Center. Any opinions expressed in the chapters are those of the authors. Whilst Emerald makes every effort to ensure the quality and accuracy of its content, Emerald makes no representation implied or otherwise, as to the chapters' suitability and application and disclaims any warranties, express or implied, to their use.

British Library Cataloguing in Publication Data
A catalogue record for this book is available from the British Library

ISBN: 978-1-78714-880-2 (Print)
ISBN: 978-1-78714-879-6 (Epub)
ISBN: 978-1-78743-941-2 (Online)
ISBN: 978-1-78754-244-0 (Paperback)

INVESTOR IN PEOPLE

Contents

List of Contributors   *vii*

Introduction: Mobile Technologies in Language and Literacy Practice and Learning in Preschool and Primary School Children
Grace Oakley   *1*

Chapter 1   Young Children's Imaginative Play and Dynamic Literacy Practices in the Digital Age
Sara Sintonen, Kristiina Kumpulainen and Jenni Vartiainen   *15*

Chapter 2   A Gallery of Practices – Mobile Learning, Language, Literacy and the Arts (K-6)
Kathy Rushton and Jon Callow   *29*

Chapter 3   Introducing Coding as a Literacy on Mobile Devices in the Early Years
Chris Walsh and Claire Campbell   *51*

Chapter 4   Digital Storytelling as a Pedagogy to Develop Literacy and Twenty-first Century Competencies in a Singapore Primary School: Teachers as Designers
Mohamed Melwani, Lee Yong Tay and Cher Ping Lim   *67*

Chapter 5   Mobile Devices and Multimodal Textual Practices
Amy Hutchison and Beth Beschorner   *83*

Chapter 6   Mobile Tools for Literacy Learning across the Curriculum in Primary Schools
Jan Clarke   *99*

Chapter 7   Mobilising Critical Literacies: Text Production in Children's Hands
Lisa Kervin, Annette Woods, Barbara Comber and Aspa Baroutsis   *119*

Chapter 8 Personalised Learning with Digital Technologies at Home and School: Where is Children's Agency?
Natalia Kucirkova 133

Chapter 9 Supporting Children's Literacy Learning in Low- and Middle-income Countries Through M-learning
Grace Oakley and Umera Imtinan 155

Index 177

List of Contributors

Aspa Baroutsis	Faculty of Education, Queensland University of Technology, Australia
Beth Beschorner	University of Minnesota, Mankato, USA
Jon Callow	Sydney School of Education and Social Work, University of Sydney, Australia
Claire Campbell	Victoria University, Australia
Jan Clarke	Association of Independent Schools of Western Australia (AISWA)
Barbara Comber	School of Early Childhood and Inclusive Education, Queensland University of Technology; School of Education, University of South Australia, Australia
Amy Hutchison	George Mason University, USA
Umera Imtinan	Graduate School of Education, University of Western Australia, Australia
Lisa Kervin	School of Education Early Start, Faculty of Social Sciences, University of Wollongong, Australia
Kristiina Kumpulainen	University of Helsinki, Finland
Natalia Kucirkova	University College, London Institute of Education, UK
Cher Ping Lim	Department of Curriculum and Instruction, The Education University of Hong Kong, Hong Kong
Mohamed Melwani	Department of Development, Research & Technology, Beacon Primary School, Singapore
Grace Oakley	Graduate School of Education, University of Western Australia, Australia
Kathy Rushton	Sydney School of Education and Social Work, University of Sydney, Australia
Sara Sintonen	University of Helsinki, Finland
Lee Yong Tay	Office of Education Research, National Institute of Education, Singapore
Jenni Vartiainen	University of Helsinki, Finland
Chris Walsh	College of Arts & Education, Victoria University, Australia
Annette Woods	Faculty of Education, Queensland University of Technology, Australia

Introduction: Mobile Technologies in Language and Literacy Practice and Learning in Preschool and Primary School Children

Grace Oakley

I.1. Purpose of This Book

The broad aim of this book, *Mobile Technologies in Children's Language and Literacy: Innovative Pedagogy in Preschool and Primary Education*, is to attempt to make a contribution to the advancement of theory and practice in relation to the use of mobile technologies for learning and teaching literacy, with a focus on children up to the age of 12. Although there are substantial bodies of literature about the teaching and learning of literacy, and a growing body of research on the use of mobile technologies for language and literacy learning (Oakley, Pegrum, Faulkner, & Striepe, 2012; Pegrum, Oakley, & Faulkner, 2013), there is a need for connections between mobile learning (m-learning) and children's literacy learning to be highlighted, examined, problematised, theorised and researched. Clearly, the ways in which mobile technologies might fundamentally change literacy definitions and practices cannot be ignored, and such transformations are also considered in this book.

The chapters in this book explore how children from preschool to the end of their primary (elementary) school years develop and learn literacy, and the ways in which mobile technologies and associated digital cultures may contribute to, change, or even disrupt this learning. Also explored is the impact this 'mobile turn' may have on learning environments; student, parent and teacher roles and interactions; power relations; and social and material interactions, among other things. It is acknowledged that this book only goes so far; there is ample scope for more exploration and discussion than is possible within the confines of one book. Issues such as curriculum and society, and how educators might harness mobile technologies to equip literacy learners for the twenty-first century are also touched on in this book, as are global issues including the information and communication technology (ICT) for development (ICT4D) movement, and the role of mobile technologies in improving equitable access to literacy opportunities for disadvantaged groups, such as girls and children of poverty. However, these issues deserve more attention by researchers in the future.

This introductory chapter endeavours to set the scene by providing a broad overview of research in the areas of mobile learning (m-learning), learning with mobile technologies and the literacy practices and learning of preschool and primary school children. Brief summaries of, and commentaries on, each of the chapters in the book are then offered.

I.2. M-learning and Literacy Issues

I.2.1. Pervasiveness of Mobile Devices

In recent years, there has been a rapid increase in the use of mobile devices such as smartphones and tablets by children, their families and their educators, both inside and outside early childhood education and care (ECEC) centres and primary (elementary) classrooms (Kabali et al., 2015; Marsh, 2016). The affordability of mobile devices has increased in many parts of the world, alongside their affordances, or the technological characteristics which affect how they might be used (Pegrum, 2014). There has also been a rapid increase in the range and quality of software or apps that can be run on these devices as well as improvements in connectivity. Mobile devices such as mobile phones and tablets have therefore become prevalent among adults and children alike, most notably in the developed world. In the USA, for example, the vast majority of children have used mobile devices before they reach the age of four, including children from low-income groups, and increasingly large numbers of children actually own a mobile device (Kabali et al., 2015). Mobile technologies now pervade many aspects of people's lives and are used for a wide variety of purposes including social, entertainment, healthcare, education and professional purposes. Having access to mobile technologies can facilitate learning 'on the move' (Park, 2011), learning across time and place (Kukulska-Hulme, 2010) and can enable innovative ways of participating in collaborative learning. This pervasiveness has changed the ways in which learning, teaching and literacy can be 'done', both inside and outside the classroom – indeed, it has opened up new 'in between' learning spaces, bridging the classroom and outside the classroom, formal and informal learning and teaching and learning (see Potter & McDougall, 2017; Schuck, Kearney, & Burden,2017). This has significant implications for literacy and may open up more 'third space literacies', as discussed by Potter and McDougall (2017).

I.2.2. M-learning and Literacy Learning in Children

An increasing body of research exists on mobile learning and how it can support social, authentic, lifelong and contextual learning (Kearney, Schuck, Burden, &

Aubusson, 2012; Traxler, 2011), not to mention new ways of finding, generating and communicating knowledge. It should be acknowledged, however, that not all uses of mobile devices for learning are considered to be examples of 'm-learning', according to current m-learning theories, because merely using mobile technologies may not be construed as m-learning if the users themselves are not mobile (for example, if they are sitting at desks).

Much of the existing research on m-learning and literacy is concerned with older students and adults, rather than children in preschool and primary school settings, and there is certainly a need for more research and theorising on the relationships between mobile learning and literacy learning in children in their early years and primary school years. For young children in preschool settings and primary classrooms, there are many considerations and constraints that need to be taken into account when designing learning using mobile technologies, such as limited access to mobile technologies in some settings, restricted freedom of young children to move around different physical spaces and physical safety and cyber safety concerns (Oakley, 2017). Furthermore, in many learning situations, young children need considerably more face-to-face scaffolding than older students, and in early childhood settings there are distinct pedagogical approaches such as play-based learning which may render some aspects of existing m-learning theory and research less applicable – new or modified theoretical perspectives and frameworks may need to be developed. For example, notions of flexibility in the use of time and space are central to m-learning (Kearney et al., 2012). It is not difficult to see how opportunities for flexibility in these dimensions may be curtailed somewhat in the context of young children.

This book brings together thinking and insights from academics and expert practitioners from around the world, whose chapters should prompt readers to consider innovative practices and pedagogies using mobile technologies in the context of early childhood and primary language and literacy learning and teaching. It is also an aim of this book to stimulate discussion about curriculum design, home−school relationships and the very nature of texts and how they are constructed and used. The book necessarily engages with the ever-changing nature of literacy and how this interfaces with culture/s and technologies.

I.3. Defining Literacy

Conceptions of what literacy is and what it is for, and how it is done, are shifting. As Mills (2016) has pointed out, there are many ways of looking at literacy; she has described social-cultural, critical, multimodal, socio-spacial, socio-material and sensory literacies. Consideration of multiple and expansive literacy theories seems crucial when discussing mobile technologies and how they might be used by children, educators, families and the communities that they inhabit. The chapters in this book connect with several of these lenses on literacy. Particularly interesting in the context of doing literacy with mobile technologies are the socio-spacial and socio-material lenses on literacy. The socio-spacial lens draws attention to literacy as being situated in social spaces, while the socio-material lens encourages us to think about the materiality of literacy practice – how material objects like books, tablets, phones and even people's bodies cannot be ignored as they are integral to making meaning (Mills, 2016). It is also worth emphasising that the construction and communication of multimodal texts (Walsh, 2017) can be facilitated yet complicated in the context of mobile technologies.

Clearly, digital literacies are highly relevant when thinking about the role of mobile technologies in young children's literacy learning. Although there are many ways of defining digital literacy, some of which emphasise knowing how to use digital technology, a narrower definition of digital literacies is taken by most authors in this book, in line with that of Levy, Yamada-Rice, and Marsh (2013, p. 333), where the term is used 'to refer to reading, writing and meaning-making mediated through new technologies'.

In an attempt to overcome the conceptual difficulties associated with multiple and shifting definitions of literacy, Potter and McDougall (2017) have posited the term 'dynamic literacy', which is an umbrella term that encompasses many other literacies and presumably has the capacity to incorporate others as they come along. In Chapter 1 of this book, the authors frame literacy as dynamic.

I.4. Defining Mobile Technologies

Simply put, mobile technologies involve hardware (*devices* like smartphones and tablets), software (such as apps and web-based platforms) and also the technologies that enable connectivity such as 4G, Bluetooth and wifi. However, it is beyond the scope of this book to delve further into the intricacies of the technologies themselves. It does seem necessary to clarify what is meant by mobile devices although, as UNESCO (2013) has stated, it would be unwise to try and provide a definitive definition due to rapid changes in technologies and what they can be used for. Thus, following UNESCO's lead, a broad definition is taken in this book: "UNESCO chooses to embrace a broad definition of mobile devices, recognizing simply that they are digital, easily portable, usually owned and controlled by an individual rather than an institution, can access the internet, have multimedia capabilities, and can facilitate a large number of tasks, particularly those related to communication (UNESCO, 2013, p. 6)". Mobile devices obviously include smartphones and tablet computers but may also include other portable, networked devices such as e-readers, wearables and some robotic devices. Smaller and more mobile laptops are becoming available, especially 2-in-1 devices which serve as both laptops and tablets. Mobile devices can connect to the Internet and to each other via cellular connections, Bluetooth, wifi and other technologies. With GPS, they are also location aware and able to provide contextual information that is relevant to the location. They often have built-in a gyroscope and accelerometer to detect the direction and speed of the user's movement, not to mention a host of other tools such as a camera, audio recorder and the ability to run a wide range of apps, including Augmented Reality apps which can superimpose a layer of digital information onto the real world. Mobile devices often have haptic features such as touchscreen and vibrate, which can be very appealing to young children and change the ways in which they create and interact with texts (Piotrowski & Krcmar, 2017).

I.5. M-learning Definitions and Theory

UNESCO (2013, p. 6) has suggested that: "Mobile learning involves the use of mobile technology, either alone or in combination with other information and communication technology (ICT), to enable learning anytime anywhere. Learning can unfold in a variety of ways: people can use mobile devices to access educational resources, connect with others, or create content, both inside and outside the classroom." Since this definition was offered, the notion of 'with anyone' has been added to discussions to reflect the fact that mobile technologies have enabled learners to connect with each other and engage in social learning. It is posited that in the not too distant future, the term m-learning may become superfluous because it is likely that learning with mobile technologies and all this entails will become widespread and normal – an accepted and taken-for-granted part of learning – so much so that Kukulska-Hulme (2010, p. 5) has argued that we could soon be thinking of m-learning as 'just learning'. However, there is an argument that there are some distinct characteristics of m-learning that may contribute to transformation of learning and where, when, how, why and with whom it takes place.

To date, several definitions of m-learning have been offered, all of which have their strengths and limitations. Like definitions and theories of literacy, definitions and theories of m-learning have evolved, and are still evolving, to take into account new technologies and practices. Early definitions of m-learning tended to be somewhat technocentric, with much emphasis on the device itself, rather than the learning processes or the social interactions, learning spaces or new ways of thinking. For example, Traxler (2005, n.p.) defined mobile learning as 'any educational provision where the sole or dominant technologies are handheld and palmtop devices'. He later suggested that mobile learning involves: 'the personalised, connected, and interactive use of handheld computers' (Traxler, 2007, p. 3). Sharples, Taylor, and Vavoula (2007, p. 4) suggested that mobile learning is: 'the processes of coming to know through conversations across multiple contexts amongst people and personal interactive technologies'. Here, the idea of m-learning being a *process* is introduced, and the importance of conversations and context are highlighted.

Similarly, Koole (2009, p. 26) defined m-learning as 'a process resulting from the convergence of mobile technologies, human learning capacities, and social interaction'. Later definitions place more focus on the mobile *learner*, rather than the mobile device itself (Cochrane, 2013; Kukulska-Hulme, 2016), and the mobile learning experiences or tasks that students engage with (Pegrum, 2016).

Traxler (2011, pp. 6–7) summarised how mobile technologies might present teaching and learning opportunities, such as: *contingent learning*, which involves students being able to react to the environment that they are in and respond to the contingencies that arise at the time; *situated learning*, which is learning that occurs in the place or context in which the knowledge is meaningful and useful to the activity or situation at hand; *authentic learning*, where learning experiences and tasks and goals are meaningful to the students – often this means there is some 'real life' relevance; *context aware learning* involves being able to access information that is relevant to the specific location, for example, being able to find out about the history or access data about a particular place; and *personalised learning*, 'where learning is customised for the interests, preferences and abilities of individual learners or groups of learners (Traxler, 2011, p. 7). These types of mobile learning can overlap. As well as the types of learning outlined above, Traxler (2011) has noted that mobile technologies can facilitate game-based learning and new ways of assessing student learning.

Park (2011) proposed a pedagogical framework for mobile learning that highlighted *transactional distance* and *social learning* as two key elements. In this pedagogical framework, Park built on Moore's (1997, 2007) important work on Transactional Distance (TD) theory. TD could be described as the 'cognitive space' or psychological distance (Shearer, 2007) between those involved (learners and teachers) in the process. Moore defined TD as: the: 'interplay of teachers and learners in environments that have the special characteristics of their being spatially separate from one another' (Moore, 2007, p. 91). The social nature of learning, or the second dimension in Park's framework, is the extent to which a learning activity involves interaction with others. The attention here is not on the mobile technology but on space, time and social interaction.

Park's model has four quadrants. These reflect four categories of mobile learning: high transactional distance socialised m-learning (HS), high transactional distance individualised m-learning (HI), low transactional distance socialised m-learning (LS) and low transactional distance individualised m-learning (LI) (Park, 2011, n.p.). It might be argued that activities that allow movement between the different types of learning may make the most of what mobile learning has to offer, while honouring the multiple environments that children inhabit and allowing educators to meet the needs of individual students within specific learning situations, drawing in an appropriate mix of resources and pedagogical strategies.

Another framework for mobile learning that has considerable potential for guiding early childhood and primary literacy educators in planning and implementing mobile learning for literacy learning is the *Mobile Pedagogical Framework* (MPF), developed by Kearney et al. (2012). This framework highlights the importance of personalisation, authenticity and collaboration as three key aspects of learning that can be facilitated through the use of mobile technologies, with learners being untethered from space and time constraints associated with timetabled, classroom learning. Authenticity means that learning experiences are meaningful and have real life relevance to learners – for example, students may be in a museum when engaging with historical texts, or visiting a farm and preparing a presentation on farm animals using their mobile device. Collaboration may involve conversation, which may not be face-to-face conversation but some kind of online discussion/interaction. It also involves data sharing, which includes the sharing of artefacts such as photographs, texts and so on. Personalisation is about using the affordances of the device to promote choice, agency and self-regulation in learners. Mobile technologies can facilitate the customisation or tailoring of learning activities, tools and resources to meet the individual needs and interests of learners.

Kearney and colleagues have further developed the MPF into the *iPAC framework*, which retains the central concepts of personalisation, authenticity, collaboration (PAC) and the space-time flexibility. The notion of 'signature' pedagogies around PAC is a feature of this framework, which can be seen in full at the Mobile Learning Toolkit website at http://www.mobilelearningtoolkit.com/ipac-framework.html. This differs from the MPF in that the PAC elements are refined. Authenticity is defined in terms of setting, task and tool. Personalisation replaces customisation as one of the three central concepts, and customisation is relegated to an aspect of personalisation, along with agency. Collaboration means working with networks of people. 'The networking capability of mobile devices creates shared, socially interactive environments allowing students to easily communicate multi-modally with peers, teachers and other experts, and to exchange information. Learners consume, produce and exchange an array of "content", sharing information and artefacts across time and place (n.p.) (see Figure I.1)'.

A concept that draws attention to the power of mobile technologies to bridge or blur boundaries or distances in learning is *seamless learning* (Looi et al., 2010). Looi et al. state that 'seamless learning environments bridges private and public learning spaces where learning happens as both individual and collective efforts and across different contexts (such as in-school versus after-school, formal versus informal)' (p. 156). Building on this, Wong (2012) has provided *10 dimensions of mobile seamless learning*: (MSL1) encompassing formal and

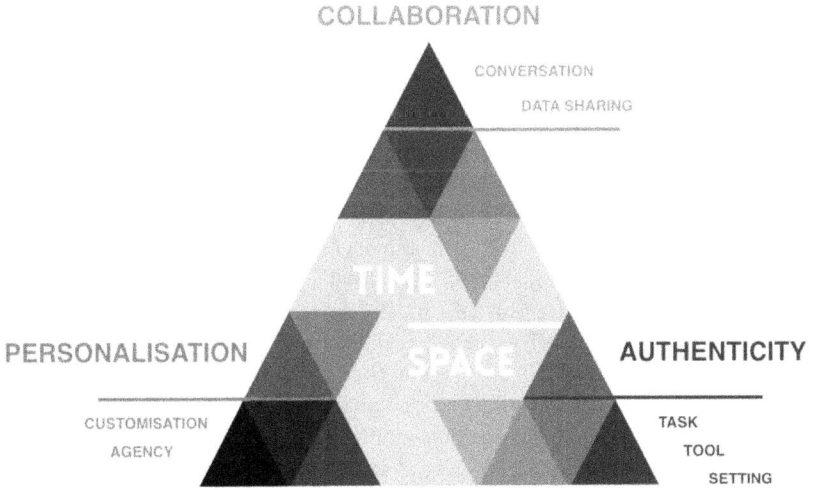

Figure I.1: The iPAC Framework. *Source*: Kearney *et al.*(2012).

informal learning, (MSL2) encompassing personalised and social learning, (MSL3) across time, (MSL4) across locations, (MSL5) ubiquitous knowledge access, (MSL6) encompassing physical and digital worlds, (MSL7) combined use of multiple device types, (MSL8) seamless switching between multiple learning tasks, (MSL9) knowledge synthesis and (MSL10) encompassing multiple pedagogical or learning activity models. Many of the dimensions may be applicable to language and literacy learning and practice in primary school students, but perhaps less so for children in their earlier years.

It is important to mention the concept of *ubiquitous learning* or u-learning, which can be defined as follows: '[U]biquitous learning (u-learning) involves learning in an environment where "all students have access to a variety of digital devices and services, including computers connected to the Internet and mobile computing devices, whenever and wherever they need them' (van't Hooft, Swan, Cook, & Lin, 2007, p. 6). Here, technology is seen as almost invisible because it is pervasive and ubiquitous in people's everyday lives. This concept overlaps considerably with the concept of seamless learning.

There are many other perspectives, theories and frameworks relating to m-learning that have not been discussed here because of space limitations. Nevertheless, it is hoped that the key concepts and frameworks presented will be sufficient to enable readers of this book to think about implications for literacy practice and pedagogy in relation to children in early childhood settings and primary school.

I.6. Implications for Teacher Professional Learning?

Within this context of constant technological change and concomitant redefinitions of literacy, traditional models of professional learning for literacy educators may no longer be adequate. More and more educators are engaging in networked professional learning and sharing via social media to find out about and contribute to emerging practices (Krutka & Carpenter, 2016). While this may be an increasingly necessary part of the professional learning mix, educators need to be able to sift through and critically evaluate the myriad ideas (some of which are created by commercial entities) presented online. To be able to do this, having a command of relevant theory and research seems critical (Oakley, 2018). It would be true to say there is almost an oversupply of online information for early childhood and primary educators on how to use mobile technologies such as iPads in the classroom. Unfortunately, the quality of the information available is varied with much of the information being somewhat superficial, in the form of '7 ways to use iPads' or '10 ten tips for flipping classrooms and mobile learning', on blogs and sites such as virtual pin board sites (Oakley, 2018). This kind of information can certainly inspire educators to innovate and connect with each other in communities of practice (Wenger, 1998), but there is some danger that, in some cases, it may lead to superficial and incoherent professional learning for teachers, resulting in fragmented pedagogical practices and, potentially, superficial learning for children. Some ideas spread extremely quickly online and become extraordinarily popular, and resultant learning could be termed 'viral learning' (Oakley & Pegrum, 2015). Here, there may not be time for ideas to be fully assessed and critiqued, let alone rigorously researched, before they are taken on board by practitioners. Although there may certainly be benefits associated with the kind of professional learning associated with rapid spread and uptake of new ideas, there may also be risks to children's learning if gimmicky practices that have not been adequately thought about and evaluated are being implemented at scale. An aim of the book is to help foster coherent and effective pedagogical approaches in the classroom and preschool, through attention to theory and research, without giving the impression that there is 'one best way' to do things.

I.7. Overview of the Chapters in this Book

It is gratifying to have the work of distinguished scholars and practitioners from around the world represented in this book. The contributing authors have brought their expertise and particular perspectives to bear on how mobile technologies and literacy practices and learning in children might interconnect. Although the authors do not always explicitly refer to the m-learning theories outlined earlier, readers will certainly be able to reflect on these while reading the chapters.

Chapter 1, by Sara Sintonen, Kristiina Kumpulainen and Jenni Vartiainen (Finland) discusses young children's imaginative play and literacy practices as mediated by digital technologies and media. Drawing on socio-cultural theory and the notion of dynamic literacies, the chapter considers how digital technologies including mobile technologies can interact with, and potentially expand children's imaginative play, linking to dynamic literacy practices. In this chapter, children are viewed as active agents in their own learning. Sintonen and her colleagues propose several pedagogical principles that can be applied to using mobile technologies in play-based early childhood education in support of young children's creative thinking, storytelling and dynamic literacy practices, both indoors and outdoors.

Chapter 2, by Kathy Rushton and Jon Callow (Australia), focuses on the interconnections between the arts and literacy, and how the use of mobile technologies can be used to build and transform literacy learning in and through the arts. In this chapter, literacy and the arts are viewed as socio-cultural practices. Rushton and Callow present a gallery of resources and practices to support authentic and engaging learning experiences for children, that encourage collaboration, agency and creativity in children.

Chapter 3, by Chris Walsh and Claire Campbell (Australia), considers the relatively new literacy of coding. The idea that coding is a literacy that all children will need to learn in order to function and succeed in the future has been posed by several commentators, such as Vee (2017), who suggests that coding is becoming an increasingly important literacy as a reading-writing tool. However, this idea has not yet been widely accepted by practitioners. In this chapter, Walsh and Campbell explore the idea that coding is a literacy and discuss how young children might be scaffolded to learn simple coding concepts in meaningful, play-based ways. They then describe how mobile technologies can support this endeavour.

Chapter 4, by Mohamed Melwani, Lee Yong Tay and Cher Ping Lim (Singapore and Hong Kong), discusses the case of a school in Singapore to demonstrate how the process of digital storytelling can expand and deepen children's literacy repertoires as well as their twenty-first century competencies through activities involving acquisition, inquiry, practice, production, discussion and collaboration. Melwani et al. argue that, in the ecology of digital and non-digital tools used to create and share digital stories, mobile technologies are becoming increasingly useful. A learning design framework consisting of Laurillard's 'conversational framework' (Laurillard, 2012), as well as Puentedura's (2014) Substitution, Augmentation, Modification and Redefinition (SAMR) framework is used by the authors to examine the technology-infused teaching and learning activities in the school.

Chapter 5, by Hutchison and Beschorner (USA), discusses the role of digital technologies, including mobile devices, in enabling transformation in the creation and sharing of multimodal texts. Fundamental changes in the ways in which young children 'do' literacy are signposted – and the authors acknowledge the importance of the home, the community and various environments in stimulating and supporting these changes. In this chapter, the authors describe how an increase in authenticity can enhance children's motivation to write. They also share their research on instructional planning with mobile technologies and multimodal text, namely the Technology Integration Planning Cycle for Literacy Language Arts.

Chapter 6, by Jan Clarke, (Australia), outlines a range of practices in use in Independent schools in Western Australia, using mobile technologies, which aim to promote the development of literacy across the curriculum. It is known that the use of mobile technologies helps learners and educators cross and minimise boundaries of time, space (Looi et al., 2010) and culture, and Clarke illustrates how they can also be used to cross curriculum boundaries for children across the year groups in primary schools.

Chapter 7, by Lisa Kervin, Annette Woods, Barbara Comber and Aspa Baroutsis (Australia) is concerned with critical literacy and how affording children agency with regards to materials, spaces and interactions with adults can assist them in becoming critical consumers and creators of digital texts. The authors argue that critical literacy involves 'repositioning students as researchers of language, respecting minority language practices and problematising texts' (p. 119). Moreover, the authors explore how mobile technologies can alter socio-spacial power relations that exist in schools, which are institutions that can either constrain or enable the ways in which literacy learning proceeds through the structures, procedures and relationships that they uphold. The authors draw on data collected as part of a larger study on learning to write in the early years of school and examine some instances of 'disruption', where teachers and children were engaged in practices outside normal routines.

In Chapter 8, Natalia Kucirkova (UK) examines the role of mobile technologies in personalising literacy learning in primary school children. As in several of the other chapters in this book, the concept of agency is highlighted. It is acknowledged by the author that children's learning experiences are mediated by adults and that there are various constraints (such as time and technologies available) that impact on personalisation of learning using mobile technologies. Drawing on research carried out in one UK primary school, Kucirkova outlines her 5As of personalisation – five variables with agency at the core. In this chapter, Kucirkova makes the important point that adults who mediate children's technology use for literacy practice and learning need to find ways to create opportunities for children's agency, instead of imposing barriers.

Chapter 9, written by Grace Oakley and Umera Imtinan (Australia), concerns the use of mobile technologies in low- and middle-income (LMI) countries. The authors describe and critique a range of programmes and interventions that have been implemented in many of these less economically advantaged countries with the aim of raising literacy levels. In this chapter, the programmes are discussed with reference to mobile learning and literacy theory and research. It is concluded by Oakley and Imtinan that the use of mobile technologies to improve literacy opportunities for children in LMI countries has considerable potential but that there are limitations in pedagogical design and implementation practices, not to mention restricted views of what literacy is and might be for children in these locations, which hamper such efforts.

I.8. Concluding Comments

It has been the intention in this chapter to provide an introduction to key concepts and theoretical frameworks underpinning this book and to briefly describe the contents and aims of the individual chapters. Without a doubt, some of the concepts and insights in this book will all too quickly become outmoded because of rapid developments in technologies and practices. However, it is hoped that they will still be useful and important stepping stones to future work. It is not the intention of this book to be an authority on how to 'do' or teach literacy in the context of mobile technologies; rather, to stimulate innovation and professional discourse and to promote a mindset that embraces multiplicity and dynamism. It is clear from the chapters in this book that promoting agency and authenticity in children's literacy learning are particularly valued by educators, and attempts to reconceptualise and retain play-based learning in the context of mobile technologies is also a priority for early childhood educators and researchers.

References

Cochrane, T. (2013). A summary and critique of m-learning research and practice. In Z. L. Berge & L. Y. Muilenburg (Eds.), *Handbook of mobile learning* (pp. 24–46). New York, NY: Routledge.

Kabali, H. K., Irigoyen, M. M., Nunez-Davis, R., Budacki, J. G., Mohanty, S. H., Leister, K. P., & Bonner, R. L. (2015). Exposure and use of mobile media devices by young children. *Pediatrics, 136*(6), 1044. doi:10.1542/peds.2015-2151

Kearney, M., Schuck, S., Burden, K., & Aubusson, P. (2012). Viewing mobile learning from a pedagogical perspective. *Research in Learning Technology, 20*(1), 1–17. doi:10.3402/rlt.v20i0/14406

Koole, M. L. (2009). A model for framing mobile learning. In M. Ally (Ed.), *Mobile learning: Transforming the delivery of education and training*. Athabasca, AB: Athabasca University Press.

Krutka, D. G., & Carpenter, J. P. (2016). Participatory learning through social media: How and why social studies educators use Twitter. *Contemporary Issues in Technology and Teacher Education, 16*(1), 38–59.

Kukulska-Hulme, A. (2010). Mobile learning as a catalyst for change. *Open Learning: The Journal of Open and Distance Learning, 25*(3), 181–185.

Kukulska-Hulme, A. (2016). *Personalization of language learning through mobile technologies: Part of the Cambridge Papers in ELT series*. Cambridge: Cambridge University Press. Retrieved from http://www.cambridge.org/elt/blog/wp-content/uploads/2017/06/CambridgePapersinELT_M-learning_2016_ONLINE.pdf. Accessed on September 1, 2017.

Laurillard, D. (2012). *Teaching as a design science: Building pedagogical patterns for learning and technology*. New York, NY: Routledge.

Levy, R., Yamada-Rice, D., & Marsh, J. (2013). Digital literacies in the classroom. In K. Hall, T. Cremin, B. Comber, & L. Moll (Eds.), *International handbook on research on children's literacy, learning and culture* (pp. 333–343). Chichester: Wiley.

Looi, C.-K., Seow, P., Zhang, B., So, H.-J., Chen, W., & Wong, L.-H. (2010). Leveraging mobile technology for sustainable seamless learning: A research agenda. *British Journal of Educational Technology, 41*(2), 154–169. doi:10.1111/j.1467-8535.2008.00912.x

Marsh, J. (2016). The digital literacy skills and competences of children of pre-school age. *Media Education, 7*(2), 197–214.

Mills, K. A. (2016). *Literacy theories for the digital age: Social, critical, multimodal, spacial, material and sensory lenses*. Bristol: Multilingual Matters.

Moore, M. G. (1997). Theroy of transactional distance. In D. Keegan (Ed.), *Theoretical principles of distance education* (pp. 22–38). New York, NY: Routledge Studies in Distance Education.

Moore, M. G. (2007). The theory of transactional distance. In M. G. Moore (Ed.), *Handbook of distance education* (pp. 89–105). Mahwah, NJ: Lawrence Erlbaum Associates.

Oakley, G. (2017).Teaching teachers how to go mobile: What's happening in Australia? *Keynote presentation at the MTeach Conference*, 27–29 June, Guilin, China.

Oakley, G. (2018). Mobile technologies, language and literacy in early childhood and primary education: 10 cool considerations for professional learning. *MiTE Conference*, 18–19 February, 2018, Galway, Ireland.

Oakley, G., & Pegrum, M. (2015). Engaging in networked learning: Innovating at the intersection of technology and pedagogy. *Education Research and Perspectives*, *42*, 397–428.

Oakley, G., Pegrum, M., Faulkner, R., & Striepe, M. (2012). *Exploring the pedagogical applications of mobile technologies for teaching literacy*. Retrieved from http://www.education.uwa.edu.au/research/social-foundations/?a=2195652

Park, Y. (2011). A pedagogical framework for mobile learning: Categorizing educational applications of mobile technologies into four types. *The International Review of Research in Open and Distributed Learning*, *12*(2), 78–102.

Pegrum, M. (2014). Balancing affordability and affordances in the design of mobile pedagogy. Paper presented at the UNESCO Mobile Learning Symposium 18–19 February, Paris, France. Retrieved from http://www.unesco.org/education/MLW2014/R9WAMB3-MarkPegrum.pdf. Accessed on September 1, 2017.

Pegrum, M. (2016). Why mobile devices aren't enough: Learning languages, building communities and exploring cultures. Paper presented at EUROCALL 24–27 August, Limassol, Cyprus. Retrieved from http://eurocall2016.org/wp-content/uploads/2016/09/EUROCALL_2016_Keynote_Pegrum.pdf. Accessed on September 1, 2017.

Pegrum, M., Oakley, G., & Faulkner, R. (2013). Schools going mobile: A study of the adoption of mobile handheld technologies in Western Australian independent schools. *Australasian Journal of Educational Technology*, *29*(1), 66–81.

Piotrowski, J. T., & Krcmar, M. (2017). Reading with hotspots: Young children's responses to touchscreen stories. *Computers in Human Behavior*, *70*(Supplement C), 328–334. doi:10.1016/j.chb.2017.01.010

Potter, J., & McDougall, J. (2017). *Digital media, culture and education: Theorising third space literacies*. London: Palgrave MacMillan.

Puentedura, R. (2014). SAMR and curriculum redesign. Retrieved from http://www.hippasus.com/rrpweblog/archives/2014/08/30/SAMRAndCurriculumRedesign.pdf

Schuck, S., Kearney, M., & Burden, K. (2017). Exploring mobile learning in the Third Space. *Technology, Pedagogy and Education*, *26*(2), 121–137. doi:10.1080/1475939X.2016.1230555

Sharples, M., Taylor, J., & Vavoula, G. (2007). A theory of learning for the mobile age. R. Andrews & C. Haythornthwaite (Eds.), *The Sage handbook of elearning research* (pp. 221–247). London: Sage Publications.

Shearer, R. (2007). Instructional design and the technologies: An overview. In M. G. Moore (Ed.), *Handbook of distance education* (pp. 219–232). Mahwah, NJ: Lawrence Erlbaum Associates.

Traxler, J. (2005). Mobile learning:It's here but what is it? *Interactions*, *9*(1). Retrieved from https://warwick.ac.uk/services/ldc/resource/interactions/issues/issue25/traxler/. Accessed on August 31, 2018.

Traxler, J. (2007). Defining, discussing and evaluating mobile learning: The moving finger writes and having writ…. *The International Review of Research in Open and Distance Learning*, *8*(2). Retrieved from http://www.irrodl.org/index.php/irrodl/issue/view/29. Accessed on August 31, 2018.

Traxler, J. (2011). Introduction. In J. Traxler & J. Wishart (Eds.), *Making mobile learning work: Case studies of practice* (pp. 4–12). Bristol: ESCalate. Retrieved from http://escalate.ac.uk/downloads/8250.pdf. Accessed on September 1, 2017.

UNESCO. (2013). Policy guidelines for mobile learning. Retrieved from http://unesdoc.unesco.org/images/0021/002196/219641E.pdf. Accessed on August 31, 2018.

van't Hooft, M., Swan, K., Cook, D., & Lin, Y. (2007). What is ubiquitous computing? In M. van't Hooft & K. Swan (Eds.), *Ubiquitous computing in education*. Mahwah, NJ: Lawrence Erlbaum Associates.

Vee, A. (2017). Introduction: Computer programming as literacy. In *Coding literacy: How computer programming is changing writing* (pp. 1–42). Cambridge, MA: MIT Press. Retrieved from http://www.jstor.org.ezproxy.library.uwa.edu.au/stable/j.ctt1s476xn.5

Walsh, M. (2017).Multiliteracies, multimodality, new literacies and …. What do these mean for literacy education? In M. Milton (Ed.) *Inclusive principles and practices in literacy education* (Vol. 11, pp. 19–33). Bingley: Emerald Publishing. Published online: 18 Jul 2017. https:doi.org/10.1108/S1479-363620170000011002

Wenger, E. (1998). *Communities of practice: Learning, meaning, and identity*. Cambridge: Cambridge University Press.

Wong, L.-H. (2012). A learner-centric view of mobile seamless learning. *British Journal of Educational Technology*, *43*(1), E19–E23. doi:10.1111/j.1467-8535.2011.01245.x

Chapter 1

Young Children's Imaginative Play and Dynamic Literacy Practices in the Digital Age

Sara Sintonen, Kristiina Kumpulainen and Jenni Vartiainen

Abstract

This chapter discusses children's imaginative play and literacy practices as mediated by mobile digital technologies and media. In this chapter, drawing on sociocultural theory and the notion of dynamic literacies, we consider how digital technologies including mobile technologies interact and potentially expand children's imaginative play, leading to dynamic literacy practices and learning opportunities. Based on this understanding, we will propose some pedagogical principles that can be applied to play-based early childhood education in support of young children's creative thinking, storytelling and dynamic literacy practices, both indoors and outdoors.

Keywords: Imaginative play; literacy; early childhood education; mobile digital technologies; creative thinking; dynamic literacies

1.1. Introduction

Eeli is a seven-year-old Finnish boy who, like many other children today, enjoys playing with Lego. Eeli's favourite Lego series is Ninjago. His reason for liking Ninjago so much is strengthened by a children's TV programme about Ninjago, which Eeli watches every week. He has many Lego Ninjago building blocks at home, and he builds constructions according to both available instructions and his own imagination. In addition to watching the TV series and playing with Lego blocks, Eeli engages in imaginative play marked by remarkable bodily expressions. His imaginative play does not include any objects but rather many

Ninja-like moves, battle sounds, running and jumping. At times, Eeli stops his imaginative play and retrieves his tablet device. He opens the online Lego Ninjago catalogue and scans over it. He uses the catalogue to inspire his imaginative play. After a few minutes, he returns to his own imaginative play mode and continues acting out a world of play that is invisible to other people.

Eeli's Ninjago play is one example of a contemporary type of play characterised by dynamic literacy practices and seamlessly combining traditional and ascetic (solitary) imaginative play with digital resources (see also Marsh, Plowman, Yamada-Rice, Bishop, & Scott, 2016; Potter & McDougall, 2017). Agile shifts in the child's imaginative play between TV, Lego blocks and pictorial content enable him to engage in several important literacy practices. These include acting as *the recipient and meaning-maker* (TV), *the producer* (Lego building), *the creator* (imaginative play) and *the developer* (imaginative play enriched with tablet content).

In this chapter, we consider how digitally enriched imaginative play and the roles and positions children take in their play activity can nurture their literacy learning in dynamic and holistic ways. By dynamic literacies, we refer to hybrid literacy practices in which various tools and practices meet and intersect (see Potter & McDougall, 2017). The chapter considers how pedagogy in children's early years can purposefully harness their imaginative play via digital technologies and media to promote their literacy practices and early education. In the approach advocated by our work, children's imaginative play is not separated from their use of digital technologies and media (see also Fleer, 2011), but is instead seen as a natural part of the cultural toolkit children can use to create, build and make meaning of the world and of themselves. Hence, the chapter argues against consumer-focused positioning of young children with digital technologies and media (see also Selwyn, 2003; Sorin, 2005, pp. 13–18), and proposes that children should be viewed as active agents in using digital technologies and media in their imaginative play as a form of dynamic literacy practices.

1.2. Imaginative Play

Researchers have long identified imaginative play as a vital component in the normal development of a child (Bergen, 2002; Garvey, 1993; Vygotsky, 1976). Imagination differs from normal reality, the material environment and the social presence of others and, as such, can widen our experience of the world (Zittoun & Cerchia, 2013). Imagining creates a new space or form of thinking with which children can surpass their own level of understanding and create a zone of proximal development for themselves (Vygotsky, 1962). Zittoun and Gillespie (2016, p. 2) define imagination as 'the process of creating experiences that escape the immediate setting, which allow exploring the past or future, present possibilities or even impossibilities'. Imagination feeds on a wide range of experiences people have with or through the cultural world, through diverse senses, combined, organised and integrated in new forms (Zittoun & Gillespie, 2016).

Similarly, Russ (2004, p. 141) noted that imaginative play helps children solve problems, especially in a creative fashion, and can assist children in reducing anxiety and fear. He argued that when we leave some space for imagination, it is easier to cope with the constant flux of the world. For Brown and Vaughan (2009), imagination allows individuals to create 'simulated realities that [they] can explore without giving up access to the real world' (p. 86). Also, Egan (1997, 2009) highlighted the importance of imagination for human development more generally, suggesting that imagining enables children to think beyond actuality to potentialities. He regarded imagination as the originator of invention, the novel and the flexible, while also underlining its role in rational thought. Overall, imagination is a fascinating phenomenon. It is more embodied than we often give it credit for. For example, imagination can be used in rehabilitation from strokes: imagining movement activates the same brain areas as actually physically moving (e.g. Mulder, 2007).

Walker and Gopnik (2013) suggested an interesting purpose for children's imaginative play: to provide children with the opportunity to practise the cognitive skills necessary for causal cognition or the ability to think about cause–effect relationships. As they stated: "Pretend play and counterfactual reasoning involve the same cognitive machinery: The ability to consider unreal events, to separate representations of those events from reality, and to think about the outcomes of those events as if they had occurred" (Walker & Gopnik, 2013, p. 43). Play can be portrayed as a learning instrument with which children can practise developing skills.

Despite arguments that the digital age is depriving children of opportunities for imaginative play (Bodrova & Leong, 2010; Karpov, 2005; Singer & Singer, 2005; Smirnova, 2011), current research has provided evidence of children's agency in their play and interactions with digital technologies and media. In fact, existing research has demonstrated dynamic literacy practices in children's digitally enriched play activities, whereby children seemingly weave together and merge online and offline play (Marsh, 2010; Plowman, McPake, & Stephen, 2010, 2012). For instance, in her study of the play preferences of Australian children aged 20 months to five years, Edwards (2013) revealed how parents described their children's active remixing of play activities, in which more traditional roles and pretend play using dolls and teddy bears actively interacted with narratives associated with experiences gained from technology use involving watching popular programmes on television, DVDs or online.

With respect to this association, Potter and McDougall (2017) introduced the notion of the 'third space' (see also Bhabha, 1994), which they defined as a dynamic literacy space in which diverse meanings and learnings are negotiated through the agentive activity of individuals – be they children or adults – in interaction with the social and material environment. In this chapter, we are interested in how such third spaces are created in children's engagement in creative play in which more traditional play is remixed with their experiences of and with digital content, tools and media. We see great educational potential in such hybrid spaces for children's dynamic literacy practices and literacy learning.

1.3. Imaginative Play, Dynamic Literacies and Literacy Learning

Imaginative play is also known to form a basis for children's literacy development. For instance, children can practise language through pretend play with others; they can use their toys more symbolically, creating narratives and making rules and roles they can act out (White, 2012). Listening, reading, enacting and playing stories foster imagination as well. Stories inspire, evoke emotions and help children to retain information (Lawrence & Paige, 2016). Storytelling involves connection and sharing. In a live situation, stories are created in the presence of recipients. Storytelling is a social activity as well as a communal process; the listener's role is as important as the narrator's. From a cultural perspective, stories are central to many cultures, as 'storytelling provides a platform and medium for retaining information that needs and should be retained' (Pattakos, 2011). Similarly, storytelling is important for children growing up in a culture insofar as it maintains a cultural continuum. As Brown and Vaughan (2009, p. 67) claimed, storytelling 'occupies a central place in early development and learning about the world, oneself, and one's place in it'.

According to Brown and Vaughan's (2009) typology of play, narrative play, of which storytelling is a prime example, encourages people to 'make up stories about why things are the way they are, which becomes our understanding of the world. Stories are a way of putting disparate pieces of information into a unified context" (p. 92). Similarly, Palmer (1996) described talking as playing because storytelling constitutes one form of children's play: "Language is the play of verbal symbols that are based in imagery. Imagery is what we see in our mind's eye, but it is also the taste of a mango, the feel of walking in a tropical downpour, the music of Mississippi Masala. Our imaginations dwell on experiences obtained through all the sensory modes, and then we talk" (p. 3).

In Brown and Vaughan's (2009) typology, narrative play has much in common with imaginative play (creating simulated realities, immersion in imaginary worlds and events, moving freely back and forth between reality and fiction) and creative play – the transformation towards the unknown. Moreover, social play, which comprises playing and sharing with others, overlaps with narrative, imaginative and creative play.

Contextualising play and storytelling in early childhood education is not a novel approach. Over 25 years ago, Paley (1990) wrote about play and storytelling as the primary realities in preschool and kindergarten. Likewise, for Hendy and Toon (2001), play emerges from a shared creative activity in which stories and tales are entwined with the play environments built according to children's ideas and wishes. Overall, children's imaginative play and dynamic literacy practices can be viewed as social practices in the literacy cultures created for and by the children. Participation in such cultures, including acting, playing and learning together, mediate and develop both children's and adults' interest in new phenomena, skills and knowledge, creating new forms of interaction and establishing new relationships.

Contextualising play, storytelling and literacy development in the digital era have been a challenge for researchers. Extant research has problematised digital technologies as either negatively impacting the quality of children's play (Singer & Singer, 2005) or threatening children's imaginative capacity to play (Smirnova, 2011). More research is needed to understand the full potential of children's imaginative play, volitional storytelling and digital production (Edwards, 2013; Marsh, 2010). As Bird and Edwards (2015) reported, rather than being concerned over young children's use of technology in early childhood education settings, researchers should re-approach digital devices as catalysing a change in children's innovative and symbolic activities. According to Bird and Edwards (2015), such devices are associated with promoting children's social interactions, fostering thinking and laying the foundations for literacy learning – in other words, dynamic literacy. Another project, from Hill (2005), revealed that the traditional content of reading and writing needs to be broadened to include the use of multiple sign systems that represent meaning. Young children have always used constructions, drawings or illustrations, movements and sounds to represent meaning. In this respect, newer technologies merely add to children's choice of mediums with which to represent ideas and comprehend meanings in a range of texts.

Research also suggests that providing a playful context wherein children can freely and agentively create and replay their story elements instead of following adult-led activities leads to more structured and creative stories (Whitebread & Jameson, 2010). The future of reading and writing is closely tied to the future of digital technologies. Children already gain substantial experience with digital, multimodal texts at home. If we ignore new technologies and prevent young children from accessing them, we risk disconnecting them from the world in which they live, as Yelland (1999), among others, mentioned almost two decades ago.

Supporting young children's imaginative play and literacy practices with digital technologies can be considered a playful, embodied and creative action among young learners. It is important to combine play, imagination, creativity and embodiment with digital learning in early childhood education (Sintonen, Ohls, Kumpulainen, & Lipponen, 2015). The advantage of mobile devices is that they can be easily used when needed. In addition, mobile devices can be adapted to activities, bearing in mind that the activities are not dependent on these devices. This requires careful and innovative pedagogical design: the learning activities of young children should not be limited to digital devices and other new technologies and media, but should be augmented and supported *through* them, according to pedagogical guidelines.

For example, a smartphone can be taken along on a nature excursion and used to identify the names of flora and fauna that children find interesting; photographs can also be taken depending on the moment and interests of the children. Photography is one of the basic functions of mobile learning that young children can use. Children can practise using cameras and recording their observations. For children, recording observations in more diverse ways than only by verbal expression makes it possible to return to the experiences more effectively. Pictures and videos, for instance, trigger children's memory and help them to process experiences further. From the adult point of view, offering children with versatile documentation tools and memory stimulants for storytelling, would enable adults to better comprehend matters of significance to children worth recording.

1.4. Towards a Pedagogy of Dynamic Literacies in Early Childhood Education

The pedagogical principles advocated by our recent development efforts in Finland to promote young children's dynamic literacies are multisensory, playful and story-like, and they encourage children to use their imagination, be creative and collaborate with each other (Kumpulainen, 2018; see also the work of Jacobs, 2013 and Leander & Boldt,2013). These principles entail rich textual environments where the culture produced by children and the culture produced for them, such as fairy tales and stories, rhymes and poetry, music, TV programmes and films, digital games and applications, come into dialogue. Creating a rich, multimodal textual environment is aimed at inviting children to investigate, interpret, use and produce texts for various purposes and audiences. Learning environments are designed to generate flexible, pedagogically coherent and continuous entities (themes, phenomena) across the curriculum, drawing on children's social ecologies, including home cultures and literacies. The learning environments for multiliteracy learning can be situated in outdoor and indoor spaces, nearby nature areas, parks and cities, as well as in cultural institutions and digital and virtual spaces. Shifts in different learning environments and contexts are considered important in learning multiliteracies, and therefore, children's free time and home cultures cannot be overlooked.

As multiliteracy also includes media and digital literacies, a range of texts are introduced in digital modes and environments. Children are familiarised with various digital tools, media, applications and games in meaningful, playful and creative ways, and attention is paid to the significance and safe use of these tools in their everyday lives. Digital technologies and media are utilised to produce a wide range of content and meaning. Digital documentation also plays an important role as an element of meaning making, experimentation, production and knowledge exchange across children's social ecologies, such as at home and school (see Potter & McDougall, 2017).

Early years pedagogy addressing dynamic literacies can depend on children's play, creative thinking and storytelling. This approach integrates digital technologies intrinsically and naturally in children's everyday activities. Teachers are encouraged to use a variety of interactions with texts, including digital texts, and to choose the most suitable texts for various learning goals, especially those encompassing dynamic literacy practices. Children are encouraged to express themselves in multisensory, playful ways by using digital technology and creating their own content. When the concept of literacy is more widely considered from the point of view of children's imaginative play and dynamic literacy, and digital tools and mobile devices become a more integral part of education (including early childhood education), a collaborative, inclusive and multimodal environments reflecting contemporary digital culture can be created, as described in the points below.

(1) The co-production of content, creativity, sharing, peer learning, advising and helping others and immediate feedback are activities that are characteristic of, and familiar to, participants in digital cultures. Such activities could also serve as the basis for learning dynamic literacy practices in early childhood education.
(2) The use of a multitude of different forms of expression and tools can make both producing and receiving content more intriguing and meaningful to children. Multimodality challenges the traditional 'monomodal' pedagogy and materials in a positive way.
(3) Several methods exist for documenting and storing children's play interactions and their use and creation of artefacts. These can be used to indicate learning and improvement, to strengthen the feeling of ownership, for storytelling, as support material and to help in archiving memories.
(4) Not everything needs to be completed at once and by oneself; content can evolve, take different shapes and adjust to various situations, needs and participants. Adaptability and remixing are key for digital content creation.
(5) Digitisation has enabled visits to, and perusals of places, worlds and possibilities that are analogically inaccessible. This cultivates imagination and can form a basis for storytelling.

In sum, mobile technologies can be used to stimulate children's own creative production in a variety of ways. For instance, mobile devices such as tablets and smartphones can be used to make, record and share personal observations, thoughts, views and stories. In early childhood education, creative production can refer to, for example, digital stories, photos and photo collages, books (fairy tale books, nonfiction books and diaries), movies and other videos, music or games, made alone or collaboratively (Sintonen et al., 2015).

1.5. Dynamic Literacies Approach in Early Years Pedagogy: An Example

The following is an example of our development work regarding pedagogies and learning materials for early years education, drawing on children's imagination, imaginative play, storytelling and dynamic literacies and enriched by digital technologies and media. *Whisper of the Spirit* is a set of activity cards with the educational aim of encouraging children to exercise their imagination and take an interest in Finnish nature and ancient myths from a variety of perspectives and modalities. The activity card tasks encourage children to imagine, observe, collaborate, reflect, innovate and experiment in many ways, both indoors and outdoors (see Figure 1.1).

Nature has always been especially important to Finnish people, as the country's four seasons make for a rich and varied environment. It is thus unsurprising that the natural climate and geography of Finland has long kindled the imagination of the Finnish people and served as the source of many beliefs. For example, shooting stars were once believed to be cracks in the sky through which the Gods could peer down at the Earth. Similarly, forests and their spirit denizens were an essential part of the culture and way of life of Northern Finland, as forests were a critical food source.

Myths are culturally shared stories and beliefs about entities, events and places no one has seen or experienced but which are nonetheless held to be true. In the ancient past, Finnish myths often had their origins in observations of nature. The natural world inspired and fostered interaction by the Finnish people, who experienced a completely different relationship to nature than their modern descendants. As Lawrence and Paige (2016, p. 66) noted, myths possess a unique form of storytelling significance and value:

> The elements of a great story are imagination, believability and content. In terms of the content, it is all about the problem, resolution and moral of the story. Moreover, a well-told story of the distant past can illustrate the value and importance of the myths we invent and how they serve to hold cultures together and empower individuals to build their lives around these experiences. (Lawrence & Paige, 2016, p. 66)

The pedagogical material, *Whisper of the Spirit*, is currently widely used in Finnish early childhood education settings. The activities teachers have voluntarily developed around the material connect hands-on activities to digital production, documentation and remixing. For example, in one case, a teacher motivated preschool children (aged 5–6) with an image she had produced by using a mobile app called *ChatterPix* by Duck Duck Moose. She took a photo of a rock, drew a line to make a mouth and recorded the question, 'Would you like to hear my story?' with a lowered voice. She downloaded the talking image to *ThingLink* (www.thinglink.com), on which she had already uploaded one page from *Whisper of the Spirit* as a background image. After showing the materials to the group, the teacher asked the children whether they wanted to visit the rock in a forest nearby and create their own stories. The children used their own documentation (digital photos, videos taken during the trip using mobile devices) and experiences (sensory experiences and observations in the woods and samples collected from nature), as well as their own imagination (individual and shared storytelling and voice-recorded narration) to create digital stories through, for example, an application called *BookCreator* by Red Jumper Ltd.

Figure 1.1: The Pedagogical Material *Whisper of the Spirit*, Two Sample Pages.

The children were allowed to use the media of their choice. Finally, all the material was gathered on the same *ThingLink* page the teacher had originally created. After a week of working with *Whisper of the Spirit*, the children asked to look at the *ThingLink* page several times, and they also wanted to re-visit the rock in the forest on several more occasions. This helped the children to develop their dynamic literacies by exploring and learning about the natural world around them, albeit in different ways, through imagination and make-believe.

If ready-made content, such as various materials, images and stories are utilised in mobile literacy learning, they must be pedagogically appropriate and of high quality. They must also both interest children and support their learning. Manufacturers of such products should also be cognisant of the impact they have on children; from the perspective of early childhood education, it is vital that the content produced for children is high quality, ethically and aesthetically sustainable and suitable for use on mobile devices. It should also leave enough space for children's own thoughts.

1.6. Closing Thoughts

Imagination and storytelling are an essential part of children's play activities and should be included in literacy and learning practices in formal early childhood education. Open-ended activities, such as creative play, instead of prescriptive activities, foster diverse thinking among children. Digital devices and media should not be regarded as antithetical to creative play and learning but rather as an integral part of children's dynamic literacies in the twenty-first century. As Paley (1990) noted some time ago, storytelling is the primary reality in preschool and kindergarten. The same reality still exists nowadays. However, contemporary storytelling is rooted in much richer communication than verbal expression alone.

As our examples of Eeli's Ninjago play and *Whisper of the Spirit* show, contemporary digital devices can expand children's imaginative play and storytelling, positioning children within hybrid literacy practices that entail acting as *the recipient and meaning-maker* (TV), *the producer* (Lego building), *the creator* (imaginative play) and *the developer* (imaginative play enriched with tablet content). Moreover, new technologies provide a wide variety of possibilities for children to share and document the processes and products of their imaginative play, in turn broadening their audiences. For example, pictures and videos of Lego creations can be uploaded in an application, and then shared with and reviewed by other Lego builders. These new extensions, mediated by digital technologies and media, demonstrate a kind of 'third-space': a hybrid space in which several meanings and learnings are shared, negotiated and represented through the agentive activity of children in interaction with the social and material environment.

Below, we summarise some practical advice and pedagogical principles to promote young children's imaginative play and dynamic literacy practices in early childhood education, using digital technologies including mobile devices:

- Let children try out different digital tools and technologies at a very young age in various contexts. Carry such tools with you as a part of your ordinary, day-to-day life and take inspiration from the situations, moments and places where you use them.
- Inspire and encourage children to create their own content, to be creative with digital devices. Relate imaginative and creative play to digital production. Learn to recognise what constitutes natural and positive creative moments from the children's viewpoint.
- Use a various range of modalities (e.g. visual, aural, etc.) in content production and create diverse texts – for example, images and soundtracks – containing the same information.
- Supply a wide range of digital devices and content when possible, as being restricted to one tool or type of content also restricts what can be accomplished. There is no need to buy everything: you can also borrow, exchange or share. Let your children know about your media history and the devices you have used in the past.
- Learn about different digital technologies, tools and various applications together with colleagues, children and parents. Many great features of devices and production environments often go unused when adults have not acquainted themselves with them. Allow the children to take the role of an expert now and then.
- Show interest and take part in the digital worlds of children as well as their creative experiments and offer them diverse opportunities for creative play and learning. Discuss with children the content they have created, ask them questions and share your remarks.
- It is a good idea to take part in child-led activities that make use of mobile devices. Show your interest and be excited by the content they are producing. Also, try out new things for yourself and let children give you instructions.
- When you comment or give feedback to children, always have something positive to say and explain your views. Consider what you see and experience in their productions, and discuss with them how different audiences might respond to these productions.
- Encourage sustained play and resilience in children's creative productions and work. Remember that the actual process of creation is as meaningful and important as the final product.

Being creative, playful and imaginative in early education is not always a pleasant experience for teachers but occasionally demanding, difficult and confrontational. At the same time, it can be very rewarding. It raises – and should raise – questions about the fundamental structures of power, authority and resistance in our society (see Sefton-Green et al., 2015). If imagination and creativity are conceptual tools with which children adapt to change and handle the unknown and unpredictable, why are children not given opportunity to dynamic literacy practices and tools for their bodily sense making and production of their world? Dynamic literacy of young children should not be limited by digital mobile devices but to be considered as a playful, embodied, creative and imaginative actions with and through them.

References

Bergen, D. (2002). The role of pretend play in children's cognitive development. *Early Childhood Research and Practice, 4*, 1–12.
Bhabha. (1994). *The location of culture*. New York, NY: Routledge.
Bird, J., & Edwards, S. (2015). Children learning to use technologies through play: A digital play framework. *British Journal Education Technology, 46*(6), 1149–1160. doi:10.1111/bjet.12191
Bodrova, E., & Leong, D. J. (2010). Curriculum and play in early child development. In R. E. Tremblay, R. G. Barr, R. De, V. Peters, & M. Boivin, (Eds.), *Encyclopedia on early childhood development* [online] (pp. 1–6). Montreal, Quebec: Centre of Excellence for Early Childhood Development. Retrieved from http://www.child-encyclopedia.com/documents/Bodrova-LeongANGxp.pdf
Brown, S., & Vaughan, C. (2009). *Play: How it shapes the brain, opens the imagination, and invigorates the soul*. New York, NY: Avery.
Edwards, S. (2013). Digital play in the early years: A contextual response to the problem of integrating technologies and play-based pedagogies in the early childhood curriculum. *European Early Childhood Education Research Journal, 21*(2), 199–212. doi:10.1080/1350293X.2013.789190
Egan, K. (1997). *The educated mind: How cognitive tools shape our understanding* (p. 299). Chicago, IL: University of Chicago Press.
Egan, K. (2006). *Teaching literacy: Engaging the imagination of new readers and writers*. Thousand Oaks, CA: Corwin Press.
Fleer, M. (2011). Technologically constructed childhoods: Moving beyond a reproductive to a productive and critical view of curriculum development. *Australasian Journal of Early Childhood, 36*(1), 16–25.
Garvey, C. (1993). *Play*. Cambridge, MA: Harvard University Press.
Hendy, L., & Toon, L. (2001). *Supporting drama and imaginative play in the early years*. Buckingham, UK: Open University Press.
Hill, S. (2005). *Mapping multiliteracies: Children in the new millennium. Report of the research project 2000–2004*. Adelaide: University of South Australia. Retrieved from http://www.unisanet.unisa.edu.au/staff/suehill/mapping_multiliteracies.pdf
Jacobs, G. E. (2013). Reimagining multiliteracies: A response to Leander and Boldt. *Journal of Adolescent & Adult Literacy, 57*(4), 270–273.
Karpov, Y. V. (2005). *The neo-Vygotskian approach to child development*. Cambridge: Cambridge University Press.
Kumpulainen, K. (2018). *Promoting multiliteracies from early years onwards: Insights to an ongoing educational reform effort in Finland*. Manuscript submitted for publication.
Lawrence, R. L., & Paige, D. S. (2016). What our ancestors knew: Teaching and learning through storytelling. *New Directions for Adult and Continuing Education, 2016*(149), 63–72.

Leander, K., & Boldt, G. (2013). Rereading "a pedagogy of multiliteracies": Bodies, texts, and emergence. *Journal of Literacy Research, 45*(1), 22–46. doi:10.1177/1086296X12468587

Marsh, J. (2010). Young children's play in online virtual worlds. *Journal of Early Childhood Research, 8*, 23–39.

Marsh, J., Plowman, L., Yamada-Rice, D., Bishop, J., & Scott, F. (2016). Digital play: A new classification. *Early Years, 36*(3), 242–253. doi:10.1080/09575146.2016.1167675

Mulder, T. (2007). Motor imagery and action observation: Cognitive tools for rehabilitation. *Journal of Neural Transmission, 114*(10), 1265–1278. doi:10.1007/s00702-007-0763-z

Paley, V. G. (1990). *The boy who would be a helicopter*. Cambridge, MA: Harvard University Press.

Palmer, G. B. (1996). *Toward a theory of cultural linguistics*. (1st ed.). Austin, TX: The University of Texas Press.

Pattakos, A. (2011). *Modern storytelling and the search for meaning*. [Blog] Huffpost. Retrieved from http://www.huffingtonpost.com/alex-pattakos/storytelling-culture-meaning_b_814798.html. Accessed on September 7, 2018.

Plowman, L., McPake, J., & Stephen, C. (2010). The technologisation of childhood? Young children and technologies at home. *Children and Society, 24*(1), 63–74.

Plowman, L., McPake, J., & Stephen, C. (2012). Extending opportunities for learning: The role of digital media in early education. In S. Suggate & E. Reese (Eds.), *Contemporary debates in child development and education*. (pp. 95–104). London: Routledge.

Potter, J., & McDougall, J. (2017). *Digital media, culture and education. Theorising third space literacies*. London: Palgrave Macmillan UK.

Russ, S. W. (2004). *Play in child development and psychotherapy*. New York, NY: Routledge.

Sefton-Green, J., Kumpulainen, K., Lipponen, L., Sintonen, S., Rajala, A., & Hilppö, J. (2015). *Playing with learning*. Helsinki: University of Helsinki. Retrieved from https://helda.helsinki.fi/handle/10138/158664

Selwyn, N. (2003). 'Doing it for the kids': Re-examining children, computers and the 'information society'. *Media, Culture & Society, 25*(3), 351–378.

Singer, D. G., & Singer, J. L. (2005). *Imagination and play in the electronic age*. Cambridge, MA: Harvard University Press.

Sintonen, S., Ohls, O., Kumpulainen, K., & Lipponen, L. (2015). *Mobile learning and the playing child*. Helsinki: University of Helsinki, Playful Learning Center. Retrieved from https://helda.helsinki.fi/handle/10138/155512

Smirnova, E. (2011). Character toys as psychological tools. *International Journal of Early Years Education, 19*(1), 35–43.

Sorin, R. (2005). Changing images of childhood:Reconceptualising early childhood practice. *International Journal of Transitions in Childhood, 1*(1), 12–21.

Vygotsky, L. S. (1962). *Thought and language*. Cambridge: MIT Press.

Vygotsky, L. S. (1976). Play and its role in the mental development of the child. In J. Bruner, A. Jolly, & K. Sylva (Eds.), *Play: Its role in development and evolution* (pp. 76–99). New York, NY: Basic Books.

Walker, C. M., & Gopnik, A. (2013). Pretense and possibility: A theoretical proposal about the effects of pretend play on development: Comment on Lillard et al. (2013). *Psychological Bulletin, 139*(1), 40–44.

White, R. (2012). *The power of play: A research summary on play and learning.* St. Paul, MN: Minnesota Children's Museum.

Whitebread, D., & Jameson, H. (2010). Play beyond the foundation stage: Storytelling, creative writing and self-regulation in able 6-7 year olds. In J. Moyles (Ed.), *The excellence of play.* (3rd ed., pp. 95–107). Maidenhead, UK: Open University Press.

Yelland, N. (1999). Technology as play. *Early Childhood Education Journal, 26*(4), 217–220.

Zittoun, T., & Cerchia, F. (2013). Imagination as expansion of experience. *Integrative Psychological and Behavioral Science, 47*(3), 305–324. doi:10.1007/s12124-013-9234-2

Zittoun, T., & Gillespie, A. (2016). *Imagination in human and cultural development.* London: Routledge.

Chapter 2

A Gallery of Practices – Mobile Learning, Language, Literacy and the Arts (K-6)

Kathy Rushton and Jon Callow

Abstract

While visual arts, drama, dance and music have been used to enhance literacy learning for many decades in preschool and primary classrooms, engaging with mobile learning can also provide many opportunities for young learners to explore and develop language and literacy. The use of mobile devices is of particular interest as technology has an impact on pedagogy and the mobility of digital devices provides many opportunities for engaged and meaningful literacy learning when teamed with the arts. In this chapter, we define the arts and their relationship with literacy learning before exploring a number of resources and practices for integrating their use in early learning settings.

Keywords: Multimodality; mobile technology; creative arts; literacy; language; TESOL

2.1. Introduction

Engaging with mobile learning and the arts opens many opportunities to explore and develop language and literacy with young learners. Visual arts, drama, dance and music have been used to enhance literacy learning for many decades in preschool and primary classrooms. The affordances of mobile devices can prompt us to revisit these practices, given the increasing role of digital technology in children's social and cultural lives. As with the arts, language and literacy are socio-cultural practices that can only be made sense of in terms of their development within particular societies and cultures. All cultures have cultural artefacts, shared beliefs and ways of doing things and members of cultural groups have roles. Thus, 'digital cultures' in childhood might be broadly construed as the ways in which groups of children develop literacy through the affordances offered by the use of technology such as mobile devices. The use of mobile devices is of particular interest as the use of technology has an impact on pedagogy and the mobility of digital devices provides many opportunities for engaged and meaningful literacy learning when teamed with the arts. The following sections first define the arts and their relationship with literacy learning before moving to explore a number of resources and practices for integrating their use in early learning settings.

2.2. Exploring the Arts and Literacy and Language Development

Understanding the role of the arts in literacy and language learning first requires us to explain the terms and concepts we are working with when we use the term 'the arts'. Shenfield asserts that the arts are an 'area of imaginative and investigative inquiry that facilitates deep and considered aesthetic understanding of an art form' (Shenfield, 2015, p. 11). Many arts educators argue that the appreciation and creation of all types of artistic works offer 'aesthetic experiences that are not only pleasing, but that transform the very way we encounter our world' (Albers & Harste, 2007, p. 8). Education *in* and *through* the arts includes strategies and pedagogical practices that 'foster the capacity for creative and flexible thinking, as well as to provide a way of coming to understand and make connections across different kinds of knowledge' (Ewing, 2010, p. 7). Further, what elements make up our definition of the arts?

The arts are often defined quite broadly, drawing on a number of fields and expressive activities. Ewing (2010) argues for the definition to include dance, drama, visual arts, music, film and other media arts, as well as literature. The Road Map for Arts Education (UNESCO, 2006) sees the arts as part of human rights and cultural participation. Barton and Baguley characterise the UNESCO road map as laying 'the foundation for a balanced creative, cognitive, emotional, aesthetic and social approach for the development of people from birth to old age' (Barton & Baguley, 2017, p. 3). Similarly, the Convention on the Rights of the Child (United Nations, 1989) states in article 31 that:

- Every child has the right to rest and leisure, to engage in play and recreational activities appropriate to the age of the child and to participate freely in cultural life and the arts.
- Member governments shall respect and promote the right of the child to participate fully in cultural and artistic life and shall encourage the provision of appropriate and equal opportunities for cultural, artistic, recreational and leisure activity.

It is significant to note the role of play in the first part of article 31. Play and the arts are intertwined, with a number of theorists arguing the importance of this connection. Dewey (1934) claimed the importance of play as foundational for learning while Eisner contends that the arts provide 'in all their manifestations, are close in attitude to play' (Eisner, 2002, p. 4).

Within each of the arts areas, researchers not only affirm the value of learning about the arts in their own right but explore the benefits of each field of the arts. For example, Winner and Hetland's research suggests that musical training for young children has a 'substantial effect on auditory cortical development' (Winner & Hetland, 2000, p. 512) while Heath argues that dance generates interdependency as it 'demands the most immediate display of cooperation and literal dependence on the strength and ability of others' (Heath, 2001, p. 11). Ewing's review of the arts presents a large body of research for the impact of drama on learning. She cites a number of researchers who have utilised process drama which encourages collaboration, problem solving and self-reflection processes (Ewing & Saunders, 2016; Miller & Saxton, 2004; Neelands, 1992).

The visual arts encourages learners to not only use their visual senses to understand images and artworks but to acknowledge the emotional and personal reactions that viewers bring to pictures (Callow, 2005). Given the increasing acknowledgement of the role that visual and multimodal texts have in our contemporary culture (Jewitt, Bezemer & O'Halloran, 2016), the visual arts have a particularly important role in helping students engage, enjoy and critique all types of images and artworks.

Creativity and imagination are fostered when the arts are integrated into classroom learning experiences (Greene, 2008). The arts also offers opportunities for problem solving and collaboration (Pope, 2005), as well as evoking significant emotional responses, vital to our physical and mental well-being (Karkou & Glasman, 2004).

2.2.1. Connecting Literacy and Language Learning to the Arts

When we consider the role of the arts in literacy development, the literature suggests that the arts can both involve students in literacy learning using arts processes such as drama and drawing, as well as assist in supporting reading (vocabulary, fluency and comprehension development using drama and reader's theatre) and writing (the development of storytelling and narratives enhanced by drama and visual arts) as well as talking and listening skills (Barton, 2013; Scripp et al., 2007; Shenfield, 2015). Recent research in the area of multiliteracies and multimodality acknowledges that 'young children are capable of representing their ideas in creative, symbolic, and concrete forms with multiple media' (Hartle & Jaruszewicz, 2009, p. 188). Acknowledging that literacy learning involves multiple modes of meaning, where students use multiliteracies to shape, share and experience a variety of texts immediately resonates with the way different art forms, from visual arts to drama also draw on multiple modes.

Consider the use of puppets as part of drama, storytelling and visual arts making. Gibson and Campbell (2013) articulate how language learning is enhanced as one aspect of making and playing with puppets. Citing Linderman and Linderman (1984) work, they argue that puppets:

- Encourage communication
- Develop social expression and feelings
- Build opportunities to design, model, paint and sew
- Support oral storytelling
- Practise verbal skills and expression
- Enhance discussion and questioning between peers and with teachers

Using the arts as part of literacy learning thus offers opportunities to integrate creative, imaginative and collaborative learning as part of literacy learning. Socio-cultural models of literacy acknowledge the role of multimodal texts and experiences which include all features of the arts such as performance, drama, drawing, dance and visual media. Multimodal texts are those that combine two or more communication modes, whether live, print or screen-based (Callow, 2013). Albers and Harste contend that multimodal theory, informed by social semiotics (Jewitt et al., 2016; Kress, 2010) engages with many aspects of the arts in terms of using multiple communication modes to create meaning. Definitions of literacy have expanded to include the role of images and visual literacy (Narey, 2017), digital and interactive texts (Kervin, 2016) and the development of new technology influenced literacy practices (Lankshear & Knobel, 2011). These acknowledge the multiplicity of texts that are part of children's literate landscapes. encouraging educators to examine performance, drama, film and visual arts as resources for teaching and learning about English and literacy.

Puppets on Screen

Building on Gibson & Campbell's work on puppets, a variety of apps allows children to create and voice puppets or create puppets from objects they photograph (*Sock Puppets*, (Smith Micro Software Inc., 2015)) and *Chatterpix*, (Duck Duck Moose Inc., 2015), for example). These allow children to create puppet shows, talk to each other in character, take on roles and experiment with language and voice.

Emily Gravett's Monkey and Me (Gravett, 2008) is the simple rhyming story of a young girl who takes her toy monkey to the zoo. The repetitive refrain 'Monkey and me, monkey and me, we went to see…' is teamed with pictures that give clues to the reader as to what animal they will see next. The story is narrated by the young girl. The *Chatterpix* app allows any child to become the teller of the story, simply by taking a photo of themselves and then recording the refrain, allowing them to practice and hear the rhythm and rhyme. Alternatively, a soft toy or animal may become the narrator, where the child's name can be included into the refrain ('Petey and me, Petey and me, we went to see […] '). The mouth of the puppet moves in time with the spoken words (see Figure 2.1) and the final product is saved as a movie file. In this way, children are able to develop social expression, practice verbal skills and oral storytelling.

Figure 2.1: The Mouth Moves in Time as the Child Speaks and is Then Saved as a Movie. *Source:* Soft toy photo by Denisse Leon on Unsplash.

2.3. Mobile Technologies, the Arts and Literacy Learning

Bringing together the area of mobile technologies, literacy learning and the arts offers many creative possibilities for use in early childhood and school settings. The role of technology in English, literacy and arts disciplines is reflected in curriculum documents in many countries. In Australia, the *Early Years Learning Framework* (Australian Government Department of Education; Employment & Workplace Relations, 2009) and the *Australian National Curriculum – English* (Australian Curriculum Assessment and Reporting Authority (ACARA), 2011) both contain clear statements about the inclusion of technologies in curriculum delivery, as does the *Australian National Curriculum – The Arts* (Australian Curriculum Assessment & Reporting Authority (ACARA), 2015).

To explore the use of a pedagogical model for using digital technology as part of literacy and arts-based learning, a number of broader principles from recent research in the field are useful to guide the discussion (Burnett & Merchant, 2013; Dezuanni, Dooley, Gattenhof, & Knight, 2015; Flewitt, 2013; Larson & Marsh, 2013; Marsh, 2013). These include the importance of play and creativity opportunities; constructivist learning principles; appropriate and engaging content; and the importance of multimodal features.

As previously noted, play is an important part of early childhood learning experiences as well as central to the arts. Play is also a key principle when considering the use of mobile technologies in literacy and arts-based activities. Drawing on earlier reviews by Roskos and Christie (2001) on the links between play and literacy learning, Flewitt argues for the importance of extending this into the use of digital resources as part of multimodal literacy learning (Flewitt, 2013). The particular use of mobile technologies that might facilitate play and literacy learning incorporate a range of experiences. These could be including popular culture videos and movies in the classroom, using apps that allow play with voice, sound and movement when creating multimodal texts, as well as using and discussing popular apps and games, which have a play element integral to their use.

Constructivist approaches are common in early childhood education (Branscombe, 2014) and they are also important when using digital resources and mobile devices. Supporting young learners to explore and construct meaningful experiences should involve purposeful learning activities, extensive talk and collaboration as well as active choices and control of digital resources by children. There are many apps such as *Book Creator* (Red Jumper Limited, 2015) or *My Story* (Bright Bot, 2015) that allows stories to be created and then shared, either digitally or as a printable resource. Each allows a child to design a page and tell a story, using both drawing and imported photos. The creation of both drawings and photographs by the children is a key aspect in developing both artistic skills and aesthetic understanding. Knight and Dooley (2015) argue that by providing regular use of a camera on the iPad, the young children in their study developed confidence and practised aesthetic judgments in what they photographed and how they played with and manipulated framing and shot choices. Similar aesthetic choices are developed with children are able to choose various media when drawing from paper and cardboard to crayons, pencils, charcoal or paints. Teaming children's artworks with writing both values their artwork, as well as develops thinking and writing skills. Consider the creation of a simple digital book from a class visit to the zoo (Figures 2.2 and 2.3). As part of the day's activities, children can be encouraged to think about what animals they photograph and how they choose to portray them. The following day the children can be involved in creating the digital text, recounting the events of the day and adding audio comments to the photos on the screen. Teachers and children could also share the pen or keyboard to add written text or labels to the screen. Particular photos such as the close up shot in Figure 2.3 can be discussed when adding captions or comments. Having modeled the activity for the whole class, children could then use the same app independently for creating their own page to add to the class book. The final books can be printed or shared as a video with the audio commentary or as a printable PDF file. The final product displays the children's visual artworks, as well as publishing their jointly written recount.

Any digital resource used in a classroom should have appropriate and engaging content as well as opportunities to develop skills. The focus on skills is often an issue, as many educational apps (particularly literacy and maths) are likely to be drill and practice-based, rather than those with more constructivist principles (Goodwin, 2012; Highfield & Johnson, 2013; Neumann & Neumann, 2014). While it is useful to be able to develop some skills using technology, Highfield and Johnson (2013) caution that the design of these apps may only support slower-level neural development. While the interactive element of some apps may be high, the content and quality of learning also needs to be considered.

Figure 2.2: Book Creator Interface. *Source:* App: © Red Jumper Ltd.

Figure 2.3: Page Using Close-up Photo to Support Written Text. *Source:* App: © Red Jumper Ltd. Tiger photo by Nick Karvounis on Unsplash.

If we consider literature as a key element in the arts, there are many digital resources that allow children to read, view and interact with high quality literature that has been adapted for mobile devices. Reading aloud to children is a cornerstone of solid literacy instruction. Playing a YouTube video of someone else reading a story aloud is not the most helpful use of technology, as it is the teacher's knowledge of her learners and interaction with them as she reads that are critical when helping young learners to enjoy a story. Many quality texts are now available on tablets, which effectively creates electronic big books, where children can follow and listen to the story, as well as see the pictures clearly. Current authors whose work is available in digital format include Tohby Riddle, Oliver Jeffers, Emily Gravett, David Wiesner, Anthony Browne, Aaron Blabey, John Burningham, Ian Falconer and Jackie French.

Mobile technologies can also be used to explore and enhance the experience of reading a children's story. Callow, Ewing, and Rushton (2016) explored the work of Oliver Jeffers, where both a drawing app *Sketches* (Tayasui, 2017) and a presentation app *Explain Everything* (Explain Everything, 2015) were used to innovate on the Jeffer's narrative from his book *Stuck*. Children can draw their own picture of the main character Floyd, who has a disposition for throwing ever-larger objects up into a tree, where they remain stuck. Jeffer's has a particularly engaging and whimsical artistic style, which children can emulate and explore. His simple characters with stick like legs allow ease of drawing but in this story it is the outrageous oversized objects that are flung into the tree that provide insights into how visual images can convey humor and fun. Using *Explain Everything*, children can import digital or drawn pictures. This app then allows them to easily manipulate the size and placement of the objects, in similar ways to the rather surreal style which Jeffers uses in his story. Here, concepts of composition, placement and perspective are further explored in the context of a quality piece of literature.

Exploration of the visual arts in the context of literacy and mobile technologies not only encompasses relevant learning content and enjoyment of viewing but also complements the increasingly multimodal nature of literacy learning. Recent work by Gattoff and Dezuanni (2015) posited a number of principles from their research project around mobile technologies in early childhood settings when considering visual arts learning with iPads. These include the idea that technology should complement not supplant physical arts engagement, the importance of creating artworks from scratch (as opposed to using set templates), and the observation that quality learning requires intervention and redirection by adults.

Anthony Browne's work regularly references and explores the world of art. From an art gallery visit with a family in *The Shape Game* (Browne, 2003), to surrealist references in *Voices in the Park* (Browne, 1999) or having his favourite monkey Willy exploring masterpieces across the ages in *Willy's Pictures* (Browne, 2001), these stories not only introduce children to viewing and talking about fine art but can also inspire their own artworks. The app *Faces iMake* (iMagine Machine Israel LTD, 2017) provides children with many types of objects from fruit and vegetables to tools and toys, which can be used to create collaged faces. When sharing this app with a group of children, we first discussed some of the works of Giuseppe Arcimboldo, the sixteenth-century painter who used fruit and vegetables and other objects to create faces, his most famous being an image of Holy Roman Emperor Rudolf II re-imagined as Vertumnus, the Roman god of nature (Figure 2.4).

Mobile Learning, Language, Literacy and the Arts (K-6) 37

Figure 2.4: Porträtt, Rudolf II som Vertumnus. Guiseppe Arcimboldo. *Source:* Wikimedia commons.

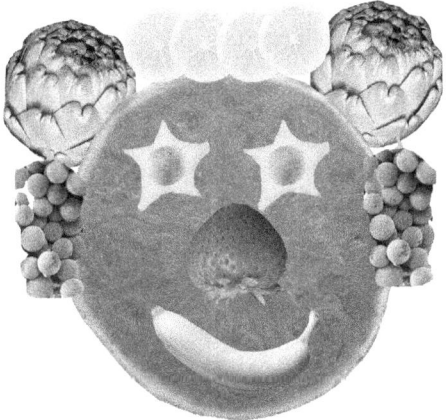

Figure 2.5: A version of Arcimboldo. *Source:* All photos from Unsplash. Watermelon by Patrick Fore; Grapes photo by Nacho Domínguez Argenta; Artichokes photo by Nacho Domínguez Argenta; Lemons and oranges photo by Brooke Lark; Banana photo by Mike Dorner on Unsplash; Strawberries photo by Hal Gatewood.

In each picture, we tried to work out what fruit or vegetable had been used to create the eyes, hair or mouth. After this, the children created their own faces using the resources in the app (Figure 2.5).

Another visual arts app is the MoMA art laboratory, which provides both blank canvases on which to draw and collage, but which also uses items from their extensive collection to teach young learners how to collage, paint, use lines, create a chance collage and create a sound poem (Museum of Modern Art, 2013).

While literature and the visual arts are but two of the wider range of arts practices, the examples used here seek to illustrate a number of the key principles when using mobile technologies with the arts and literacy learning. The importance of play and creativity is foregrounded, where free play is also balanced with guidance from a mentor or teacher, to model skills and concepts that evolve from playful experimentation. Engaging content and skills are important to consider when selecting the types of digital resources for children, whether it is a puppet show, shared reading, story writing or creating artworks. Skills focused apps have a place but in balance with apps that foster higher order thinking and learning. The following section outlines more specific examples of how literacy practices, reflecting a range of multimodal texts and apps, might be enacted in early childhood settings, the primary classroom as well as in children's homes, with the involvement of family members.

2.4. A Gallery of Practices: The Arts and Literacy Learning

In this gallery of practices, we will explore the development of literacy and some pedagogical points relating to the use of mobile technologies. This will include aspects of learning such as collaboration and the agency and creativity of the child (Ewing, 2013) as well as the focus and purpose of developing literacy and participating in the arts, as exemplified by dramatic play. The development of apps has afforded opportunities for young learners to develop their creativity through scaffolded play which encourages participation, engagement and reflection.

2.4.1. *Developing Language and Literacy through the Arts*

With the development of the internet and the introduction of technology into classrooms, many of the principles underlying a modern pedagogy such as collaboration and group work have been challenged by the physical placement of interactive whiteboards or computers which have sometimes determined how, when and where learning with modern technology will take place. Mobile technology may include laptops or keyboards which interact with interactive whiteboards and do go some way to promoting individual and small group work but it is the tablet and the development of apps which have provided educators with the opportunities to organise small group activities and to differentiate for a range of learners within the same physical space.

One of the greatest benefits is that the technology provides the opportunity for children to develop their language arts as they listen to and interact with stories (Ewing, Callow, & Rushton, 2016). For young readers, enhancing the text participant or meaning maker role (Freebody, 2005) is supported by the use of apps which allow the child to personalise the story (Kucirkova, 2017). For instance, the app *I Imagine* allows the child to choose characters and to select their appearance from skin colour to hair and clothes. The child is also able to name the characters and record the name using their own voice. As the story unfolds, the child can interact with objects and characters in the story and the written text appears on the screen as the story is told. This type of app supports reading, viewing and listening and would engage most young readers as they are able to make themselves the main character in the story, making strong connections to their own lives and experiences.

Most of the apps which provide this sort of choice allow the child to create a visual image, as in the *Playschool Playtime* app which allows the child to select items of clothing and other objects related to activities they undertake at certain times of the day. While the child is not drawing or painting, they are choosing from a selection to develop a visual image on the screen much in the way that a collage would be assembled using concrete materials. The relationship between the visual and language arts is, therefore, very clear when students are reading and interacting with picture books or when they are developing and illustrating their own stories. While younger children might use an app like *I imagine* to personalise a story provided by the app some others like *Puppet Pals* or *Playschool Artmaker* provides opportunities for children to create stories using their own imaginations and language resources. These apps provide scenes and characters to provide a framework for the story but for very young children these types of apps are best used after language has been developed through play and interaction with quality children's literature which will provide the language forms and features and the vocabulary necessary for creating a story (Jones, 1996; Painter, 2006).

For instance, using puppets to help children retell or create stories will not only support the development of language but also of dramatic play (Ewing, 2013). If children are told a story then allowed to re-enactor innovate on it using puppets they are likely to base the development of the characters on those in the story, as the story is now part of their own experience (Gibson & Campbell, 2013). They are also most likely to use the language they experienced when reading the story, especially if they have been able to interact with it independently and on several occasions. For example, they may have listened to the story on an interactive app and have also been read the story from a book (Jones, 2012).

2.4.2. Using Mobile Technology to Develop Dramatic Play

Opportunities to interact with stories in several ways will familiarise the child with many aspects of storytelling so apps such as *Hairy Maclairy* by Lynley Dodd or *Animalia* by Graeme Base are wonderful to present to children alongside the book to allow them to read the story in several ways which allows them to listen, look and interact with a story before they are able to independently decode the text. This sound basis in literature also provides the starting point for dramatic play as young children do need the support of adults in some aspects of dramatic play but after they are provided with characters, language and some familiarity with plots, settings and interactions, even very young children are able to independently innovate on a text (Ewing, 2013). Children who have been introduced to Readers Theatre (Ewing & Simons, 2016), for instance, will be able to utilise their understanding to interact with apps in playful ways.

Sometimes, these are structured by the affordances of the app but children are also able to innovate on their use of apps and the technology itself (Burnett & Merchant, 2017). As Ewing (2010) states:

> In the performing arts, well-developed interpersonal skills are needed to collaborate in creative activity, and this collaborative process is just as important as the final product. For example, consider the range of elements which together constitute the development of a script or dance: its interpretation in direction, the set design and discussion by the actors or dancers during rehearsal, the actual performance and the audience's response.
> (Ewing, 2010, p. 8)

The process of participation in the Arts and the collaboration and development of interpersonal skills can be supported by the use of mobile technology especially when children are encouraged to work collaboratively when interacting with an app. For instance, an app like *Goodnight Safari* that tells a story that is also printed on the screen supports the development of literacy but also for each event in the story the reader is invited to interact with the text. This interaction forms part of the event, such as helping to feed and bathe a baby animal which in turn leads to the next moment in the story. The reader is also in control of the pace of the story as they are able to move to the next screen by clicking on an animal footprint. This type of interactive story allows one or more students to interact with the actions and characters providing their own soundtrack or commentary for the story as they listen to it unfold. This is a highly scaffolded example of dramatic play which could provide very satisfying results for a young child and also provide valuable experiences for dramatic play with apps which provide more choices and less support such as *Puppet Pals*, *Playschool Art Maker* or *My Story*.

Mobile technologies provide affordances for collaboration and the development of language and literacy through dramatic play because of the mobility of the devices and in many cases, the ease of interaction with the app. The ability to personalise characters and settings and to develop stories using them provides young creators with plenty of opportunities to make connections to their own lives and experiences and to use their imaginations. The technology also provides the opportunity for the child to use one or more languages in the creation of a story or performance as many apps allow the user to either speak or write, and therefore, offer the opportunity for personalising the experience (Kucirkova, 2017). This ability to develop or recount stories in the first language as well as Standard Australian English is one of the greatest benefits the use of this technology can provide (Skutnabb-Kangas, 2013).

2.4.3. Using Mobile Technologies to Support Engagement with Learning

There are many apps available which not only encourage children to tell their own stories but provide opportunities for educators to connect to the child's community through the use of the first language and by making connections to the individual child's cultural heritage (Wong Fillmore, 1991) (see Figures 6 and 7).

Apps like Explain Everything or Popplet allow a child to caption a sequence of photos that may tell a story or recount an event. The captions for the photos could be recorded by a parent of community member in the child's first language as well as in English.

Storytelling in any language supports learning as the child is required to sequence ideas and events and to consider both the audience and the purpose of the text. Making a link between the home and school through story and play is an authentic, engaging activity in which parents and guardians from all walks of life and all educational backgrounds can participate (Campbell, 2013; Disbray, 2008). Storytelling is common to all cultures and can therefore provide a bridge between languages and cultures. Allowing students to listen to and interact with digital stories or stories from traditional books teaches them about structure and plot as well as developing familiarity with characters and with language. For instance, using an app like *Puppet Pals* can allow family members to upload photos of their own faces to a character and to tell a story which concerns all the family members. Very young children will need support to tell stories and the starting point is listening to stories. For bilingual children listening to stories in both the first and target language is of benefit (Gibbons, 2006) and even if this can be provided at school they will need support at home to develop a story. Using a mobile device and an app makes this much simpler as most young

Ayuda!

Aiuto!

Kokua!

Figure 2.6: Earthquake Proof Buildings.

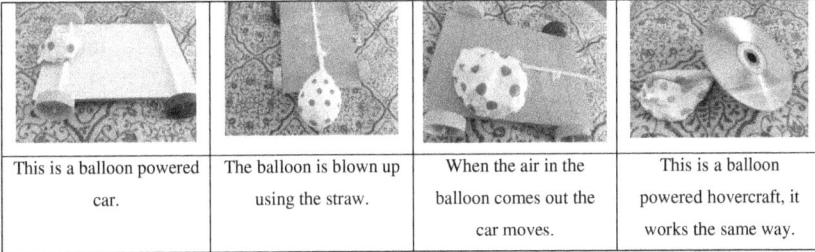

| This is a balloon powered car. | The balloon is blown up using the straw. | When the air in the balloon comes out the car moves. | This is a balloon powered hovercraft, it works the same way. |

Figure 2.7: Balloon Power.

children will be able to learn how to undertake some of these steps with help and will also be able to guide an adult who has little or no English or literacy.

2.5. Some Resources for Developing Literacy and Participation in the Arts Inside and Outside the Classroom

The Early Years Learning Framework (EYLF) 2009 states that:

> Educators honour the histories, cultures, languages, traditions, child rearing practices and lifestyle choices of families. They value children's different capacities and abilities and respect differences in families' home lives. (p. 13)

While this is an admirable goal, contemporary Australia is a multicultural, multilingual society and this may prove to be very challenging for many teachers, no matter how committed they are to honouring the many cultures and languages they may encounter. Many young learners are learning English, learning through English and learning about English (D'Warte,2014; Halliday, 2004) and it is also through language and culture that identity is developed and confirmed. In many classrooms, bilingual children are usually taught only in the medium of English but the Australian community has a minority of almost 30% of people who speak a language other than English at home (Australian Bureau of Statistics, 2011). Connections to children's families and communities are made through language as it is through language that traditions and ways of living are kept alive and it is through language that identity can be confirmed in educational settings (Compton-Lilly, 2011; Moll, Amanti, Neff, & Gonzalez,1992). The languages spoken by Australian families, including English, have links to many nations, countries and cultures across the globe. So to understand the language and cultural heritage a child brings to an educational setting it is very important to understand the language or languages and cultures a child brings to an educational setting.

Finding and using resources that may help students to explore the rich cultural heritage of their own and other Australian families is a challenge for all educators which to some extent the introduction of mobile technology has alleviated, for instance, the apps *Neomad* and *Namatjira* provide stories and experiences that help young Australians to connect to and begin to understand something about Aboriginal cultures. The number of languages spoken by Australians and the variety of cultural backgrounds that those languages reflect cannot be easily addressed by an educator. However, the use of mobile technology can allow educators to draw on the cultural and linguistic resources of the child and the child's community.

Technologies which provide multiple languages may support young bilingual learners to feel at ease, use their own language and participate in classroom talk and discussion instead of remaining silent and choosing not to respond

(Cummins, 1986; Krashen, 1992). For families with no English or with low levels of literacy in their own language and or in English, many apps can provide bilingual support (Gibbons, 2006). Parents could be offered lists of educational apps which would allow them to utilise their language as many people will have at least a phone or another device in the home. If it is within the capability of the school, mobile devices, because of their portability, can be loaded with educational apps and provided for loan to students and their families in the same way that books are borrowed from the school library or as described by Gattenhof and Dezuanni (Dezuanni et al., 2015), used in a project which links home and school by lending ipads to students for the project focused around photography.

If the stories in the apps are told in clear voices in English, they provide a great way to develop listening skills and encourage independent reading. Even better if the story is told in more than one language or has captions for bilingual learners. The arts are well supported by apps that promote story telling using both written text and oral storytelling using images and interactive characters. It is the latter that really provide a rich opportunity for cultural and linguistic development. For example, the free app *Playschool Artmaker* provides the characters from the television program *Playschool* and a variety of settings in which an interactive story can be developed using the oral language of those participating. This play can then be video recorded and stored within the app. Because of the mobility of the device, this play could be made at school or at home and shared with a class or family. This ability to connect with parents and caregivers provides an opportunity for educators to interact meaningfully and creatively with a child's community, when they are able to share their own stories in this way (Cummins, Hu, Markus, & Montero, 2015).

The following list of apps provides a range of experiences that involve facets of literacy learning as well as integrate or draw on various elements of the arts. The majority of them are free.

App	**Description**
Explain Everything	A presentation app that allows manipulation of text, pictures, drawing and digital media
Lola's Alphabet Train	Games for learning the alphabet presented in English and multiple languages including Mandarin, Japanese and several European languages
Namatjira	A Big *h*Art project developed with senior members of the Namatjira family. Paint scenes from his country in watercolour
Neomad Interactive Comic	Sci fi adventure series created by Yijala Yala Project in the Pilbara
Playschool Artmaker	Create pictures, animated movies and story slide shows with audio narration and uploading of photos

(*Continued*)

App	Description
Playschool Play Time	Guided play using playschool characters and a clock to guide the choice of play relating to the time of day
Popplet	Record and organise ideas and relationships between them with uploading of pictures
Puppet Pals Puppet Pals 2	Create puppet shows by selecting actors, backdrops and recording voices
Sketches	A drawing app offering a range of styles and drawing tools
Sock Puppets	Create lip synched videos with props, scenery and backgrounds
Story Dice	Story dice provide prompts for ideas for plot, character and setting. Useful for written and oral storytelling
The Room	A mystery game which is useful for stimulating imaginative writing
Toontastic	Draw and animate cartoons. Particularly, useful for looking at elements of narrative and narrative structure
Interactive Stories	
Kidz Story	Interactive fairy tales
Duck in the Truck	Interactive version of the picture book by Jez **Alborough**
Animalia The Waterhole	Interactive versions of the picture books by Graeme **Base**
I Imagine	**Bizzibrains** Personalise this interactive story. Choose characters, voice, appearance and clothing
Blue Hat	Interactive picture book for earlier readers. Other titles by Sandra **Boynton** also available
Dear Zoo	Interactive version of the picture book by Rod **Campbell**
Hairy Maclary from Donaldson's Dairy	Interactive version of the picture book by Lynley **Dodd** *
Olivia Acts Out	Story, video and games from the Olivia series Ian **Falconer**
The Heart and the Bottle	Interactive version of the picture book by Oliver **Jeffers**

(Continued)

App	Description
Miss Spider's Tea Party	Interactive version of the picture book by David **Kirk**
Goodnight Safari	**Polk** Street Press
PopOut! The Tale of Peter Rabbit	Interactive version of the picture book by Beatrix **Potter**
The Wonky Donkey	Interactive version of the picture book by Craig **Smith**
Don't Let the Pigeon Run this App	Based on the books by Mo **Willems**

2.6. Conclusion

This chapter has defined the arts and its relationship to literacy learning, developing insights as to how mobile technologies can be used to support participation in these areas, inside and outside the classroom. It has also explored how literacy and language can be developed through the arts, demonstrated through a gallery of practices relevant to early years contexts. Mobile technologies were presented as an avenue for developing dramatic play as well as being used to support engagement with learning. Engagement is important both in and outside the classroom and the latter sections investigated the ways in which mobile technologies may be used to provide a bridge between home and school. This connection is of special importance for families whose language is not Standard Australian English or when literacy is not well developed. The conclusion presented some resources which are appropriate for supporting literacy and the participation in the arts, as well as engaging and supporting students from a range of contexts and language experiences.

References

Albers, P., & Harste, J. C. (2007). The arts, new literacies, and multimodality. *English Education*, *40*(1), 6−20.

Australian Bureau of Statistics. (2011). *2011 Census Quick Stats*. Retrieved from 278 http://www.censusdata.abs.gov.au/census_services/getproduct/census/2011/quickstat/0

Australian Curriculum Assessment and Reporting Authority (ACARA). (2011). *The Australian Curriculum: English v3.0*. Retrieved from http://www.australiancurriculum.edu.au/English/Rationale

Australian Curriculum Assessment and Reporting Authority (ACARA). (2015). Australian curriculum: The arts-foundation to year 10 7.5. Retrieved from http://www.australiancurriculum.edu.au/download/f10

Australian Government Department of Education; Employment and Workplace Relations. (2009). Belonging, being and becoming: The early years learning frame-work for Australia. Retrieved from https://www.education.gov.au/early-years-learning-framework-0

Barton, G. (2013). The arts and literacy: What does it mean to be arts literate? *International Journal of Education & the Arts, 14*(18), 1−21.

Barton, G., & Baguley, M. (Eds.). (2017). *The Palgrave handbook of global arts education*. London: Palgrave Macmillan UK.

Branscombe, N. A. (2014). *Early childhood curriculum : A constructivist perspective* (2nd ed.). New York, NY: Routledge.

Bright Bot. (2015). My Story. Retrieved from http://mystoryapp.org

Browne, A. (1999). *Voices in the park*. London: Picture Corgi.

Browne, A. (2001). *Willy's pictures*. London: Walker.

Browne, A. (2003). *The shape game*. London: Doubleday.

Burnett, C., & Merchant, G. (2013). Learning, literacies and new technologies: The current context and future possibilities. In J. Larson & J. Marsh (Eds.), *The SAGE handbook of early childhood literacy* (2nd ed., pp. 575−587). London: Sage Publications.

Burnett, C., & Merchant, G. (2017). Opening the case of the iPad: What matters, and where next? *The Reading Teacher, 71*(2), 239−242.

Callow, J. (2005). Literacy and the visual: Broadening our vision. *English Teaching: Practice and Critique, 4*(1), 6−19.

Callow, J. (2013). *The shape of text to come: How image and text work*. Newtown, NSW, Australia: Primary English Teaching Association Australia (PETAA).

Callow, J., Ewing, R., & Rushton, K. (2016). PETAA Paper 206. Two weeks with Oliver Jeffers: Developing early language and literacy with literature. Newtown: PETAA.

Campbell, V. (2013). Playing with storytelling. In R. Ewing (Ed.), *Creative arts in the lives of young children: Play, imagination and learning* (pp. 114−128). Camberwell: ACER Press.

Compton-Lilly, C. (2011). Literacy and schooling in one family acros time. *Research in the Teaching of English, 45*(3), 24−251. doi:849266511

Cummins, J. (1986). Empowering minority students: A framework for intervention. *Harvard Educational Review, 56*(1), 18−36.

Cummins, J., Hu, S., Markus, P., & Montero, M. K. (2015). Identity texts and academic achievement: Connecting the dots in multilingual school contexts. *TESOL Quarterly, 49*(3), Sept 2015, 555−581.

Dewey, J. (1934). *Art as experience*. New York, NY: Minton.

Dezuanni, M., Dooley, K., Gattenhof, S., & Knight, L. (2015). *iPads in the early years: Developing literacy and creativity*. London: Routledge.

Disbray, S. (2008). Storytelling styles: A study of adult-child interactions in narrations of a picture book in Tennant Creek. In J. Simpson & G. Wigglesworth (Eds.), *Children's language andmultilingualism:Indigenous language use at home and school* (pp. 56−78). London: Continuum International Publishing Group.

D'Warte, J. (2014). Exploring lingusitic repertoires: Multiple language use and multimodal literacy activity in five classrooms. *Australian Journal of Language and Literacy, 37*(1), 21-20.

Duck Duck Moose Inc. (2015). Chatterpix: Duck Duck Moose, Inc. Retrieved from http://www.duckduckmoose.com

Eisner, E. W. (2002). *The arts and the creation of mind.* New Haven, CT: Yale University Press.

Ewing, R. (2010). *The arts and Australian education: Realising potential.* Melbourne, Australia: Australian Council for Educational Research.

Ewing, R. (2013). Imaginative play in the lives of young children. In R. Ewing (Ed.), *Creative arts in the lives of young children: Play, imagination and learning* (pp. 7–18). Melbourne: ACER Press.

Ewing, R., Callow, J., & Rushton, K. (2016). *Language and literacy development in early childhood.* Port Melbourne: Cambridge University Press.

Ewing, R., & Saunders, J. N. (2016). *The school drama book: Drama, literature and literacy in the creative classroom.* Sydney: Currency Press.

Ewing, R., & Simons, J. (2016). *Beyond the script 3: Drama in the English & literacy classroom.* Newtown: PETAA.

Explain Everything. (2015). Explain Everything. Retrieved from http://explaineverything.com

Flewitt, R. (2013). Multimodal perspectives on early childhood literacies. In J. Larson & J. Marsh (Eds.), *The SAGE handbook of early childhood literacy* (2nd ed., pp. 295–311). London: Sage Publications.

Freebody, P. (2005). Hindsight and foresight: Putting the four roles model of reading to work in the daily business of teaching. In A. Healy & E. Honan (Eds.), *Text next: New resources for literacy learning* (pp. 3–17). Sydney: Primary English Teaching Association.

Gattenhof, S., & Dezuanni, M. (2015). Arts education and iPads in the early years. In M. Dezuanni, K. Dooley, S. Gattenhof, & L. Knight (Eds.), *IPads in the early years: Developing literacy and creativity* (pp. 30–43). London: Routledge.

Gibbons, P. (2006). *Bridging discourses in the ESL classroom: Students, teachers and researchers.* London: Continuum.

Gibson, R., & Campbell, V. (2013). Playing with puppetry. In R. Ewing (Ed.), *Creative arts in the lives of young children: Play, imagination and learning* (pp. 114–128). Melbourne: ACER Press.

Goodwin, K. (2012). Use of tablet technology in the classroom. *NSW Department of Education and Communities.*

Gravett, E. (2008). *Monkey and me.* London: Macmillan Children's.

Greene, M. (2008). Education and the arts: The windows of imagination. *Learning Landscapes, 2*(1), 17–21.

Halliday, M. A. K. (2004). Three aspects of children's language development: Learning language, learning through language, learning about language. In J. J. Webster (Ed.), *The language of early childhood: M.A.K. Halliday* (pp. 308–326, Ch. 14). New York, NY: Continuum.

Hartle, L., & Jaruszewicz, C. (2009). Rewiring and networking language, literacy, and learning through the arts: Developing fluencies with technology. In M. Narey (Ed.), *Making meaning constructing multimodal perspectives of language, literacy, and learning through arts-based early childhood education* Boston, MA: Springer

US. Retrieved from http://ezproxy.uws.edu.au/login?url=http://dx.doi.org/10.1007/978-0-387-87539-2 SpringerLink

Heath, S. B. (2001). Three's not a crowd: Plans, roles, and focus in the arts. *Educational Researcher, 30*(7), 10–17.

Highfield, K., & Johnson, K. (2013). Do educational apps enhance your child's learning? ABC Health and Wellbeing. A. Retrieved from http://www.abc.net.au/health/talkinghealth/factbuster/stories/2013/10/24/3874488.htm

iMagine Machine Israel LTD. (2017). Faces iMake-Right Brain Creativity: iMagine Machine Israel LTD. Retrieved from https://itunes.apple.com/au/app/faces-imake-right-brain-creativity/id439641851?mt=8

Jewitt, C., Bezemer, J., & O'Halloran, K. (2016). *Introducing multimodality*. New York, NY: Taylor & Francis.

Jones, M. (2012). ipads and kindergarten students literacy development. *SCAN, 31*(4), 31–40.

Jones, P. (Ed.) (1996). *Talking to learn*. Newtown: PETAA.

Karkou, V., & Glasman, J. (2004). Arts, education and society: The role of the arts in promoting the emotional wellbeing and social inclusion of young people. *Support for Learning, 19*(2), 57–65. doi:10.1111/j.0268-2141.2004.00321.x

Kervin, L. (2016). Powerful and playful literacy learning with digital technologies. *Australian Journal of Language and Literacy, 39*(1), 64–73.

Knight, L., & Dooley, K. (2015). Visual arts learning with iPads. In M. Dezuanni, K. Dooley, S. Gattenhof, & L. Knight (Eds.), *IPads in the early years: developing literacy and creativity* (pp. 103–122). London: Routledge.

Krashen, S. (1992). *Fundamentals of language education*. New York, NY: McGraw-Hill.

Kress, G. (2010). *Multimodality: A social semiotic approach to contemporary communication*. London, UK: Routledge.

Kucirkova, N. (2017). How can digital person(ized) books enrich the language arts curriculum? *The Reading Teacher*, 0.0.1–10.

Lankshear, C., & Knobel, M. (2011). *New literacies everyday practices and classroom learning* (3rd ed.). Maidenhead: Open University Press.

Larson, J., & Marsh, J. (2013). *The SAGE handbook of early childhood literacy* (2nd ed.). London: Sage.

Linderman, E. W., & Linderman, M. M. (1984). *Arts & crafts for the classroom* (2nd ed.). New York, London: Macmillan, Collier Macmillan.

Marsh, J. (2013). Early childhood literacy and popular culture. In J. Larson & J. Marsh (Eds.), *The SAGE handbook of early childhood literacy* (2nd ed., pp. 207–223). London: Sage Publications.

Miller, C. S., & Saxton, J. (2004). *Into the story: Language in action through drama*. Portsmouth, NH: Heinemann.

Moll, L., Amanti, C., Neff, D., & Gonzalez, N. (1992). Funds of knowledge for teaching: Using a qualitative approach to connect homes and classrooms. *Theory Into Practice, 31*(2), 132–141. doi:10.1080/00405849209543534

Museum of Modern Art. (2013). MoMA Art Lab: Museum of Modern Art. Retrieved from http://momadesignstudio.org/Art-Lab-App

Narey, M. J. (Ed.). (2017). *Multimodal perspectives of language, literacy, and learning in early childhood : The creative and critical "art" of making meaning*. Pittsburgh, PA: Springer International Publishing.

Neelands, J. (1992). *Learning through imagined experience: The role of drama in the national curriculum*. London: Hodder & Stoughton.

Neumann, M. M., & Neumann, D. L. (2014). Touch screen tablets and emergent literacy. *Early Childhood Education Journal, 42*(4), 231–239. doi:10.1007/s10643-013-0608-3

Painter, C. (2006). Preparing for school: Developing a semantic style for educational knowledge. In. F. Christie (Ed.), *Pedagogy and the shaping of consciousness*. London: Continuum.

Pope, R. (2005). *Creativity: Theory, history, practice*. Abingdon: Routledge.

Red Jumper Limited. (2015). Book creator: Red Jumper Limited. Retrieved from http://www.redjumper.net/bookcreator/

Roskos, K., & Christie, J. (2001). Examining the play–literacy interface: A critical review and future directions. *Journal of Early Childhood Literacy, 1*(1), 59–89. doi:10.1177/14687984010011004

Scripp, L., with Burnadord, G., Bisset, A., Pereira, S., Frost, S., & Yu, G. (2007). *Developing early literacy through the arts (DELTA): A final report*. Chicago, IL: Chicago Arts Partnerships in Education.

Shenfield, R. (2015). Literacy in the arts. *Literacy Learning: The Middle Years, 23*(1), 47–53.

Skutnabb-Kangas, T. (2013). Today's indigenous education is a crime against humanity: Mother tongue based multilingual education as an alternative? *TESOL in Context, 23*(1&2), 82–124.

Smith Micro Software Inc., I. (2015). Sock Puppets. Retrieved from https://itunes.apple.com/us/app/sock-puppets/id394504903?mt=8

Tayasui. (2017). Sketches. Retrieved from http://tayasui.com/sketches/

United Nations. (1989). *Convention on the Rights of the Child*. Retrieved from http://www.austlii.edu.au/cgi-bin/sinodisp/ au/other/dfat/treaties/ATS/1991/4.html

UNESCO. (2006, 6–9 March 2006). Road map for arts education. Paper presented at the World Congress on Arts Education, Lisbon, Portugal.

Winner, E., & Hetland, L. (2000). The arts in education: Evaluating the evidence for a causal link. *Journal of Aesthetic Education, 34*(3/4), 3–10.

Wong Fillmore, L. (1991). When learning a second language means losing the first. *Early Childhood Research Quarterly, 6*(3), 323–346. Retrieved from http://www.sciencedirect.com.ezproxy2.library.usyd.edu.au/science/journal/08852006/6/3

Chapter 3

Introducing Coding as a Literacy on Mobile Devices in the Early Years

Chris Walsh and Claire Campbell

Abstract

This chapter explores how to introduce young children to coding as a literacy using mobile devices. Learning how to code is changing what it means to be literate in the twenty-first century and, increasingly, early years educators are expected to teach young children how to code. The idea that coding is a literacy practice is relatively new, and this chapter first presents strategies for introducing coding without technology. It then explores how to scaffold young children's coding literacy proficiencies through programming and coding robotic toys. When young children have become familiar with coding and solving challenges using concrete materials and robotic toys, it is possible to introduce mobile devices, apps and humanoid robots in playful ways. This chapter explores how this can be done.

Keywords: Coding as a literacy; robotics; mobile technologies; early years; tablets

3.1. Introduction

Increasingly, mobile technologies, particularly touch screen tablets like the iPad, are used to teach literacy in the early years (Aliagas & Margallo, 2017; Bates et al., 2017; Merchant, 2015; Neumann, 2014, 2016; Neumann & Neumann, 2014; Paciga, 2015). Because mobile technologies and apps are used to teach the more traditional literacies of reading and writing (e.g. Moo-O, Aesops Quest, Learn With Homer, Super Hero Comic Book Maker, etc.), it makes sense to use these same technologies to teach young children coding as a literacy practice. The idea that coding is a literacy practice is relatively new, but quickly gaining traction, even in the early years. Australia's Queensland Government (2015) went so far as to state: 'Coding is the new literacy and must have for every student' (p. 5) and, 'The movement to teach coding from the early years through to the senior years of schooling is gaining momentum' (p. 9). Similar movements are underway in Canada, the United Kingdom and Sweden to name a few (Dredge, 2014; Julie, 2017; Roden, 2017). Early years teachers do not generally view coding as a type of literacy similar to reading and writing that is taught across the curriculum but this view will likely change as coding as a literacy practice takes hold and more early years teachers become responsible for teaching coding. Annette Vee (2017) argues:

> Coding is a type of literacy (noun) and programming is re-coding literacy (verb). That is, computer programming is augmenting an already diverse array of communication skills important in everyday life, and because of the computer's primary role in all digital literacies, programming's augmentation of literacy fundamentally reconfigures it. Literacy becomes much larger, and as it grows, the relationships and practices it characterizes change. When literacy includes coding, the ways we experience, teach, and move with our individual skills, social paradigms, communication technologies, and information all shift. (Kindle Locations, pp. 208–211)

When coding is recognised as a literacy, politicians and the public may begin to legitimise supporting it as an educational initiative. This is because the term literacy serves as 'a cipher for the kind of knowledge a society values' (Vee, 2017, Kindle Location 173). When a large education system like Queensland's identifies coding as a 'must have' for all children, early childhood educators will become responsible for teaching coding, even when they may have had no or little preparation and training to do so.

The envisioned place of coding in large school systems as a 'must have', is shaping perceptions of coding as equally important as the literacy practices of reading and writing. Coding is no longer seen as confined to the domain of computer science. Australia's Prime Minister Malcolm Turnbull, similar to a move made by then US President Barack Obama, recently backed Code Club Australia and stated:

> Coding is not just about learning a new skill – it's about learning how to think critically and solve problems…These are the most important skills to have in the 21st century, so I commend Code Club Australia for their very important work and for equipping our children with the skills to have a bright and prosperous future. (Redrup, 2015, para. 6)

Such statements have serious implications for all educators. When governments, politicians and leading technology figures like Bill Gates (Microsoft) and Mark Zukerburg (Facebook) promote learning to code as fundamental, then coding is increasingly viewed as equally important to teach as the literacy practices of reading and writing. Even if educators cannot agree as to whether or not coding is a literacy, Vee (2017) argues that coding 'presents a more complex idea of what literacy *should* be' (2017). In this sense, learning how to code is changing what it means to be literate in the twenty-first century.

When coding is viewed as one of the most important literacy skills or a 'must have' in the twenty-first century, similar to reading and writing, then teaching coding becomes too important to be left to the later years of schooling and computer science clubs that generally operate after school (Hour of Code, Code Club Australia, CoderDojo, Girls Who Code, etc.). Because it is also widely believed that by learning to code, young children engage in computational thinking or critical problem-solving skills and habits (Bers, Flannery, Kazakoff, & Sullivan,2014), the call for early years literacy teachers to also be teachers of coding, is beginning to take hold. Given the media and political rhetoric coupled with the increasing number of coding apps (Code Karts, Think & Learn Code-a-pillar, ScratchJr, etc.) and robotic toys or robots for young children (WowWee Elmoji, Blue-Bot, Cubetto, Kibo, Alpha, etc.), early years educators, by default, are suddenly responsible for introducing the new literacy of coding to young children. However, many of these educators have had limited exposure to the idea that coding is a type of literacy. This is because most early childhood teacher education programmes do not include the teaching of coding as part of literacy subjects and computer science subjects are generally only taught in upper primary and secondary schools. Furthermore, accredited professional development for early years educators around incorporating the teaching of coding into their classrooms is virtually non-existent.

3.2. Introducing Coding as a Literacy in the Early Years

It can be daunting to know where to start when planning and implementing learning experiences to teach young children coding as a literacy, particularly using mobile technologies. Some early years educators do not believe they have the right resources. Others wonder at what point babies, toddlers and young children can begin to grasp not only the foundational concepts of coding but also how to use mobile technologies and their apps. Research highlights that mobile technologies and apps work well in language and literacy teaching (D'Agostino, Rodgers, Harmey, & Brownfield, 2016; Merchant, 2015), but it is not clear how children learn to use mobile technologies through play-based learning (Bird & Edwards, 2015; Edwards, 2016), the basis for pedagogy in the early years. Understanding how to integrate mobile technologies with play-based learning is still largely unexplored in the research literature. The limited research that explores how technological devices impact young children's play highlights that it is often negative (Smirnova, 2011), or works to bring about new forms of play (Bird & Edwards, 2015).

This chapter provides an example of how mobile technologies can be used to teach the literacy of coding within a holistic play-based approach that supports the latter. Central to this approach is using mobile technologies to teach young children coding *after* using concrete resources such as symbol cards and robotic toys to teach the fundamental concepts of coding as a literacy through play. This chapter advocates using these resources in the first instance with small groups of children, rather than starting with children using mobile technologies on their own. This is because using mobile devices such as tablets or phones to teach coding as a literacy, without scaffolding from more capable others, may impede children from actively engaging with other children and the educator, as well as objects and representations foundational to play-based learning. The approach outlined here is designed to teach children foundational understandings of coding as a literacy through computational thinking or problem solving, intrinsic motivation, exploration, cause and effect, problematising and social interaction (Verenikina & Kervin, 2011) in technologies-rich early years environments.

For early years educators to feel motivated and confident to use mobile technologies to teach coding as a literacy, they first need an introduction to the basics of coding. They also need information that explains how teaching coding as a literacy dovetails with play-based learning and teaching other forms of literacy aligned with local, state and national curriculum documents. This chapter aims to first explore play-based learning strategies educators can use *without* mobile technologies to teach young children the fundamentals of coding as a literacy through inquiry-based education (Campbell & Walsh, 2017; Wang, Kinzie, McGuire, & Pan, 2010). These play-based learning experiences provide the foundation for the later use of mobile technologies, particularly tablets and smartphones, to engage in the more sophisticated block coding of humanoid robots and using programmes like Scratch Jr (Massachusetts Institute of Technology and Tufts University, 2004). ScratchJr is a popular app that teaches young children foundational coding and programming concepts to design their own interactive stories and games on tablets. Recent research highlights the success of using ScratchJr to not only keep young children engaged and exploring coding to solve problems but also the fundamental process of programming (Portelance, Strawhacker, & Bers, 2016).

The sections that follow draw on research conducted with pre-service Bachelor of Education (Early Childhood Education) students and Early Childhood educators in Australia and Singapore. Illustrations are provided to assist educators in integrating coding in ways that are playful. The chapter aims to be practical and provides ideas that can be taken up or adapted across global settings with the goal of building educators' confidence and capabilities to teach coding as a literacy. The chapter also illustrates how educators can introduce coding as a literacy in much the same way they introduce the literacy practices of reading, writing and viewing.

3.3. Starting with the Child and Introducing Coding as a Literacy

Introducing young children to coding as a literacy can be achieved with nothing more than the children themselves, symbols printed on laminated paper cards and the educator. Something as familiar as a challenge to successfully navigate an obstacle course can be a computational foundation for understanding how coding as a literacy or 'symbols and pattern systems' work (COAG, 2009, p. 43). In numerous early childhood education and care (ECEC) services around the world, the use of an obstacle course is common. In these settings, educators often complement their obstacle courses with some variation of A4-sized symbol cards that act to support children in understanding the directions 'forward', 'backward', 'left', 'right', 'hop' and 'jump'. Using printed symbols to provide directions is similar to sequenced instructions. The symbol cards provide information to children about what direction they need to head in to successfully navigate the obstacle course. Teaching coding as a literacy builds on this idea and uses the symbols (←↑→↓) that children will later encounter as buttons on top of the Blue-Bot robot. In this way, children can become familiar with aspect of Blue-Bot's programming language before they begin using the robots (Figure 3.1). Educators begin teaching coding as a literacy when they initiate a group discussion on what the symbols are, and what they might be used for. Children and educators then take turns role-playing what actions the symbols on the various cards might represent. The focus is on exploring, having a go, inquiring and making hypotheses to be tested out. Children can then go on to incorporate these symbol cards in their play, for example, in the sandpit, while using chalk on concrete or together with blocks. Children are also encouraged to incorporate the symbols into their play just as they would use traffic signs and other symbols. By completing this first, very simple, step of presenting and discussing the symbol cards, educators have familiarised children with simple code

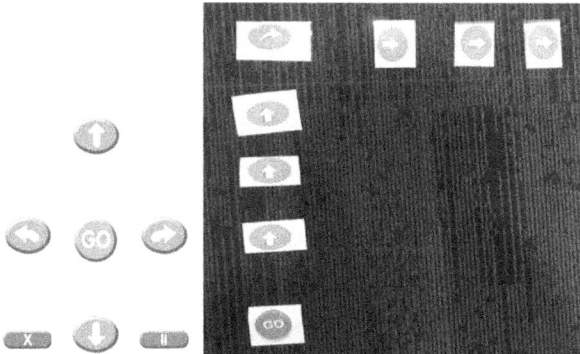

Figure 3.1: Blue-Bot Programming Language on Educator-made Laminated Symbol Cards.

and a programming language that provides instructions. This is a foundational understanding of coding as a literacy.

Once children understand that the symbols represent actions and give directions to move a certain way, educators can support them to apply what they know to 'write' a programme for themselves to follow in the familiar context of the classroom. At this point, the educator provides explicit support to the child and uses the concrete materials of the symbol cards to scaffold their understanding. Afterwards, children are given a simple design brief: 'Use the symbol cards to make yourself move like a robot'. Young children are supported to 'write' code by placing up to three symbols (for very young children) or seven symbols (for early primary school children) in a sequence. Then they follow the code or programme by moving in the directions on the cards like a robot in a playful manner using sounds they imagine a robot makes.

In follow-up sessions, the children are further challenged when presented with the design brief: 'Use the symbol cards to make your friend move like a robot'. Design briefs work extremely well for introducing coding as a literacy as part of playful inquiry and challenge-based approaches to early childhood education. In the examples above, the design brief outlines the activity and provides specification. But it also allows educators to combine guided play and adult-led learning with child-directed play and learning. Using this or a similar approach, early years educators can plan and implement three to ten sessions on teaching young children coding as a literacy using the programming language of the Blue-Bot robotic toy. This sequence scaffolds young children's learning, enabling them to more readily transfer their coding as a literacy practices to robotic toys and mobile devices. It is critical that young children experience tangible coding, through the concrete symbol cards, which can be seen, touched and moved. Learning to code a robot like Blue-Bot – without first manipulating 'code you can touch' – can be difficult for young children because it's too abstract. The children cannot 'see' the code once they've pushed the buttons on top of the Blue-Bot. They also cannot watch the Blue-Bot execute the coded sequence they entered alongside the symbols, nor understand how their coding was entered incorrectly if the Blue-Bot does not go where they wanted it go.

3.4. Introducing Robots to Teach Coding as a Literacy

The introduction of robotics, although still largely unexplored in early years settings except for a few small studies (Bers, 2010; Bers et al., 2014; Kazakoff, Sullivan & Bers, 2013), offers a concrete way of introducing literacy as coding to young children. Following on from using the symbol cards with design briefs and moving from the familiar to the more unfamiliar, the next set of lessons would introduce children to Blue-Bot and its already familiar programming language from the previously discussed activities. Initiating a discussion about the additional 'Go', 'Clear' and 'Pause' button allows children to draw on their out-of-school digital literacies knowledge and practices with mobile devices and other technologies to hypothesise what these buttons or commands may mean.

3.5. Moving from the Symbol Cards to Blue-Bot Robots

Similar to the lesson with the flash cards, children are given a design brief where they explore coding as a literacy through play. The open-ended design brief, 'Play with Blue-Bot and make it move,' provides children with opportunities to transfer their prior knowledge of coding using the concrete symbol cards to a new context, coding a robot using its symbol buttons. Blue-Bots are by far the cheapest and most common robot in early years settings, so they are illustrated here. Through play-based learning, children can discover, create, improvise and imagine as they play with the Blue-Bot, other children and the educator to hypothesise, code and then test out their ideas and programming. They also collaborate in playful ways to challenge each other's thinking and build new extended understandings about coding as a literacy. As children play with the Blue-Bots, educators should regularly prompt them to explain what they are doing and what they are thinking as they interweave the language of computer science. Children's talk is supported and extended by educators to foster deeper understandings of the literacy practices of coding. When a child explains, 'I pressed the buttons and then pressed the green button and the Blue-Bot went over there', the educator can respond by paraphrasing and helping children to deepen their thought processes: 'You did an excellent job of programming the Blue-Bot to turn left then right, then go straight ahead to get to where it is now. That was an excellent program'! In working with early years practitioners it is common to witness children picking up the language of computer science quickly as they confidently state, 'I coded the Blue-Bot to go over there'!

When early years educators use design briefs and robots this way, they are creating a play-based learning context where young children begin to move from the familiar and concrete, to the unfamiliar and abstract as they learn to code Blue-Bot through fun, hands-on experiences. This is then followed up with more detailed and challenging design briefs that ask children to, 'Make a program for the Blue-Bot to travel from the wall to the bookshelf' using the same print flashcards or the Blue-Bot TacTile Reader. The TacTile Reader is a hands-on device that allows the children to programme a sequence of moves in much the same way they would with the symbol cards. The reader is a unique, tactile programming device to control Blue-Bot with tiles representing each Blue-Bot command. Importantly, educators always ask the children to verbalise what and how they made Blue-Bot move. By using design briefs as part of play-based learning, early years educators can plan carefully sequenced, scaffolded, purposeful, and playful teaching and learning experiences through and with robots. Playing with the robots, inputting programs by pressing the buttons and simply engaging with the device (whether as a robot, as a toy, or otherwise) are examples of children familiarising themselves with digital devices, developing their understandings of robots, and learning how to code or the literacy practices of coding.

3.6. Cubetto and Kibo – Robots with Concrete Code that Children can Touch

Following well-established notions of best practice in early childhood, this approach to teaching coding as a literacy as outlined in this chapter has a strong focus on using concrete, tangible materials to support young children in building their fluency in coding as a literacy practice. This is because coding robots like Blue-Bot, without the use of cards or the tactile reader as a visual guide, is too abstract a practice for young children. As noted above, once the child has pressed the buttons and entered the code, there is no 'written' code for them to see or look at as they watch the Blue-Bot execute the programme. If the Blue-Bot does not go where the child planned, figuring out the coding mistake is not easy without a visual reference; it is important for young children to be able to see the code or programme they have inputted. Having access to perceptual cues and concrete materials is how children learn best (Baldwin, 1980; Ginsburg & Opper, 1988; Piaget, 1970). For this reason, the Cubetto (Primo Toys, 2017) and Kibo (KinderLab Robotics, 2017) robots (Images 3 and 4) are well suited to introduce young children to coding as a literacy.

Cubetto is a screen-free, app-free, Montessori-approved, friendly-looking robot that is based upon a classic early childhood resource, the wooden block. Many young children are drawn to Cubetto and find the robot and its control panel easy to use (see Figure 3.2). Cubetto does not require children to have the ability to read or be proficient in a particular coding language to use it as part of their play. Cubetto requires no set-up or preparation. The pack from Promo Toys includes the Cubetto robot, a control board, coding tiles, a fabric map, an instruction booklet and an educational story booklet that matches the mat. Therefore, early years educators can quickly and easily introduce Cubetto into their settings. Cubetto's educational story booklet is a useful resource as

Figure 3.2: A Young Child, Cubetto, Mat, Control Panel and Coding Tiles.

educators can read the story that matches the images on the mat (e.g. *Cubetto' class trip* and *Cubetto leaves Earth*) to scaffold children to programme Cubetto to move around the mat as they read the story. This is a useful combination of traditional and new literacies in action. Children can enjoy the familiar literacy of reading a book and at the same time they can begin to experience coding as a literacy in a subtle, seamless and playful manner. While the storybook included with Cubetto is carefully crafted to teach educators and children how to use Cubetto, the traditional storybook and coding as a literacy practice partnership is a valuable one to build upon. For example, educators could innovate upon this idea and co-construct new stories with children to match the mat included with Cubetto or the other maps available for purchase. Educators and children can also design their own bespoke mats that illustrate familiar places like where the children live to scaffold their coding as a literacy learning. This teaching and learning experience powerfully combines traditional and new literacies, encourages children to think creatively, hypothesise and problem solve, all while discreetly developing their understandings of robots, computational thinking, and coding literacy practices. To programme Cubetto, children place the coding blocks on the control board, which is self-correcting in that the light beside the block will only illuminate if the blocks have been inserted correctly. Children are able to easily plan, review, edit, execute, and then reflect upon their programming as it is visible and tangible. The panel has also been designed so children can explore coding loops or a sequence of code.

Kibo (KinderLab Robotics, 2017) is also a screen-free and app-free robot, but it is more 'robotic' in its appearance and functionality than those described above. Kibo is available in a variety of kits, with the main components being the robot with an inbuilt scanner and sensors and programming blocks with a barcode that is read by Kibo's scanner. Kibo is similar to the early childhood classic wooden block in that its programming blocks are wooden, and they have the ability to link together to form a sequence that children can look at, reflect upon and manipulate. Kibo's programming blocks, while tangible, are more advanced than the coding tiles included with Cubetto. They are more complex as they have an image, a barcode and text on them. Therefore, it is critical that young children are supported to understand what the images and text mean. Kibo's programming blocks also cover a wider range of functions including conditional blocks such as 'wait for clap' and 'end if'. With Kibo, young children learn more advanced concepts such as cause-and-effect, sequencing and loops though a hands-on approach. To effectively and independently use Kibo, children need to possess a reasonable level of fine motor control and hand/eye coordination. Kibo's inbuilt scanner needs to be placed within close proximity to the blocks, and progressively moved along each block in the sequence, to read each block and sequence the series of commands to create a programme for Kibo. To programme Kibo, children place the programming blocks in a sequence, which must feature the 'start' and 'end' blocks at the appropriate place. As they do this, they are actively engaged in coding as a literacy practices to author a bespoke programme. Then, the children move Kibo to scan the barcode on each block using the inbuilt scanner. Once all blocks have been scanned, children press the green light button (which only lights up if the robot has been programmed correctly) and Kibo will execute the programme. Similar to Cubetto, with Kibo, children are able to easily plan, review, edit, execute, and then reflect upon their programming as it is visible and tangible on the wooden programming blocks. While empirical research is yet to be conducted on children's use of Cubettos and Kibo, the principles and practices underpinning the design of these products aligns with the play-based pedagogies of early childhood as well as teaching coding as a literacy.

3.7. Coding as Literacy with a Mobile Device

When young children have become familiar with coding and solving challenges using concrete materials, design briefs and robotic toys like Blue-Bot, Cubetto and Kibo, the next step is to introduce mobile devices, apps and more advanced robots in playful ways. In moving from the concrete to the more abstract, educators embark on teaching more advanced coding as literacy practices when they introduce mobile devices and block coding. The use of humanoid robots works extremely well with young children because children enjoy not only using tablets to control the robot but also watching how the robot does much more than move forwards, backwards and make turns. Humanoid robots dance perform martial arts and even demonstrate yoga moves children can then practice in unison with the robot, their educators and each other.

Alpha 1 (UBTECH, 2017) is a reasonably affordable humanoid robot ($799 AU) that works well within a play-based learning approach. Alpha is easily programmed through the use of the Alpha1 app on an Apple or Android mobile devices (Figure 3.3). Unlike Cubetto and Kibo, the programming of Alpha 1 requires familiarisation with mobile devices. Working with early childhood educators in Australia, the authors of this chapter witnessed young children responding very positively to Alpha 1 as they learned more advanced coding.

Figure 3.3: Children Programming Alpha to Dance.

With its human-like features, children often connect with Alpha 1 as a friend or classroom companion and sometimes give it a name. There are three key ways that Alpha can be used to teach coding in the early years. Young children can physically move parts of Alpha, such as manipulating Alpha's arm up and then down again and then adding the action to a sequence or programme they can execute on Alpha using the tablet. A second way young children can code Alpha 1 is by selecting the icons or pictorial representations of Alpha 1 doing a 'kick', 'wave', 'salute', 'dance move' and so on. When the child touches the icon, Alpha demonstrates the movement and then the child can decide whether or not to add it to a sequence or programme of moves. Finally, similar to the block coding used by the ScratchJr app, young children can 'snap' together graphical programming blocks to make characters move, jump, dance and sing (for example, 'walk' for '10 seconds' at the speed of 'fast').

When children already possess coding literacy skills, they can transfer this prior knowledge to coding Alpha 1 on their mobile devices. A simple and effective design brief for children learning to code Alpha using a mobile device is, 'Meet Alpha and identify and describe its features'. Once young children are familiar with Alpha, its head, arms, legs and the mobile device (tablet or smartphone) that controls it, they can be given a design brief that includes some engaging and meaningful links to their lifeworlds to ensure sensitivity to, and inclusion of, their abilities, interests and learning needs. A design brief that has worked well with Australian early childhood educators observed by the authors of this chapter is: 'Program Alpha 1 to dance', after outlining a problem or challenge for the children to solve:

> Yesterday I was talking with my friend Alpha and she was very, very sad. She told me he had been invited to a holiday party, but she was worried about going to the party. I was surprised and asked Alpha why she was worried about going because that sounds like something really fun to do! Alpha then explained she did not know how to dance. I told Alpha I know some children in my Early Learning Centre classroom who know how to program dance using an iPad. I also told Alpha I think they would really like to help her learn a new dance. What do you think? Do you think we can help Alpha learn a new dance for the party using your coding skills and the app on the iPad?

This scenario was immediately engaging – the children were excited to programme Alpha 1 to dance and use the app on the tablet. Young children anywhere can complete this challenge-based design brief using any of the three ways that Alpha can be coded. For introductory teaching and learning experiences, it can be helpful to start with Alpha 1's second coding method, the selection of icons and symbols that indicate particular movements that Alpha can do. The continuity of the use of symbols is a helpful scaffold for children who are learning to code on mobile devices.

When completing the design brief, 'Program Alpha to dance', children can be scaffolded to first select a song they like from Alpha 1's music library. On the mobile device interface, there is an icon with a musical note on it and, in observations of classroom practice conducted in writing this chapter, almost every child instantly recognised this as the icon to tap on to choose and listen to one of Alpha's songs. Once children listened to and selected a song, they added the one that they liked to the programme sequence which displays across the bottom of the screen (Figure 3.3). Most children then readily recognised the 'action' icon as the one to select in order to sequence a variety of actions that will comprise Alpha 1's dance programme. The design of the app is intuitive in that children select a move based on a photograph of Alpha doing the move. However, unless the action is added to the programme sequence by children pressing the 'add' button on-screeen, the action won't appear in Alpha 1's execution of the programme. That is, if children cannot see the icon in the sequence displayed at the bottom of the screen, the move is not included in the programme. This functionality provides children with valuable opportunities to preview, predict, hypothesise, reflect upon and edit their programme before, during and after Alpha's execution of it.

It is not mandatory for children to first experience the earlier teaching and learning experiences facilitated through the challenge-based design briefs of the play-based learning approach described in this chapter to experience success in using mobile devices to learn coding. However, children who do have relevant knowledge and skills to draw upon, as well as confidence and familiarity with using robotic toys first, will be better placed to experience success when coding with mobile devices. There is an increasing need for young children to acquire coding as a literacy proficiency prior to school, as part of successfully transitioning to school. The approach outlined in this chapter provides early years educators with a viable means of supporting children to learn coding in playful ways that are simultaneously sensitive and responsive to them and their lifeworlds.

3.8. Conclusion

Learning to code robots in prior to school settings provides young children with twenty-first century skills that include coding as a literacy practice. Through learning the literacy practice of coding, in much the same way they learn the literacy practices of reading and writing, young children also develop computational thinking skills where they engage in problem-solving (Lawanto, Close, Ames, & Brasiel, 2017). As has been illustrated in this chapter, learning to code on mobile devices can be scaffolded for young children by teaching coding as a literacy with symbol cards and robotic toys before they are introduced to mobile devices. Young children need ongoing play-based opportunities coupled and intentional teaching of technologies (Edwards, 2017; Razfar & Gutiérrez, 2013), including coding as a literacy. This will not only assist them in becoming familiar with a range of hardware and software but also in understanding that coding is an important communication skill—like reading and writing—in their everyday lives (Vee, 2017). The recognition that children need ongoing play-based opportunities with technologies signals that early childhood educators need to create equally technologies-rich environments, similar to print-rich environments. Digital technologies knowledge, understanding and skills, such as the literacy of coding, will form the foundation of the digital literacies practices that young children will draw upon as they transition to school. Critically, introducing early years learners to coding as a literacy through and with robotics provides a catalyst to introduce them computational thinking, algorithmic thinking and project management. Incorporating coding literacy into the early years can help educators to 'turn around' to technologies and children (Walsh & Kamler, 2013) in ways that positively challenge reported lack of progress with regard to early years educators' use of technology in the curriculum (Lui, 2016; Thorpe et al., 2015).

The demands of the twenty-first century and expanding understandings of literacy, including coding as a literacy, signals the need for a shift in early year educators' professional identities. Early year educators need to view themselves as teachers of the literacy practices of coding in much the same way they teach the literacy practices of reading and writing. Teaching the coding as a literacy invites early years educators to take on new roles and interactions with children that connect their playful activities to content-based technologies knowledge and skills. By incorporating mobile devices and robotics into their teaching repertoires, early years educators can create technologies-rich environments that place children's digital play at the centre, with the goal of assisting them to acquire coding as a literacy proficiencies. Teaching coding as a literacy is not an add-on to the teaching and learning of conventional literacies; rather, it is an expansion of literacy education to incorporate the new literacy of coding on children's terms, as part of their play.

References

Aliagas, C., & Margallo, A. M. (2017). Children's responses to the interactivity of storybook apps in family shared reading events involving the iPad. *Literacy*, *51*(1), 44–52. doi:10.1111/lit.12089

Baldwin, A. L. (1980). *Theories of child development* (2nd ed.). New York, NY: John Wiley & Sons.

Bates, C. C., Klein, A., Schubert, B., McGee, L., Anderson, N., Dorn, L., ... Ross, R. H. (2017). E-Books and E-Book apps: Considerations for beginning readers. *The Reading Teacher*, *70*(4), 401–411. doi:10.1002/trtr.1543

Bers, M., Flannery, L., Kazakoff, E., & Sullivan, A. (2014). Computational thinking and tinkering: Exploration of an early childhood robotics curriculum. *Computers & Education*, *72*, 145–157. doi:10.1016/j.compedu.2013.10.02

Bers, M. U. (2010). The TangibleK robotics program: Applied computational thinking for young children. *Early Childhood Research and Practice*, *12*(2). Retrieved from http://ecrp.uiuc.edu/v12n2/bers.html

Bird, J., & Edwards, S. (2015). Children learning to use technologies through play: A digital play framework. *British Journal of Educational Technology*, *46*(6), 1149–1160. doi:10.1111/bjet.12191

Campbell, C., & Walsh, C. (2017). Introducing the 'new' digital literacy of coding in the early years. *Practical Literacy*, *22*(3), 10–12.

COAG. (2009). Belonging, being becoming: The early years learning framework for Australia. Retrieved from http://files.acecqa.gov.au/files/National-Quality-Framework-Resources-kit/belonging_being_and_becoming_the_early_years_learning_framework_for_australia.pdf

D'Agostino, J. V., Rodgers, E., Harmey, S., & Brownfield, K. (2016). Introducing an iPad app into literacy instruction for struggling readers: Teacher perceptions and student outcomes. *Journal of Early Childhood Literacy*, *16*(4), 522–548. doi:10.1177/1468798415616853

Dredge, S. (2014, September 4). Coding at school: A parent's guide to England's new computing curriculum. *The Guardian*. Retrieved from https://www.theguardian.com/technology/2014/sep/04/coding-school-computing-children-programming

Edwards, S. (2016). New concepts of play and the problem of technology, digital media and popular-culture integration with play-based learning in early childhood education. *Technology, Pedagogy and Education*, *25*(4), 513–532. doi:10.1080/1475939X.2015.1108929

Edwards, S. (2017, Jun) Play-based learning and intentional teaching: Forever different? [online]. *Australasian Journal of Early Childhood*, *42*(2), 4–11. Retrieved from https://search.informit.com.au/documentSummary;dn=946162091280073;res=IELAPA

Ginsburg, H., & Opper, S. (1988). *Piaget's theory of intellectual development* (3rd ed.). Upper Saddle River, NJ: Prentice Hall.

Julie, A. (2017, August 24). Teaching coding in Canadian schools: How do the provinces measure up? Global News. Retrieved from https://globalnews.ca/news/3693932/teaching-coding-in-canadian-schools-how-do-the-provinces-measure-up/

Kazakoff, E. R., Sullivan, A., & Bers, M. U. (2013). The effect of a classroom-based intensive robotics and programming workshop on sequencing ability in early childhood. *Early Childhood Education Journal*, *41*(4), 245–255. doi:10.1007/s10643-012-0554-5

KinderLab Robotics. (2017). *Kibo [Robotic toy]*. Retrieved from http://kinderlabrobotics.com/kibo/. Accessed on September 3, 2018.

Lawanto, K., Close, K., Ames, C., & Brasiel, S. (2017). Exploring Strengths and Weaknesses in Middle School Students' Computational Thinking in Scratch. *In Emerging Research, Practice, and Policy on Computational Thinking* (pp. 307–326). Springer International Publishing.

Lui, P. (2016). Technology integration in elementary classrooms: Teaching practices of student teachers. *Australian Journal of Teacher Education*, *41*(3). Retrieved from http://ro.ecu.edu.au/cgi/viewcontent.cgi?article=3020&context=ajte. Accessed on September 3, 2018.

Merchant, G. (2015). Keep taking the tablets: IPads, story apps and early literacy. *Australian Journal of Language and Literacy, the*, *38*(1), 3–11.

Neumann, M. M. (2014). An examination of touch screen tablets and emergent literacy in Australian pre-school children. *Australian Journal of Education*, *58*(2), 109–122. doi:10.1177/0004944114523368

Neumann, M. M. (2016). Young children's use of touch screen tablets for writing and reading at home: Relationships with emergent literacy. *Computers & Education*, *97*, 61–68. doi:10.1016/j.compedu.2016.02.013

Neumann, M. M., & Neumann, D. L. (2014). Touch screen tablets and emergent literacy. *Early Childhood Education Journal*, *42*(4), 231–239. doi:10.1007/s10643-013-0608-3

Paciga, K. A. (2015). Their teacher can't be an app: Preschoolers' listening comprehension of digital storybooks. *Journal of Early Childhood Literacy*, *15*(4), 473–509. doi:10.1177/1468798414552510

Piaget, J. (1970). *The origin of intelligence in the child* (3rd ed.). London: Routledge and Kegan Paul Ltd.

Portelance, D. J., Strawhacker, A. L., & Bers, M. U. (2016). Constructing the ScratchJr programming language in the early childhood classroom. *International Journal of Technology and Design Education*, *26*(4), 489–504. doi:10.1007/s10798-015-9325-0

Primo Toys. (2017). *Cubetto [Robotic toy]*. Retrieved from https://www.primotoys.com/. Accessed on September 3, 2018.

Queensland Government. (2015). *#codingcounts. A discussion paper on coding and robotics in Queensland schools*. Retrieved from http://advancingeducation.qld.gov.au/sitecollectiondocuments/coding-and-robotics-booklet.pdf. Accessed on September 3, 2018.

Razfar, A., & Gutiérrez, K. (2013). Reconceptualizing early childhood literacy: the sociocultural influence and new directions in digital and hybrid mediation. In J. Larson & J. Marsh (Eds.). *The SAGE handbook of early childhood literacy* (pp. 52–79). London: SAGE Publications Ltd. doi:10.4135/9781446247518.n4

Redrup, Y. (2015, November 9). *Malcolm Turnbull backs Code Club Australia. Financial Review*. Retrieved from https://www.afr.com/technology/malcolm-turnbull-backs-code-club-australia-20151106-gksfux. Accessed on September 3, 2018.

Roden, L. (2017, March 13). Swedish kids to learn computer coding and how to spot fake news in primary school. *The Local SE*. Retrieved from https://www.thelocal.se/20170313/swedish-kids-to-learn-computer-coding-and-how-to-spot-fake-news-in-primary-school

Smirnova, E. (2011). Character toys as psychological tools. *International Journal of Early Years Education*, *19*(1), 35–43.

Thorpe, K., Hansen, J., Danby, S., Davidson, C., Zaki, F. M., Grant, S., … Given, L. M. (2015). Teachers, teaching and digital technologies: reports from the early childhood classroom. *Early Childhood Research Quarterly*, *32*, doi:10.1016/j.ecresq.2015.04.001

UBTECH. (2017). *Alpha 1* [Robotic toy]. Retrieved from https://ubtrobot.com/pages/alpha. Accessed on September 3, 2018.

Vee, A. (2017). *Coding literacy: How computer programming is changing writing* [Kindle version 1.2.1]. Retrieved from Amazon.com.uk

Verenikina, I., & Kervin, L. (2011). iPads, Digital Play and Preschoolers. *He Kupu*, *2*(5 (eJournal)), 4–19.

Walsh, C. S., & Kamler, B. (2013). Teacher research on literacy: Turning around to students and technology. In K. Hall, T. Cremin, B. Comber, & L. Moll (Eds.),

International handbook of research in children's literacy, learning and culture (p. 499). Oxford: Wiley Blackwell. doi:10.1002/9781118323342.ch36

Wang, F., Kinzie, M. B., McGuire, P., & Pan, E. (2010). Applying technology to inquiry-based learning in early childhood education. *Early Childhood Education Journal, 37*(5), 381–389. doi:10.1007/s10643-009-0364-6

Chapter 4

Digital Storytelling as a Pedagogy to Develop Literacy and Twenty-first Century Competencies in a Singapore Primary School: Teachers as Designers

Mohamed Melwani, Lee Yong Tay and Cher Ping Lim

Abstract

This chapter reports on an ethnographic case study of how a group of elementary school teachers designed technology enhanced learning with mobile technology (e.g. notebooks, tablet computers and mobile phones) to facilitate students' development of literacy and twenty-first century competencies. These teachers designed the school's literacy pedagogical approach, leveraging the use of technology, namely digital storytelling. The school in this case study is one of the eight Future Schools in Singapore under the FutureSchools@Singapore program. The school has been providing one-to-one mobile computing learning devices and wireless Internet access for its students. The introduction of technology in the classroom makes it possible for twenty-first century competencies to be integrated into literacy development. The conversational framework is used as a framework to examine how the design of the digital storytelling pedagogical approach brings about the various teaching—learning activities — acquisition, inquiry, practice, production, discussion and collaboration. The use of digital storytelling as an approach to integrate information communication technology (ICT) into the classroom has not only modified how ICT is being used in the school, it has redefined how ICT could be used to engage young learners. It has fundamentally transformed conventional storytelling with the use of current state-of-the-shelf (i.e. easily and widely available) technologies. This case study also outlines the processes involved in improving the design of digital storytelling over the years by the teachers. The ecosystem of the school is also taken into consideration and described in detail. Findings suggest the importance of the collaborative efforts of the teachers in the continuous improvements made to this design. The adoption of a learning design framework, such as the one used in this study, can be beneficial to ensure a systematic approach to the design of learning. In addition, the availability of technological infrastructure and computing devices are necessary for the seamless use of technology in the classroom. The just-in-time learning approach is adopted for students to learn technology as they are developing their digital stories.

Keywords: Case study; ICT integration; design thinking; teaching-learning activities; future school; literacy; SAMR Model

4.1. Introduction

Over the past two decades, information communication technology (ICT) has permeated many aspects of our daily activities – in the social aspect, commercial and banking realm and the education arena. Educational institutions at the different levels, from elementary to tertiary, have been looking into ways to integrate ICT into teaching and learning.

This chapter reports on an ethnographic case study of how teachers from an elementary school in Singapore design writing tasks for lower and middle elementary students, incorporating the use of ICT. The teachers in the study adopted digital storytelling (Lambert, 2013) as a pedagogy to develop students' literacy and twenty-first century competencies. Literacy and twenty-first century skills are different from those in the twentieth century, largely due to the emergence of very sophisticated information and communications technologies (Dede, 2010). Students require additional skills and competencies, such as digital literacy and twenty-first century skills to navigate effectively in this new era. Creativity and innovation; communication and collaboration; information and research fluency; critical thinking, problem-solving and decision making; digital citizenship and wellness; digital literacy and understanding of technological operations and concepts are competencies that are associated with twenty-first century skills (NCREL, 2003; OECD, 2005; P21, 2006).

4.2. Digital Storytelling

There are a number of different definitions of digital storytelling. In essence, they all revolve around the idea of combining the art of storytelling with available multimedia tools – digital images, audio, video, animation and web publishing (Ohler, 2013; Robin, 2008; Robin & Pierson, 2005).

Digital storytelling is not a new concept: Joe Lambert and the late Dana Atchley helped create the digital storytelling movement in the late 1980s as co-founders of the Centre for Digital Storytelling, a non-profit, community arts organisation in Berkeley, California. Since the early 1990s, it has provided training and assistance to people interested in creating and sharing their personal narratives (Robin, 2008, p. 222). The Centre for Digital Storytelling developed seven elements of digital storytelling — point of view or the perspective of the author; a dramatic question to be answered in the story; emotional content to be put across in a personal and powerful way; the gift of your voice to better personalise the story; the power of soundtrack to further enhance the mood and tone; and economy as in keeping it simple and pacing the speed. Students learn how to gather, comprehend and synthesise information; to communicate their ideas and stories through words, images and music; and to use technology to enhance efficiency and impact when they create their stories.

In an international survey research involving 22 countries that looked into the educational uses of digital storytelling around the world, Yuksel, Robin, and McNeil (2011) highlighted the following benefits of digital storytelling — reflection, language, higher level thinking, social and artistic skills. According to this survey, digital storytelling can give students opportunities to construct their own understanding or experience in a content area, facilitate collaborative activities and discussion in small group, learn problem-solving and critical thinking skills, understand complex ideas and learn new content.

In addition, Di Blas and Paolini (2013) reported similar educational gains in another large-scale digital storytelling initiative that included students from pre-school to high school in Italy. The initiative made use of a locally designed, simple and easy-to-use online platform for students across the grade levels to create their digital stories, either individually or collaboratively. The online system allowed for student–teacher and student–student consultation and collaboration. This project highlighted the possibility of a more collaborative type of digital storytelling facilitated by the online platform where students and teachers did not need to be physically present in a formal school setting to engage in group and collaborative work.

Although there are reported educational benefits and gains, several concerns are raised when teachers use digital storytelling in their classrooms. First, students need to be taught to respect the copyrights of the resources found online. Second, access to technological hardware, software applications and Internet connection need to be considered. Finally, more time might be needed for the production of the stories in digital formats than by conventional means (Robin, 2008). More importantly, it is important to remind ourselves that the primary focus is on the storytelling and the technology is secondary (Banaszewski, 2002). The problem for many students is their focus on the power of the technology rather than the power of their stories. Some students are engaging the medium at the expense of the message, producing a technical event rather than a story (Ohler, 2006, p. 45).

4.3. Background

The school in this case study research was one of the three elementary-level future schools in Singapore that started its operations in 2008. The FutureSchools@

Singapore program was a joint project between the local Ministry of Education and Info-communications Media Development Authority. The main purpose of the project was to have schools pervasively use and leverage technology for teaching and learning. Useful practices and practical insights were then shared with the fraternity, locally and overseas.

The school started with 240 Primary 1 students (six to seven year olds) in its first year (in 2008); it then gradually took in new students every year. With the constant addition of each cohort of students, the school reached its steady state of enrolment at about 1,400 students (i.e. a total of six grade levels – Primary 1–6) in 2013, with more than 120 teaching and non-teaching staff supporting its daily operations. The school has implemented a one-to-one computing ownership programme where students are encouraged to own and use their computing devices in school and at home for school-related work. The school has also been using digital storytelling as an approach to engage its lower and middle grades students in writing and creating their own stories since 2008. The teachers at the school have been engaged in practitioner research and have been recording and evaluating the teaching practices with ICT as part of their professional development efforts over the years. Several teaching staff at the school have shared and published articles with regard to the use of digital storytelling for students' learning of literacy and twenty-first century skills – the use of collaborative digital storytelling in the teaching of Chinese mother tongue classes (Ng, Chai, Wen, & Lim, 2010) and the use of animation (Lee & Ho, 2013), drama (Wales & Mohamed, 2013) and formative assessment (Tay, Lim, & Lim, 2011) in digital storytelling.

4.4. Purpose of This Case Study

The purpose of this case study research was to document the development and design of the school's signature programme; that is the digital storytelling approach. Digital storytelling, based on the constructivist paradigm, was adopted after a lengthy discussion and deliberation among the pioneer teachers and school administrators. This pedagogical approach not only facilitated students' acquisition of digital literacy but also twenty-first century skills. The iterations to the design and educational benefits were analysed for the purpose of sharing with other practitioners and teachers who were looking for means to use and integrate ICT into their curriculum. The purpose was not to generalise, but to capture useful ideas and insights for sharing and further refinement by others.

4.5. Research Design

An ethnographic case study (Stake, 1995) approach was adopted to look into how teachers from a future school in Singapore designed technology enhanced learning and, more specifically, how teachers adapted the digital storytelling approach for students' acquisition of literacy and twenty-first century skills.

All the authors of this chapter were involved in the development of the school. The first and second authors were teachers of the school — the second author joined the school in December 2006, while the first author joined in January 2009. The third author was the research consultant of the school in the initial years. The approach that the school adopted won the school and teachers the Ministry of Education-Microsoft Professional Development Awards in 2008 and 2009. This case study was written based on the personal recounts of the first and second authors, the triangulation between the authors, significant events and school documentation (including the published manuscripts mentioned earlier).

4.6. Research Frameworks

Laurillard's conversational framework was adopted as the research framework for this case study to look into the design of the teaching—learning activities of the digital storytelling approach and its iterations over the years of implementation. Laurillard (2012) proposes the design thinking philosophy and the analysis of teaching—learning activities to examine the design of lessons. 'Increasingly, teaching is becoming viewed as a design profession, or even a design science' (Kali, McKenney, & Sagy, 2015, p. 177).

A second framework, in addition to the conversational framework mentioned earlier, was also adopted. The Substitution, Augmentation, Modification and Redefinition (SAMR) model (Puentedura, 2014) was used as a secondary framework to assess how the digital storytelling approach was being used by the teachers — whether the approach was merely used as a substitution with no functional change, augmentation with functional improvement, modification calling for significant task redesign or redefinition requiring the creation of new task that was previously not possible. The first two levels of the model, substitution and augmentation, outline how technology can be used to enhance teaching and learning; the next two levels describe how ICT can be used to transform teaching practices and learning outcomes.

4.6.1. Design Thinking

Design thinking in teaching, whether technology is involved or not, calls for the continuous improvement of practice, having a principled way of designing and testing improvements in practice, building on the works of others and representing and sharing of pedagogic practice (Laurillard, 2012). In essence, design thinking means the continuous improvement of practice to enhance the teaching and learning processes, with teachers working with one another in iterative cycles to advance each other's practices in their professional community (Cober, Tan, Slotta, So, & Könings, 2015; Koh, Chai, Wong, & Hong, 2015; Voogt et al., 2015). Design thinking in teaching and learning practice can be further analysed by looking into the teaching—learning activities.

4.6.2. Teaching–Learning activities

According to Laurillard (2012), the teacher's role in the teaching and learning context is to design learning environments and activities to bring about the learning of concepts and to regulate students' practice. Teaching–learning activities can be classified into the following six types: (1) acquisition, (2) inquiry, (3) practice, (4) production, (5) discussion and (6) collaboration (Laurillard, 2012). This classification provides a convenient conceptual framework and basis for teachers to design their lessons in terms of the use of the different teaching–learning activities. The first four types of teaching–learning activities describe individual learning, while discussion and collaboration describe social learning, where the student is engaged with at least one other learner. This framework can be used regardless of whether technology is being used or not. It is appropriate for the use of mobile technology (e.g. notebooks, tablet computers and mobile phones) for teaching and learning purposes. For learning through acquisition, as the name implies, the learner acquires and gains information through conventional, digital or online means – lectures, books, websites or videos. Learning through inquiry requires learners to search and learn more about the given contents, ideas or resources. The students play a more active role of their learning in this mode of learning. Inquiry learning could take the form of library or Internet searches, learning journeys and fieldwork. As for learning through practice, it entails the continuous doing and performing to achieve a certain level of fluency. Drill and practice, whether in the conventional paper and pencil or digital forms, is one of the most common approaches for practice. Learning through production requires students to produce a project, write an essay or a weblog (blog), for example. As for learning through discussion with peers, classmates or teachers, the teacher typically provides a topic or question to generate interest and questions to encourage students to have in-depth discourse into a topic or subject. This may be in the form of group discussions, seminars, online synchronous chat or asynchronous forums. Finally, for learning through collaboration, this mode of learning incorporates discussion, practice and production. This can take the form of a group project, wikis and knowledge-building environments.

4.7. The Design and Developments of Digital Storytelling in the School

4.7.1. Initial Considerations and Design of Digital Storytelling

The pioneer group of teachers of the school, including the second author, spent a considerable length of time, at least six months prior to the starting of the school, discussing and planning how ICT could be integrated into the curriculum to benefit the students. As we began our journey towards a twenty-first century learning environment, the pervasive use of mobile technology (e.g. notebooks, tablet computers and mobile phones) in teaching, and the need for students to acquire digital literacies, made it pertinent for us to reflect on our pedagogical practices at that time. It was our modest objective that the integration of technology should enable our students to critically analyse and learn language effectively through digital experiences.

In Singapore, English is taught as a first language; more and more families are also using English as the main medium of communication at home. Nevertheless, the transition from preschool to primary education marks a shift in how English lessons are designed; the most obvious being the nature and format of assessment – from informal to formal modes. In addition, at the lower primary levels, the teaching of English to seven- to eight-year olds requires different strategies to provide a rich experience for students. It can also be quite a challenge for teachers to design lessons that cater to students with varying academic proficiencies.

Keeping in mind the above philosophy of learning in the twenty-first century, the use of ICT and students' critical and creative skills, a pedagogical approach drawing from constructivism and with an emphasis on learning with technology (Jonassen, 2000) was adopted in the design of the ICT integrated lessons. After much deliberation, digital storytelling was adopted as the pedagogy in the lower primary curriculum for writing. It facilitated a constructivist approach which would allow for students' creativity, critical thinking and twenty-first century skills.

For digital storytelling, students used visuals to recount their personal narratives. The intention behind digital storytelling was to empower students to write in their personal voice. The goal of the writing task was not to reproduce descriptive text of places or objects but to create an immersive experience for the readers. The question was and is: how can a teacher guide students in producing an engaging story through digital storytelling?

4.7.2. Implementing Digital Storytelling at Lower Primary

The teaching and learning of digital storytelling was carried out in stages. First, the teacher would take students through an experience before discussing a topic. In the lower primary levels, the experience took the form of an outdoor excursion or hands-on activity such as a visit to the zoo, an ice-cream party at school or the school's sports day. The function of this activity was to provide sensory experiences where students would connect with the environment or objects. This was followed with the teacher modelling the writing exercise. Teacher-prompted questions relating to the topic and formed sentences using the responses made by students. Several aspects of English literacy were modelled on the spot, with the teacher editing sentence structure and spellings, for example.

Learning through modelling and practice was a strategy in our language learning. Students would also work in groups for group writing. It was observed that collaborative writing was a highlight for students in a lower primary classroom. Not only the students were given the opportunity to write but they also learned from one another as they communicated and discussed. These experiences, carefully planned and organised by the teachers, provided students with adequate ideas and vocabulary for their writing practice.

The practice of idea generation and discussion was important in the writing process. The intention was to support the students in understanding the purpose, audience and context of a writing task. Traditionally, teachers would elicit responses in the context of a class discussion. However, one-to-one computing empowers all students to contribute and articulate their thoughts visibly through a technological application. Students could refer to the online graphic organiser when they were engaged in their individual practice.

4.7.3. Making Thinking Visible at Middle Primary

The teachers were guided by more experienced and senior teachers, in the design of the writing lesson package before the implementation and facilitation of digital storytelling. Encouraging students to have a deeper understanding of story grammar required teachers to perform close monitoring and provide feedback. The middle primary teachers used a synchronous discussion platform, such as Tricider (www.tricider.com), to elicit responses from students before evaluating their work. Compared to an online graphic organiser such as Popplet (www.popplet.com/app), this platform enabled students to take different roles – a student could question peers, explain their reasoning, create assumption, make commentaries or critique their peers. In fact, a digital drama (or an intense interaction in a digital space) could even emerge where teacher and students were engaged in a discussion about their understanding of the narrative context. Students took on different roles and perspectives as if they were 'performing' in the online digital space. Their understanding of the topic would be enriched when they built on one another's ideas and reached a consensus on how the storyline should be written. The synchronous chat function available on Google Hangout enabled students to exchange their viewpoints on how the story should be written without being physically present together. After careful considerations on their storyline, online blog spaces were utilised as an avenue for students to showcase their draft narratives. The online blogs provided students the space to garner commentaries from friends and teachers on how they could improve their writing, or provide words of encouragement to their peers. They could also read writing pieces from better writers posted on the blog spaces. The main challenge for students was the individual practice, where they had to apply their receptive skills to productive use.

4.7.4. Function of Digital Storytelling

The purpose of requiring students to create digital stories was to empower them to write and represent their personal stories and experiences creatively, with not only text but also images, music and the students' own voices. It was not about teaching students how to create but to get them to learn to use visual, print and spoken text effectively with technology (i.e. conveying their personal stories to their audience effectively).

In the initial years (the first two years) of implementation, students either used Microsoft PowerPoint or Microsoft Photo Story (a free Microsoft application that allows users to create a visual story from their digital photos) to create their digital stories. We put forth our expectations to students by explaining to them the expectations in the set of rubrics we used. Teachers needed to guide students on how to approach learning with technology during the digital storytelling learning activities. The students were guided by teachers on using appropriate vocabulary, visuals and sound to achieve the intended learning outcomes, using technology. Teachers also provided feedback and monitoring to their students to keep their students on track in completing their digital stories.

Digital storytelling as an approach and pedagogy was first intended for the teaching and learning of English but after receiving positive and favourable feedback from students, parents and teachers, it was also adopted by the mother tongue languages (Chinese, Malay and Tamil). This also received similar positive comments. The teachers used group scribbles (https://groupscribbles.sri.com/software.html) where students contributed and responded to the lesson cooperatively with their teacher online. The mother tongue teachers also used other online graphic organisers such as Linoit (http://en.linoit.com/), Padlet (www.padlet.com) or Popplet (www.popplet.com/app) to monitor and facilitate students' generation of ideas for their digital stories. These useful online platforms were also used by the English teachers.

4.7.5. Iterations and Variations to the Digital Storytelling Approach

In a nutshell, the lower primary teachers incorporated digital storytelling into their classrooms using simple and manageable tasks. On top of teaching language and how to write, students were also taught the fundamentals of how to operate notebook computers, such as inserting pictures, recording and adding sounds, which were necessary for the creation of a digital story. It started off with the simple use of Microsoft PowerPoint to create digital stories, although some of the teachers started to use the Microsoft Photo Story 3 software application. The use of digital storytelling as an approach was quickly adopted for the teaching of various mother tongue languages, which included Chinese, Malay and Tamil. In the months and years that followed, variations to the digital storytelling were made by the teachers to further enhance and refine the processes.

A group of mother tongue language teachers, one of them being a former Chinese newspaper reporter, designed a digital storytelling lesson reporting the school's sports day. The students were formed into groups with different roles (i.e. reporter, interviewer, photographer and editor) to creatively produce a digital story, in the form of a newspaper report of the school event. The teachers reported that the collaborative element allowed students to be engaged in authentic experience and students could also be assigned the different roles according to the students' interest and aptitude. Teachers were positive that their design and efforts had brought about better language and reading competencies. Students were also given the opportunity to engage in collaborative work, although much guidance was necessary by the teachers (Ng et al., 2010). Instead of the use of static digital images, some teachers made use of the animation function in Microsoft PowerPoint to add the use of simple animations to the digital stories (Lee & Ho, 2013).

Digital storytelling was purposefully included as one of the compulsory alternative assignments for the lower primary levels to ensure that all students were given the chance to create their own digital stories. A formative assessment approach was adopted to facilitate students' acquisition of twenty-first century skills and competencies (Tay et al., 2011). Teachers designed a set of rubrics to further support students' learning.

Another unconventional way of presenting the digital storytelling was that students were empowered to tell their personal stories through social learning platforms, such as Edmodo or Google Classroom through their mobile learning devices. For instance, the Edmodo application could be accessed through mobile phones as well. At the upper primary level, characters from a literature book came alive when students put on the shoes of a character and got into the roles. They would engage in a discussion, debate and offer possible solutions when an issue was presented by the moderator, who was the teacher. Artefacts (e.g. books or toys) relating to the main character, as well as audio text or video footage that gave a glimpse about the chapter were posted and used as stimuli for conversation. The online social learning platform provided the avenue where conversations, discussions and storage of digital stories could take place; it provided an avenue for students to contribute their personal stories in a safe environment. Students spoke through the voice of a character which they role-played. The role play could also be brought into the studio to be enacted in front of a student audience. The recordings were reviewed and the sequence of actions of the characters were debated with a moderator (the teacher), either face-to-face in the classroom or online.

The latest variation was the incorporation of Scratch (www.scratch.mit.edu) programming into digital storytelling of the Primary grade 4 students. The main aim was to explore the use of computing programming language for integration into English, focusing on the skills of reading and viewing, represented in the form of animated digital graphics through the use of Scratch, a free programming software application. This initiative aimed to build students' capacity in basic computing in the development of an animated story.

4.7.6. *An Ecosystem That Supports Implementation of Digital Storytelling*

Parents from the lower primary levels were invited to the school for digital storytelling workshop to provide familiarisation training sessions to provide them with a first-hand experience of what their children would be doing in school with technology. This workshop was well received by parents and has been an ongoing annual event of the school. A digital storytelling challenge was also organised to invite students and parents to collaborate and create a digital story. The challenge was well received and we could see entries with different personal themes such as a holiday trip or adopting a new hobby. A digital storytelling festival was organised to celebrate and showcase the collaborative work at the end of the school year.

At the same time, the school started a programme to encourage student procurement and ownership of their own digital learning devices (notebook computers) from the middle primary levels; this has also further facilitated the use of ICT in teaching and learning in the school. It was a comprehensive programme that provided the necessary software applications and a three year onsite warranty, with additional financial support from the local infocomm media development authority for students from families who needed assistance. The wireless Internet coverage in the classrooms also facilitated the search for digital resources and the storage of students' work on the Intranet.

4.8. Design Thinking, SAMR Model and the Teaching–Learning Activities

4.8.1. Design Thinking

It seemed clear that design thinking, especially in terms of continuous improvement of practice (i.e. the digital storytelling as an approach or pedagogy) was evident, with teachers working together in iterative cycles, building on what had been done by their colleagues and predecessors. The teachers had much interest in developing students' narrative writing skills. They were creative in redesigning a conventional writing task that included class discussion and group collaboration to one that leveraged technology. The practice of consolidating students' responses and learning with technology was common among the teachers. Several variations to the digital storytelling approach were made over the years. The initial and more basic form involved the use of Microsoft PowerPoint, with the use of text, digital images and students' personal voiceovers to recount a personal authentic experience. Here, each student created individual digital stories. Teachers also experimented with having students produce their digital stories in groups, with different members of the group playing different roles that mimicked the production of a newspaper report, to collaboratively write a digital recount of the school's sports day. In later iterations, the use of animation, drama and even computer programming were introduced.

4.8.2. SAMR Model

In addition, the digital storytelling approach has fundamentally transformed the conventional forms of journal or composition writing at the school. From the SAMR model (Puentedura, 2006) perspective, teaching and learning has been modified and redefined. The addition of digital texts, images, animations, music, personal voiceover and technologies have significantly changed and transformed the nature of the conventional writing tasks and storytelling, a transformation that would not have been possible without the presence of ICT. The difference was evident not only in the final product of the writing task, but the process of sharing and discussion was transformed as it could be done remotely through online platforms.

4.8.3. Teaching–Learning Activities

Basically, the design of the digital storytelling did not require state-of-the-art type of technologies; simple, free or low-cost, readily available software applications and devices were used for the production – Microsoft PowerPoint, digital cameras or phones with image capturing function, a headphone with a mic for recording of students' voiceover and a notebook computer – nothing very elaborate. Although there were variations, the various forms of digital storytelling afforded five of the six types of teaching–learning activities mentioned (Laurillard, 2012) – acquisition, practice, production, discussion and collaboration.

Students acquired both technical and literacy skills and knowledge in the process of learning how to create their own digital stories. Students needed to learn how to use the computing devices. For instance, they learned how to use software applications (such as Microsoft PowerPoint and Photostory 3), use the computer keyboard, connect to the Internet/Intranet, save their files, edit digital images they had taken and do voice recording using their notebook computers or mobile phones. Students also improved their vocabulary, sentence structures, grammar and other language and literacy skills and knowledge.

When students were preparing their digital stories, they were required to write their stories, record their own voiceover, and handle the computer and software applications. All these provided opportunities for the students to practise their literacy and technical skills with their computing and mobile devices. For instance, lower primary students were observed to repeatedly, on their own accord, work towards perfecting their voiceover recordings. Students re-recorded their own voice recordings when they felt that their recordings were not good enough in terms of either pace, volume, intonation or pronunciation and this facilitated a 'natural' tendency to repetitively practise on their oral skills to enhance and clearly convey the meaning of their utterance.

Students were involved in producing different forms of digital stories, be they simple digital stories with just still images, texts and the student's personal voiceover or more elaborate ones involving background music, computer animation (e.g. animated gifs), dramatisation or coding (the use of computer programming software applications, such as Scratch programming). The rationale was to facilitate learning by doing.

Class discussions were conducted as part of the digital storytelling creation process following the learning journey or experience. Teachers led the students to discuss and elaborate what they had experienced during the learning journey. The discussions helped the students to better prepare what to write for their digital stories. The teacher guided students on the content, cohesion and grammar of the story. Through the discussion, students were given opportunities to share with and learn from their peers, especially in the process of writing. Some of the discussions were also conducted virtually through online platforms.

Depending on the nature and the design of the lesson, students were given the chance to collaboratively produce their digital stories. For instance, as mentioned earlier, students in their groups produced a newspaper report on the school's sports day, with students assuming different roles – photographer, editor, interviewer and reporter. Students played the different roles, according to their different abilities, to create a digital story reporting a school event. The task was authentic and also experiential.

4.9. Discussion and Conclusion

It has been about a decade since the digital storytelling approach was introduced in the school and, since then, it had undergone several refinements, iterations and variations. In essence and put simply, the focus has been on telling a story facilitated by technological enhancements, resulting in digital texts with images, animations, music and also the storyteller's individual and unique audio voice-over. Depending on a constructivist approach, students construct their individual or group digital stories according to the experiences they have had. Digital storytelling can be used as an approach for the integration of ICT into the classrooms for literacy, including digital literacy and learning of twenty-first century skills. At the school concerned, it has been found to be both effective and efficient. The approach has proven to be effective in that it takes a constructivist approach where students are actively engaged in the creation of their own personal digital stories. Through this approach, students acquire computer-related skills pertaining to how to use the relevant software applications and also how to use the hardware including operating a computer and keyboard, connecting to the wireless network and storage of their digital works locally on the computer or on the cloud. Students are also given opportunities to be exposed to various forms of teaching–learning activities. They are supported to *acquire* language, digital literacy and computer knowledge; *practice* both language and computer skills; *produce* their own digital stories with images, music and their personal voiceover; engage in *discussion* with their peers and teacher to formulate a better story plot with more interesting storyline; and also *collaborate* with peers to write a group digital story.

The approach has proven to be efficient in that it does not require extensive computing hardware or network and only requires some additional effort from school staff and students. In addition, teachers do not need to be computing experts in the creation of multimedia learning productions; common day-to-day computing skills, such as the inputting of text, inserting of images or music and the recording of voiceover are required and these skills can be learned by teachers without much effort if they really require them.

The importance of the ecosystem (i.e. the support structure provided by the community, school and teachers) cannot be overstated. Implicit in this case study was the commitment of the school administration in the use and integration of ICT into the curriculum for teaching and learning. The school management team stayed committed to its mission of creating a learning environment that leveraged technologies for teaching and learning. Following the same vein of argument, the school management also channelled the necessary financial resources in the procurement of computing hardware, working with the information technology branch from the local education ministry to setup the wireless network and the necessary engagement of technical personnel to support the endeavour. Apart from the commitment, direction and financial resources allocated by school leaders, the teachers were also enthusiastic in designing the initial and subsequent variations of the digital storytelling approach. Teachers put in effort by engaging in on-the-job training in how to use digital storytelling. They also redesigned the initial digital storytelling process and added variations to it. Parents were also invited to attend a workshop that demonstrated and showcased the usefulness of digital storytelling as a learning approach. Teachers also applied their knowledge with their children when an opportunity arose for a collaborative project organised by the school.

This ethnographic case study attempted to describe in details the design, process and ecological support system in the use of digital storytelling as an approach for students' learning of literacy and twenty-first century skills with commonly available digital technologies, including mobile technologies. Digital storytelling, in itself, is a powerful way to facilitate learning; however, it is also important to note that young learners could also use mobile technology that they are familiar with to create and to learn. In addition, the support of the ecosystem, in terms of the direction of the school, access to technologies and commitment of the teachers, cannot be overstated.

References

Banaszewski, T. (2002). Digital storytelling finds its place in the classroom. *Multimedia Schools*, *9*(1), 32–35.

Cober, R., Tan, E., Slotta, J., So, H.-J., & Könings, K. D. (2015). Teachers as participatory designers: Two case studies with technology-enhanced learning environments. *Instructional Science*, *43*(2), 203–228. doi:10.1007/s11251-014-9339-0

Dede, C. (2010). Comparing frameworks for 21st century skills. *21st century Skills: Rethinking How Students Learn*, *20*, 51–76.

Di Blas, N., & Paolini, P. (2013). Beyond the school's boundaries: PoliCultura, a large-scale digital storytelling initiative. *Educational Technology & Society*, *16*(1), 15–27.

Jonassen, D. H. (2000). *Computers as mindtools for schools: Engaging critical thinking*. Upper Saddle River, NJ: Merrill.

Kali, Y., McKenney, S., & Sagy, O. (2015). Teachers as designers of technology enhanced learning. *Instructional Science*, *43*(2), 173–179. doi:10.1007/s11251-014-9343-4

Koh, J. H. L., Chai, C. S., Wong, B., & Hong, H.-Y. (2015). *Design thinking for education*. Singapore: Springer Singapore.

Lambert, J. (2013). *Digital storytelling: Capturing lives, creating community (4th ed.)*. New York, NY: Routledge.

Laurillard, D. (2012). *Teaching as a design science: Building pedagogical patterns for learning and technology*. New York, NY: Routledge.

Lee, S. Q. Y., & Ho, C. (2013). 'I Can Animate!' Project. In L. Y. Tay & C. P. Lim (Eds.), *Creating holistic technology-enhanced learning experiences: Tales from a Future School in Singapore* (pp. 93–116). Rotterdam: SensePublishers.

Ng, S., Chai, C., Wen, L., & Lim, S. (2010). Advancing students' language competency through collaborative digital storytelling. In L. Y. Tay, C. P. Lim, & M. Khine (Eds.), *A school's journey into the future* (pp. 71–88). Singapore: Pearson.

North Central Regional Educational Lab (NCREL). (2003). *EnGauge 21st century skills: Literacy in the digital age*. Chicago, IL. Retrieved from http://pict.sdsu.edu/engauge21st.pdf. Accessed on March 21, 2017.

OECD. (2005). *The definition and selection of key competencies: Excutive summary*. Paris, France. Retrieved from https://www.oecd.org/pisa/35070367.pdf. Accessed on February 20, 2017.

Ohler, J. (2006). The world of digital storytelling. *Educational Leadership, 63*(4), 44–47.

Ohler, J. (2013). *Digital storytelling in the classroom: New media pathways to literacy, learning, and creativity (2nd ed.)*. Thousand Oaks, CA: Corwin Press.

Partnership for 21st century skills (P21). (2006). *A state leader's action guide to 21st century skills: A new vision for education*. Tucson, AZ. Retrieved from http://www.p21.org/storage/documents/stateleaders071906.pdf. Accessed on March 21, 2017.

Puentedura, R. (2006). *Transformation, technology, and education*. Presentation given August 18, 2006 as part of the Strengthening Your District Through Technology workshops, Maine, US. Retrieved from http://hippasus.com/blog/archives/date/2006/11. Accessed on April 8, 2017.

Puentedura, R. (2014). SAMR and curriculum redesign. Retrieved from http://www.hippasus.com/rrpweblog/archives/2014/08/30/SAMRAndCurriculumRedesign.pdf. Accessed on February 21, 2017.

Robin, B. (2008). Digital storytelling: A powerful technology tool for the 21st century classroom. *Theory into Practice, 47*(3), 220–228.

Robin, B., & Pierson, M. (2005). *A multilevel approach to using digital storytelling in the classroom*. Paper presented at the Society for Information Technology & Teacher Education International Conference, Phoenix, AZ. Retrieved from https://www.learntechlib.org/p/19091

Stake, R. E. (1995). *The art of case study research*. Thousand Oaks, CA: Sage Publications.

Tay, L. Y., Lim, S. K., & Lim, C. P. (2011). Exploring alternative assessments to support digital storytelling for creative thinking in primary school classrooms. In *Technology for creativity and innovation: Tools, techniques and applications* (pp. 268–284). Hershey, PA: IGI Global.

Voogt, J., Laferrière, T., Breuleux, A., Itow, R. C., Hickey, D. T., & McKenney, S. (2015). Collaborative design as a form of professional development. *Instructional Science, 43*(2), 259–282. doi:10.1007/s11251-014-9340-7

Wales, P. E., & Mohamed, M. (2013). Digital storytelling and drama in the English language classroom. In L. Y. Tay & C. P. Lim (Eds.), *Creating holistic technology-enhanced learning experiences: Tales from a Future School in Singapore* (pp. 59–73). Rotterdam: SensePublishers.

Yuksel, P., Robin, B. R., & McNeil, S. (2011). *Educational uses of digital storytelling around the world*. Paper presented at the Proceedings of Society for Information Technology & Teacher Education International Conference, Nashville, TN. Retrieved from https://www.learntechlib.org/p/36461

Chapter 5

Mobile Devices and Multimodal Textual Practices

Amy Hutchison and Beth Beschorner

Abstract

Children's emerging conceptions about literacy and its functions are influenced by their experiences with a wide range of written and oral literacies, including the use of digital technology, in their homes and communities. Now that mobile technologies have become intuitive to use, relatively inexpensive, small and easy to move around and networked, they have provided an entry point for transformations in the creation and sharing of texts – they are changing the way young children 'do' literacy. In this chapter, the authors discuss the ways that children learn about multimodal texts; how mobile technology can facilitate the reading, creation and sharing of multimodal texts in preschool and primary classrooms; the literacy skills necessary for reading multimodal texts, and; strategies for planning instruction into which multimodal texts and mobile devices are integrated. Examples of how children may engage in multimodal reading and writing in and out of the classroom are also provided.

Keywords: Multimodal; digital literacy; instructional planning; mobile learning; early literacy; new literacies

5.1. Emerging Conceptions of Literacies and Multimodality

Children develop knowledge of the meaning of, and purposes for, literacies as they engage with the world around them, in their homes, schools and communities (Marsh, Hannon, Lewis & Ritchie, 2017; Purcell-Gates, 1996), i.e. children's understandings of literacies emerge as they are exposed to an expansive range of written and oral literacies and through '…exploration, young children actively construct their knowledge of reading and writing' (Neumann, 2016, p. 61). Therefore, to understand how children come to know about the meaning and purpose of text, it is essential to consider the ways that they and the adults around them use different types of tools, both digital and paper-based, for reading, writing, listening and speaking both at home and at school. In this chapter, we discuss how multimodal texts, viewed and created on mobile devices, influence young children's conceptions of literacy and can help students learn to use a range of modalities, such as speaking, listening and viewing, to understand information and communicate for different audiences and purposes.

Numerous scholars have described the ways that children develop literacies with traditional tools and practices such as shared storybook reading (Bus, van IJzendoorn, & Pellegrini, 1996), engaging with environmental print (Neumann, Hood, Ford & Neumann, 2011) and through oral storytelling (Isbell, Sobol, Lindauer, & Lowrance, 2004). However, the ways that digital technologies influence young children's emerging conceptions of literacy also require attention, considering that most children are immersed in a media and technology-rich environment from birth (Marsh et al., 2017; Marsh et al., 2015). Specifically, children are surrounded by adults ubiquitously using mobile digital technology throughout daily life (Smith, 2017) and have rapidly increased their own time spent using digital technology (Common Sense Media, 2013; Marsh et al., 2017; Ofcom, 2014). Further, the mobile nature of many devices that young children use, such as phones and tablets, coupled with the increased availability of the Internet, have widened the spaces and places where young children can engage in digital literacy practices, such as in cars, shops, restaurants and libraries (Marsh, 2014). While some scholars have argued that children's use of digital technology can have negative consequences (e.g. Subrahmanyam, Kraut, Greenfield & Gross, 2000), digital tools have influenced the ways that children come to understand the use of, and purpose for, literacies. In particular, children are increasingly gaining exposure to and experience with multimodal texts (Levy, 2009). Multimodal texts can consist of images, sounds, videos, colour, physical spaces, printed text and movement, and usually include a combination of those modalities.

Evidence suggests that children themselves are actively engaging with multimodal literacies using mobile devices in multiple ways (Beschorner & Hutchison, 2013b; Hutchison, Beschorner & Schmidt-Crawford, 2012). They are also observing family members and other adults using mobile technology for a variety of purposes and participating in digital intergenerational literacy practices with other family members (Marsh et al., 2017). For example, in a typical day a child might see others sending and receiving texts or emails that may include a combination of printed text, images, emojis, annotated photographs and more. Similarly, they may observe adults socially interacting with photographs, avatars or content on social media sites. They might witness adults using their phones to obtain directions to a local museum or library, for accessing a train or bus schedule, trying a new recipe or reading the news. Family members might also use social media to read and write multimodal messages. As children witness adults and other family members using digital technology in these ways, it is likely that their conceptions about communication, reading, writing, listening and speaking are influenced in ways that might contribute to their own literacy practices.

5.2. Exploring Skills for Reading and Writing Multimodal Texts with Mobile Devices

Given the increasingly diverse range of communication modes and text types through which adults, and accordingly children, communicate, it is important to consider the literacy skills necessary for effective multimodal communication and the implications for classroom instruction. A unique aspect of multimodal reading and writing is that children do not necessarily have to be able to decode traditional (alphabetic) text to read and write multimodal texts. Multimodal texts can consist of images, sounds, videos, colour, places and more, and usually include a combination of those modalities. Although children may not be reading alphabetic text, they are able to analyse and make meaning of information conveyed through images, videos, icons and emojis.

As children improve their abilities to read traditional alphabetic text, they must become competent at searching for and locating information online and evaluating the validity and reliability of that information (Leu, Castek, Henry, Coiro & McMullan, 2004). To locate this information, readers must be able to navigate a digital device and understand a variety of contexts, vocabulary and norms that are not typically associated with print-based texts. They must also be able to generate appropriate and useful search terms. Additionally, readers and writers must understand how to combine multiple modes of text to create an effective message.

In addition to knowing how to navigate multimodal texts and digital devices, children must also be adept at understanding which type of text or tool to use for which purpose. Lankshear and Knobel (2007) suggest that literacy "is not a matter of knowing how to read and write a particular kind of script. Rather, it is a matter of 'applying this knowledge for specific purposes in specific contexts of use' (ibid.)" (p. 4).

In the case of multimodal texts, young children must learn the various purposes and uses for different modes of texts. For example, they must be taught the purposes for sending text messages, sharing photographs and viewing websites.

Readers and writers today must engage with an increasingly diverse range of multimodal texts that require an increasingly diverse range of skills and strategies that must be included in classroom literacy instruction (Hutchison, Woodward & Colwell, 2016).

5.3. Mobile Devices Widen the Spaces for Developing Multimodal Literacies

In addition to creating new opportunities for communication with multimodal texts, the mobility of digital devices also expands the spaces and places where children can engage in literate practices. The portability of mobile devices allows for opportunities to read, write, listen and speak virtually anywhere (Ciampa & Gallagher, 2013; Swan, van't Hooft, Kratcoski & Unger, 2005). For example, mobile devices provide opportunities for authoring at home or in the community through the use of text, photographs and the ability to record audio and video. For instance, as a family walks through their neighbourhood, their child may take pictures on a phone or tablet of flowers and animals that they encounter. These photographs could then be sent as text messages or emails to other family members, used as artefacts for a child's oral storytelling recounting the walk, or inserted into a digital story that describes the sights and sounds of the neighbourhood. Additionally, the child could make audio and video recordings to describe what they see and hear.

This expansion of places for engaging in literacy also extends to the classroom. A teacher might use these digital features to collect environmental print in the community for use in the classroom. For example, as children are learning about vowel sounds, they might take a walk around the school and try to find as many letters representing vowel sounds in the school as possible. Photographs could be taken of the words containing letters with vowel sounds that are found. These photographs could be taken back to the classroom where children might annotate them, drawing on the image to indicate the vowels, or use them to create a digital class book using one of the many digital book creation apps that are available for mobile devices. Older children might use mobile devices as they prepare to write an informational or persuasive text by collecting survey data from other students throughout the school or recording answers to interview questions. In these cases, the mobility of the device allows children to collect data from their participants anywhere in the school or community.

Finally, the mobile nature of phones or tablets allows these devices to become tools that can be easily transported between home and school (Rowe & Miller, 2016). When a mobile device is transported between home and school, children can take photographs to be used later for creating multimodal projects, record audio clips of their family members or work with other members of the family to record family events or stories. Further, these homes literacies can be used, shared and valued at school in ways that honour the multiple languages and dialects used in home and communities (Rowe & Miller, 2016). Conversely, when a child brings a mobile device home, the family becomes an authentic audience for the multimodal writing projects created at school. Thus, the mobility of some devices affords a purposeful connection between home and school.

5.4. A Wider Audience for Sharing Work

In addition to widening the places and spaces for engaging in multimodal text production, digital technology also expands the number and variety of people with whom children can share their multimodal texts. The Internet serves as a platform for children to read and write for a broader audience outside of the home or classroom (Levy, Yamada-Rice & Marsh, 2013), which may motivate children to produce higher quality writing (Karchmer, 2001). Many teachers have created a classroom blog or website and have used it to not only communicate information to stakeholders but as a space to publish children's own multimodal texts (Karchmer, 2001). One authentic reason for students to blog is to respond to reading, perhaps in the form of a synopsis or review of literature (e.g. Leu et al., 2004) or through a virtual book club (Castek, Bevans-Mangelson & Goldstone, 2006). This practice allows children to have a purpose for their reading and an authentic audience for their writing (Levy et al., 2013), which expands beyond the four walls of the classroom and might include other children in different schools, states or countries. Further, readers of a blog can add comments on children's posts, which creates the possibility of engagement and communication with an unknown or unfamiliar audience (Levy et al., 2013).

Similarly, social media platforms, such as Twitter or Instagram, allow children to create, share and consume multimodal text with/from other users from around the world and from anywhere they are located in the world. For example, children might create a persuasive text highlighting the dangers of global warming and post a link to the presentation on Twitter using a relevant hashtag to connect the presentation to Twitter-users globally that might be interested in a similar topic. Further, readers of the presentation could reply to the tweet, creating an authentic opportunity for children to have purposeful digital communication. Similarly, children can use social media to search for information relevant to specific topics or to learn from experts that post information.

Educators can also utilise the affordances of the wider audiences for sharing work that mobile devices afford, particularly by capturing and sharing children's work with parents. Specifically, educators can take photographs or videos of practices that occur at school and, thus, cannot easily be shared, and then quickly and easily send them via email to families or other stakeholders (Beschorner & Hutchison, 2013b). Educators might also consider using some of the digital platforms discussed previously, such as a blog or social media, to communicate with families and share student work. However, when educators make these decisions about sharing student work, children's privacy and safety on the Internet must be examined and appropriate measures taken.

5.5. Planning Instruction with Mobile Devices and Multimodal Text

Instruction around multimodal texts and use of mobile technology will look different at every grade level and in every classroom. In the past, teachers have

88 Amy Hutchison and Beth Beschorner

consistently reported that, even when they are familiar with digital technologies, they have difficulty planning literacy instruction that integrates digital technology (Hutchison & Reinking, 2011). This difficulty in planning is why Hutchison and Woodward (2014b) created the Technology Integration Planning Cycle (TIPC). The TIPC is designed to support teachers in designing instruction that integrates digital technology and supports the development of multimodal reading and writing skills. As can be seen in Figure 5.1, The TIPC involves seven guiding elements, described subsequently.

5.5.1. Identifying the Instructional Goal

Rather than being guided by a sense of wanting to integrate technology or a desire to try a new digital tool, every lesson should begin and end with the teacher's instructional goal, which is determined by a teacher's instructional standards, knowledge of students' skills and experience with digital technology and understanding of students' current literacy skills. It is important to have an understanding of students' traditional and digital literacy skills before beginning instruction so that the teacher can build on those skills and ensure that any

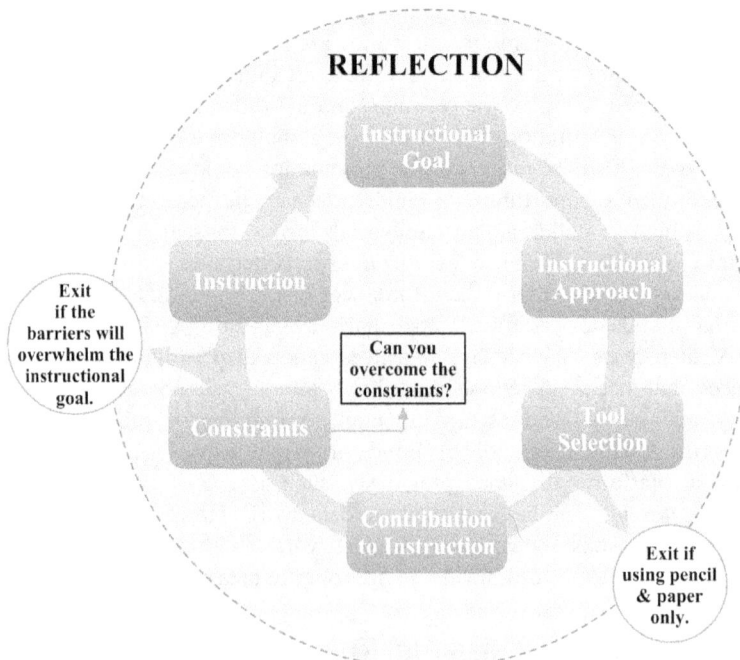

Figure 5.1: The Technology Integration Planning Cycle for Literacy and Language Arts. *Source*: Figure from Hutchison and Woodward (2014b). Reprinted with permission.

difficulties students have are not related to challenges with navigation of the digital device or a lack of understanding about the mode of text being presented. If those aspects of the instruction present challenges, teachers should provide explicit instruction on those skills because they are an essential part of reading and writing with multimodal text using mobile devices. Instruction on the navigational and digital aspects of reading with mobile devices is often overlooked. Thus, it is important to understand students' traditional *and* digital skill levels prior to designing instruction.

5.5.2. Determining the Instructional Approach

Another step in designing instruction that integrates multimodal literacy practices with mobile devices is to determine an appropriate instructional approach for the learning goals that have been identified based on standards and student skill levels. According to Hutchison and Woodward (2014b, p. 460), teachers can do this by considering the extent to which the learning should: (1) be teacher or student centered; (2) be convergent or divergent (should students develop similar understandings or draw their own conclusions?); (3) involve relevant prior experiences with the topic and with the technology that will be used; (4) facilitate a more surface-level or deep understanding of the topic − this decision may vary by the phase of instruction and within a lesson; (5) be longer or shorter in duration; (6) involve more or less structured learning; (7) take place in a whole group, small group, or individual configuration; and (8) involve additional resources. These are important considerations when designing multimodal instruction for mobile devices because this type of instruction will likely be significantly different from instruction that does not involve digital devices and multimodal text production.

5.5.3. Identify Digital Resources

Next, the teacher should identify the digital devices, apps, websites, or other resources that will help address the instructional goal using the instructional approach that was determined most useful for instruction. For example, a teacher may determine that the instructional goal would be best supported by having students use the built-in camera on an iPad to search for real-life examples of a concept in their immediate environment or local community. Alternately, the instructional goal may be best taught by augmenting the surrounding environment with supplementary information with the use of an augmented reality app. Augmented reality apps allow users to superimpose images on a user's view of the real world to supplement the physical environment. Thus, it would be necessary for the devices that students use to be highly mobile and able to host the necessary augmented reality app. These are only two minor examples of the types of considerations teachers should take into account. Fortunately, the mobility of digital devices provides endless opportunities for enhancing instruction in and out of the classroom. However, these endless opportunities also create a need to carefully design instruction with mobile devices.

5.5.4. *Determining the Contribution to Instruction*

After teachers have determined how they will use mobile technology to support students in reading and designing multimodal text, it is important to consider the contribution that the technology will make to the instruction. This part of the process involves determining if the teacher is maximising the instruction by helping students learn the skills, strategies and dispositions needed for not only reading but also producing, multimodal text. As discussed previously, to read and write digitally, students must engage with an increasingly diverse range of multimodal texts that require an increasingly diverse range of skills and strategies that must be included in classroom literacy instruction. By considering in advance how the planned instruction will strategically support students in developing these skills, teachers can ensure that they are maximising the potential benefits of mobile technology.

5.5.5. *Determining the Constraints of the Digital Resources*

After considering how to maximise the benefits of mobile technology to support students in reading and writing multimodal text, teachers should also consider the possible constraints of the digital resources that will be used. By considering the possible constraints prior to instruction, teachers may be able to develop solutions for possible challenges or constraints. An example of a possible constraint may be something like limited storage capacity on mobile devices. For example, a teacher may plan instruction in which the students will use iPads on a community walk to capture videos of various workers in the community to create a video presentation of the jobs held by people in their community. In this case, it is possible that there may not be enough storage space on the device for multiple videos. By considering this possible constraint in advance, the teacher could develop another method for storing the videos, such as a cloud-based storage solution. Again, this is only one example of the many potential constraints of teaching with mobile technology. Thus, considering these possible constraints in advance is essential for ensuring that the use of digital technology is more helpful than disruptive.

It is also important to consider that the constraints of using mobile technology may, in some cases, be more distracting than they are helpful. In these cases, the digital tool should not be used in the way planned. Rather, the teacher should continue to consider possible solutions or go back in the planning cycle to select different digital resources. If the teacher is unable to select appropriate digital resources, then perhaps digital technology should not be used in the lesson being planned. At this point, the teacher should exit the planning cycle if he or she is unable to overcome the constraints of using the digital tool. It is important to remember that many digital tools may have challenges, but those challenges may only improve by gaining experience with the tools and finding potential solutions. However, this type of problem-solving should be balanced with the goals of instruction.

5.5.6. *Instructional Considerations and Reflection*

The final components of the planning cycle are instruction and reflection. As part of the final phases of instructional planning, teachers should consider the aspects of instruction that will need special consideration because of the use of mobile technology for multimodal reading and writing. For example, it may be the case that students need special instructions about the boundaries of the places they can explore if they are taking their devices outside of the classroom. Alternately, students may need instruction on the special features of the apps they will be using, such as how to annotate images within the app or how to save and export work. It is common for teachers to forget to consider the necessity for instruction around these topics when teaching with mobile technology (Hutchison & Woodward, 2014a) because such instruction is typically unnecessary when teaching without digital technology.

Finally, as the instruction is being implemented, and after it is completed, teachers should reflect on the lesson to determine if they met the instructional goals identified at the beginning of the planning process. When successful, teachers should consider which aspects of instruction contributed to the success of the lesson. If the use of mobile technology led to a scenario in which the technology distracted students from accomplishing the lesson objectives, teachers should consider why that happened and which aspects of instruction to change in the future to minimise such distraction.

By using the TIPC to plan instruction, teachers can ensure that they are carefully designing their instruction to ensure that they are maximising the potential benefits of mobile technology and meeting their goals for supporting students in learning to read and write multimodal text.

5.6. Classroom Examples of Reading and Writing Multimodally with Digital Technology

Because mobile technology expands the types of text children can create, the variety of places where they can create them, the audience with whom they can share them and the skills needed for reading and writing, it is essential to consider the applications of mobile technologies for multimodal text consumption and production in the classroom. Some classroom examples in this section.

5.6.1. *E-books*

Common multimodal texts that children encounter in the classroom are e-books. There are many e-book apps for mobile devices, which often include audio of the text and interactive features such as animations. Some research suggests that these features can be distracting for the reader (Neumann & Neumann, 2016). However, there is evidence that e-books can support vocabulary learning, engagement and story comprehension (Miller & Warschauer, 2014) and that young children can retell e-books that they listen to independently, often engaging with the text in ways that are similar to how they have read print-based text with adults (DeJong & Bus, 2004). Further, many e-books provide numerous multimodal options for students to learn through features, such as text-to-speech that will read an unknown word to the reader, hyperlinks that support vocabulary knowledge and possibilities for annotating the text.

Additionally, when teachers have students reading e-books on mobile devices, students often have access to a wide range of books at different difficulty levels, from different genres and covering a number of high-interest subjects that they can read anywhere, inside or out of the classroom. This range of books is often more expansive than a teacher's classroom library of print-based texts because of the cost and space limitations of paper books. Further, having students read e-books allows more than one student to read a particularly popular book at a time, which capitalises on the social nature of literacies and may encourage children to discuss and recommend books to one another. Students may also use features of e-books that can provide assistance with reading (Cavanaugh, 2002). Thus, e-books are promising for classroom use. However, teachers must also consider that it can be difficult to monitor what students are reading on their screens around a classroom, and how they will model the appropriate use of the features available within an e-book to ensure they will be used to aid in comprehension rather than as a distraction.

5.6.2. Drawing and Composing

In addition to reading and listening to e-books on mobile devices, children can also use drawing or composing apps to write in emergent and conventional ways using scribbling, writing and by copying words (Neumann, 2016) but also through the use of digital stickers, 'paint', photographs and text (Beschorner & Hutchison, 2013a). These types of apps can be used by children to author multimodal products that incorporate photographs, drawings, audio recordings and print (Lynch & Redpath, 2014). Thus, multiple modes of representation can be incorporated into the composing process using a host of multimodal tools (Rowe & Miller, 2016).

The wide range of multimodal tools provides nearly endless possibilities for meaningful literacy instruction. For example, at the beginning of the year, children might write about their family using an app that incorporates text, images and drawings and record themselves explaining their writing using audio. Then, other children could read these multimodal texts about their peers' families to get to know them. This instructional practice could allow children to make connections between print and its meaning and creates opportunities for the teacher to scaffold each individual child's emerging knowledge of multimodal text by supporting concepts of word, letter-sound knowledge, use of high frequency words, using or creating images, etc. as children write. After the children's writing is complete, the children or teacher could then share the writing with families via email or a class blog to create a meaningful multimodal text for children to share with their families.

Older students might use mobile devices to take photographs of a plant at different stages of growth during a science unit. These photographs could then be annotated to label parts of the plant each day over time as the plant grows. Further, students could make audio recordings to explain their observations of the plant each day. At the end of the unit, students would have labelled photographs and a detailed account of their observations as the plant grew over time. This information could then be captured in a digital book or presentation to be shared with younger children learning about plants, with their families or with interested groups online.

5.6.3. Video Viewing and Production

Children can also use mobile devices to view and create videos. For example, young children might use apps to watch shows that introduce specific content or ideas related to the curriculum (such as PBS Kids) or search the Internet for short video clips or other media that highlight favourite characters (O'Mara & Laidlaw, 2011). It is also possible for children to use mobile devices to record and share their own videos, which can be done in a variety of ways. Specifically, videos can be stored on the device, can be accessed and viewed immediately, or can be shared via email, text message or via a social media platform (e.g. YouTube and Vimeo), often with just one touch of the screen. Children can not only create videos of their activity and environment but can also create videos to tell a story using household objects or to record their own reading and commentary (O'Mara & Laidlaw, 2011). Additionally, children can use video to participate in video calls with family and friends, which can scaffold 'children's understanding about literacy, or in this case multimodal communication, as a social practice' (Marsh et al., 2017, p. 58) by providing authentic opportunities to use multiple modes of communication with a range of communicative practices and tools.

Many of these uses for video have multiple possibilities for classroom instruction. First, teachers can use video from the Internet to enhance their instruction by bringing information in from outside the classroom. For example, teachers might select a short video that provides background knowledge for a text that they believe students may know little about or have students include links to videos related to a specific topic when creating an informational multimodal text. Second, teachers can also have students create video for multiple instructional purposes. For instance, students might video record an interview of the Physical Education teacher or record their peers' favourite way to stay active when researching healthy living for a persuasive text they are creating. In this way, the mobility of the digital device is a critical affordance that allows the students to collect video anywhere, inside or outside of the classroom.

5.6.4. Games

In addition to the ways that children compose their own content using open content applications, they also play closed content game apps where the content has already been formatted, such as the game Fruit Ninja (Neumann & Neumann, 2016; Rowe & Miller, 2016). However, apps that are specifically marketed for their educational value often focus on a discrete set of skills, which can bore children, rather than a more expansive notion of literacy that involves of storytelling, imagination and communication (Plowman, 2013). While some of these apps undoubtedly have value in helping children learn what Paris (2005) has termed constrained skills, such as letter identification and letter-sound correspondence, teachers should limit their use of literacy-related games and, instead, make instructional decisions that encourage open-ended use of multimodal literacies.

5.7. Final Considerations

In this chapter, we have considered some of the ways that children learn about multimodal text, the skills they need to become proficient in reading and writing multimodal texts, strategies for planning instruction on reading and writing multimodal texts with mobile devices and examples of how children may be taught to read and write multimodally. Teachers can use the types of multimodal activities described in this chapter to complement or integrate with other early literacy activities designed to target reading and writing at the word level. Based on the discussion heretofore, we conclude with a few cautions and reminders for teachers who are considering the importance of teaching students to communicate multimodally and are considering the use of mobile devices for instruction.

First, teachers should be aware that it is their responsibility to model high quality use of technology for students (National Association for the Education of Young Children, 2012). Some teachers may perceive technology integration as a luxury or something extra they do to keep students motivated (Hutchison & Reinking, 2011). However, reading and writing with technology is an essential part of the Common Core State Standards ([CCSS]; CCSS Initiative, 2010) used in most states in the United States and mandated curriculum in many other countries around the world; to be fully literate, students must be digitally literate. Thus, teachers should model high quality uses of technology by planning instruction that provides opportunities for high-quality, interactive engagement and learning opportunities. Teachers should provide models of high-quality interactions with multimodal texts. Teachers should also facilitate opportunities for students to design and produce creative multimodal texts by providing instruction that enables students to take advantage of the mobility of their digital devices to create unique multimodal products.

Second, it is important to consider that geographical and income-based disparities still limit or prohibit access to digital devices and/or Internet access for a percentage of the world's population. For example, Internet access is available to only 88% of people in the United States and France, 87% of people in

Australia, 73% of people in Russia, 53% of people in China and 35% of people in India (International Telecommunication Union, 2017). Students without access to a household device or an Internet connection are likely to have fewer interactions with digital tools prior to entering skill, and therefore have less opportunities to develop basic digital literacy skills, such as device navigation. Thus, teachers should be intentional in providing opportunities for students to learn with digital devices.

Finally, it is essential that teachers provide systematic and explicit instruction to develop multimodal literacy skills. Although providing students with access and opportunities to use mobile devices for learning in and out of school is an important step, simply providing access is not enough. Teachers must be attentive to the systematic and explicit instruction and scaffolding that must accompany instruction with mobile devices. Interactive mini-lessons aimed at developing navigational and other basic digital skills may be necessary. Because mobile technologies offer unique opportunities for collaboration, it may be useful for teachers to provide feedback and instruction through apps designed for digital collaboration, and for students to digitally mentor each other, with students who have more digital experience acting as tutors for students with less experience.

By taking advantage of the opportunities afforded by mobile devices, teachers can support students in developing the critically important abilities to read and write multimodal texts. Not only must students have opportunities to develop their multimodal reading and writing skills but those opportunities must be of high-quality and must be equitable for all students, even those without devices at home, to make all students twenty-first century ready.

References

Beschorner, B., & Hutchison, A. (2013a). iPads as a literacy teaching tool in early childhood. *International Journal of Education in Mathematics, Science, and Technology*, *1*(1), 16–24.

Beschorner, B., & Hutchison, A. (2013b). iPads as tools for communication with parents. *The Oklahoma Reader,* 49(1), 17–19.

Bus, A., van IJzendoorn, M., & Pelligrini, A. (1996). Joint book reading makes for success in learning to read: A meta-analysis on intergenerational transmission of literacy. *Review of Educational Research*, *65*(1), 1–21.

Castek, J., Bevans-Mangelson, J., & Goldstone, B. (2006). Reading adventures online: Five ways to introduce the new literacies of the Internet through children's literature. *The Reading Teacher*, *59*(7), 714–728.

Cavanaugh, T. (2002). Ebooks and accommodations: Is this the future of print accommodation?*Teaching Exceptional Children*, *35*(2), 56–61.

Ciampa, K., & Gallagher, T. (2013). Getting in touch: Use of mobile devices in the elementary classroom. *Computers in the Schools*, *30*(4), 309–325.

Common Core State Standards Initiative. (2010). Common Core State Standards for English language arts and literacy in history/social studies, science, and technical subjects. Washington, DC: National Governors Association Center for Best Practices and the Council of Chief State School Officers.

Common Sense Media. (2013). *Zero to eight: Children's media use in America 2013*. Retrieved from https://www.commonsensemedia.org/research/zero-to-eight-childrens-media-use-in-america-2013#. Accessed on June 11, 2018.

DeJong, M., & Bus, A. (2004). The efficacy of electronic books in fostering kindergarten children's emergent story understanding. *Reading Research Quarterly*, *39*(4), 378−393.

Hutchison, A., Beschorner, B., & Schmidt-Crawford, D. (2012). Exploring the use of the iPad for literacy learning. *Reading Teacher*, *66*(1), 15−23.

Hutchison, A., & Reinking, D. (2011). Teachers' perceptions of integrating information and communication technologies into literacy instruction: A national survey in the United States. *Reading Research Quarterly*, *46*(4), 312−333.

Hutchison, A., & Woodward, L. (2014a). An examination of how a teacher's use of digital tools empowers and constrains language arts instruction. *Computers in the Schools*, *31*(4), 316−338. doi:10.1080/07380569.2014.967629

Hutchison, A., & Woodward, L. (2014b). A planning cycle for integrating technology into literacy instruction. *Reading Teacher*, *67*(6), 455−464. doi:10.1002/trtr.1225

Hutchison, A., Woodward, L., & Colwell, J. (2016). What are preadolescent readers doing online? An examination of upper elementary students' reading, writing, and communication in digital spaces. *Reading Research Quarterly*, *51*(4), 435−454.

International Telecommunication Union. (2017). *ICT facts and figures*. Retrieved from http://www.itu.int/en/ITU-D/Statistics/Pages/facts/default.aspx

Isbell, R., Sobol, J., Lindauer, L., & Lowrance, A. (2004). The effects of storytelling and story reading on the oral language complexity and story comprehension of young children. *Early Childhood Education Journal*, *32*(3), 157−163.

Karchmer, R. (2001). The journey ahead: Thirteen teachers report how the Internet influences literacy and literacy instruction in their K-12 classrooms. *Reading Research Quarterly*, *36*(4), 442−466.

Lankshear, C., & Knobel, M. (2007). *A new literacies sample*. New York, NY: Peter Lang.

Leu, D., Castek, J., Henry, L., Coiro, J., & McMullan, M. (2004). The lessons that children teach us: Integrating children's literature and the new literacies of the Internet. *The Reading Teacher*, *57*(5), 496−503.

Levy. (2009). 'You have to understand words...but not to read them': Young children becoming readers in the digital age. *Journal of Research in Reading*, *32*(1), 75−91.

Levy, R., Yamada-Rice, D., & Marsh, J. (2013). Digital literacies in the primary classroom. In K. Hall, T. Cremin, B. Comber, & L. Moll (Eds.), *International handbook of research on children's literacy, learning, and culture* (pp. 333−343). Chichester: John Wiley & Sons.

Lynch, J., & Redpath, T. (2014). Smart technologies in early years literacy education: A meta-narrative of paradigmatic tensions in iPad use in an Australian preparatory classroom. *Journal of Early Childhood Literacy*, *14*(2), 147−174.

Marsh, J. (2014, December). *Young children's online practices: Past, present, and future*. Paper presented at the National Conference of the Literacy Research Association, Marco Island, FL.

Marsh, J., Hannon, P., Lewis, M., & Ritchie, L. (2017). Young children's initiation into family literacy practices in the digital age. *Journal of Early Childhood Research, 15*(1), 47–60.

Marsh, J., Plowman, L., Yamada-Rice, D., Bishop, J. C., Lahmar, J., Scott, F., ... Winter, P. (2015). *Exploring play and creativity in preschoolers' use of apps: Final project report.* Retrieved from www.techandplay.org

Miller, E., & Warschauer, M. (2014). Young children and e-reading: Research to date and questions for the future. *Learning, Media, and Technology, 39*(3), 283–305.

National Association for the Education of Young Children. (2012). *Technology and interactive media as tools in early childhood programs serving children from birth through age eight.* Washington, D.C.

Neumann, M. (2016). Young children's use of touch screen tablets for writing and reading at home: Relationships with emergent literacy. *Computers and Education, 97*, 61–68.

Neumann, M., Hood, M., Ford, R., & Neumann, D. (2011). The role of environmental print in emergent literacy. *Journal of Early Childhood Literacy, 12*(3), 231–258.

Neumann, M., & Neumann, D. (2016). The use of touchscreen tablets at home and preschool to foster emergent literacy. *Journal of Early Childhood Literacy, 17*(2), 203–220.

Ofcom. (2014). *Children and parents: Media use and attitudes report.* Retrieved from https://www.ofcom.org.uk/research-and-data/media-literacy-research/childrens/children-parents-oct-14

O'Mara, J., & Laidlaw, L. (2011). Living in the iworld: Two literacy researchers reflect on the changing text and literacy practices of childhood. *English Teaching: Practice and Critique, 10*(4), 149–159.

Paris, S. (2005). Reinterpreting the development of reading skills. *Reading Research Quarterly, 40*(2), 184–202.

Plowman, L. (2013). Digital media and the everyday lives of children. In L. Whitaker (Ed.), *The children's media yearbook* (pp. 133–140). London: The Children's Media Foundation.

Purcell-Gates, V. (1996). Stories, coupons, and the TV guide: Relationships between home literacy experiences and emergent literacy knowledge. *Reading Research Quarterly, 31*(4), 406–428.

Rowe, D. W., & Miller, M. (2016). Designing for diverse classrooms: Using iPads and digital cameras to compose ebooks with emergent bilingual/biliterate four-year-olds. *Journal of Early Childhood Literacy, 14*(4), 425–472.

Smith, A. (2017). *Record shares of Americans now own smartphones, have home broadband.* Retrieved from www.pewresearch.org/fact-tank/2017/01/12/evolution-of-technology/

Subrahmanyam, K., Kraut, R., Greenfield, P., & Gross, E. (2000). The impact of home computer use on children's activities and development. *Children and Computer Technology, 10*(2), 123–144.

Swan, K., van't Hooft, M., Kratcoski, A., & Unger, D. (2005). Uses and effects of mobile computing devices in K-8 classrooms. *Journal of Research on Technology in Education, 38*(1), 99–112.

Chapter 6

Mobile Tools for Literacy Learning across the Curriculum in Primary Schools

Jan Clarke

Abstract

This chapter presents the perspective of an Information and Communications Technology (ICT) integration specialist on how mobile devices and apps are being used in several Western Australian primary schools to improve students' literacy across a range of contexts and curriculum areas. In her role, the author is responsible for assisting teachers in Independent sector schools with Technologies, ICT Literacy and Science, Technology, Engineering and Mathematics (STEM) education and has worked extensively in helping teachers design rich cross-curricular tasks and programmes that harness a range of digital technologies, including mobile devices. The chapter presents several examples of how teachers in Western Australian Independent schools have used mobile tools across the curriculum in rich tasks, and how this has supported students' literacy learning. Although this chapter makes specific references to Australian curricular requirements and contexts, it is envisaged that the practical examples and insights presented will be more broadly applicable in helping practitioners use mobile technologies to enhance literacy learning across the curriculum.

Keywords: Rich tasks; mobile technologies; iPads; literacy across the curriculum; contextual literacy; productive apps

6.1. Mobile Tools for Literacy Learning through Rich Tasks

Through rich cross-curricular learning activities, many aspects of literacy and the English curriculum area can be developed, including speaking and listening, reading and writing, as well as viewing and the development of multimodal literacies. Generic literacy skills, understandings and practices that are transferable across content areas (Fisher & Frey, 2015), as well as discipline-specific literacy (Beach, 2014), can be fostered through rich cross-disciplinary learning activities – and this endeavour can be supported and enhanced by the use of mobile technologies.

Although it is acknowledged that the term 'rich task' is not always used consistently in the literature or in practice, such tasks are generally deemed to be interdisciplinary, contextually authentic, resource-intense, dynamic and generative, student-centred, reflective and collaborative (Aubusson, Burke, Schuck, Kearney, & Frischknecht, 2014; Grabinger, Dunlap, & Duffield, 1997). The term will be used fairly loosely in this chapter to reflect its use by the teachers whose practices are described. It will be demonstrated in this chapter how mobile technologies can successfully be used to facilitate and transform such tasks.

Teachers with whom I work appreciate that engaging in rich tasks can support creativity, design, persistence, problem-solving, explanation, investigation, collaboration, questioning and prediction. Many of these skills are recognised as twenty-first century skills (Scott, 2015), which are considered to be essential for success in today's workplaces. Furthermore, rich tasks are likely to appeal to students with diverse abilities, interests and learning preferences because they offer a variety of cognitive challenges and ways of participating in learning experiences.

Inherent in such tasks are opportunities for making use of a variety of digital tools – for example, the use of the mobile device's camera to capture evidence in situ, and the employment of content free or productive apps to collect and record evidence of students' learning journeys (see Table 6.1 for a list of examples). Limited research has been carried out on mobile technologies and rich tasks in the context of literacy learning in early childhood and primary contexts, and this chapter aims to provide current examples of practice that may inform practitioners and researchers. It is essential that teachers and students have access to the tools they need for engaging in rich tasks, and mobile devices are appropriate tools for many rich learning tasks and are increasingly accessible and popular. This claim will be demonstrated throughout this chapter. In my experience, the popularity among teachers of devices such as iPads can be attributed to features such as portability, size, flexibility of use, ease of access (boot up and log-in), intuitive navigation systems, the availability and affordability of a range of apps and their ability to engage students in learning. Furthermore, mobile devices are relatively easy for students to learn to use, promoting independence and agency in children. I frequently observe students assisting each other before asking teachers for help.

Mobile devices are becoming prevalent in the home and, although there are still inequities when it comes to access to technology, a large proportion of children in Australia live in homes where there is at least one mobile device. According to the Australian Bureau of Statistics (2018), 91% of connected

Mobile Tools for Literacy Learning   101

Table 6.1: A Generic List of Suggestions for Using Apps to Address Typical Aspects of the Development of a Rich Task.

Stage of project	Kind of task	App genre or kind of technology required	Some popular app examples, all platforms + web-based		
Know the design brief or the project scope; clarify the goals	Find out what you are required to do; get the resources & class notes	Shared network or cloud account (to receive docs from teacher)	iCloud Google Drive Google Docs	Edmodo OneNote Class Notebook MS Office 365 Teams	WeMap Mural Stormboard
Get organised	Manage time and track deadlines	Timer, project planner tool, shared calendar	iHourglass Clock Pro	SandTimer Google Calendar	Tools4Students Timeli, Work Flowy
Plan ways to collaborate	Work out how to share ideas/work	Apps with provision for shared workspace/text	Email, chat, sms Padlet, WeMap	OneNote Class Notebook EtherPad	Google Docs Edmodo
Research to find facts	Research the content information	Browser, subject-specific apps for content	Safari, Chrome Internet Explorer	Subject content apps Wikipanion	Var. online databases Khan Academy Kids
Research to collect opinions	Collect data about what people think	Surveys, polling tool, spreadsheet, chart tool	Survey Monkey Kahoot!, Plickers	Poll Everywhere Microsoft Forms	Google Forms Socrative
Organise the ideas and facts	Show your research, plan your project	Concept-mapping tools, graphic organisers	Popplet, Kidspiration Nova Mind	Idea Sketch, Bubbl.us Espresso Mindmap	Tools4Students StoryboardThat
Set up the carrier app used to hold content	Select a content presentation method	Presentation, journal or portfolio apps	CBB, Book Creator Explain Everything	Doceri, Google Docs OneNote, Evernote	PPT, Sway, Prezi Keynote, Pages, SeeSaw
	Take photos and screenshots	Camera, screenshot or snipping tool	Device camera In-app camera access	Screen-capture Snipping tools	Snip&Share Screen Chomp
Collect or create useful multimedia	Collect images or video created by others	Browser, YouTube, screen capture, video converter	Safari search	YouTube Wikimedia	Google Images Creative Commons
	Take video, make a screen recording	Camera, screen capture, time-lapse apps	Onboard camera MovieMakerLive	In-app functions Spark, Sway	iMovie, ScreenChomp Office Mix, Snip
	Collect or create music or audio fies	Audio recording tool, music composition	Audacity, AudioNote GarageBand	Voice Recorder In-app tools	TuneTrain, WavePad Instrument play apps
Create the text content	Collect written key points from research	Note-taking software, word processor, e-pub	NotePad WebNotes	AudioNote LITE OneNote, MS Word	Pages Google Docs
	Get familiar with new vocabulary	Word-art apps, word puzzle makers, dictionary	Visual Poetry Wordle, Tagxedo	Type Drawing Word Collage	Crossword-Creator Word Mover
	Explore other written genres	Comic strip creators, poetry, infographics	Comic Life, Easel.ly Word Collage	Strip Designer Comic Creator, KidBlog	Word Tiles, Wordle Pictochart, Venngage
	Make a quiz or an interactive element	Multiple choice quiz or poll	CBB in-app quiz Microsoft Forms	QuizJet Google Forms	Kahoot! QR maker/scanner

Table 6.1: (Continued)

Create the image or video content	Improve photo(s) by annotation or creativity	Photo layering, filters, annotation, cropping etc	Juxtaposer iPhoto	Markup Photo Skitch, Photo Editor	Canva
	Draw a diagram or flowchart	Draw app, grid feature, measures, tech tools	Draw Grafio3	In-app tools Google Drawings	Drawing Desk Diagram, Visio
	Add a map, 2D plan, 3D model	Capture or create a map or pathway	Google Earth Google Maps	Atlas app Map Distance	FingerRuler 123DSculpt+
	Paint or draw a creative image	Pen/paint brush, stickers or cut-outs;	Kidpaint DoodleBuddy	StorymakerHD Scribblify, ArtStudio	Juxtaposer SketchFlow
	Create a slideshow	Use image sequence to tell story; save as video	Sway, Toontastic PhotoStory3	Google Slides 30 Hands, Animoto	PowerPoint iPhoto slideshow
	Create a composite image	Using many images to create one montage	PicStitch, Adobe Spark PicCollage	Snap Photo Collage Strip Designer	EasyPhotoEdit Frames
	Annotate a map or image	Load an image and draw or add text	Kidpaint Express OneNote, iPhoto	Skitch PicStitch	Doodle Buddy Fresh Paint
	Make an animated explanation	Stop-motion, time-lapse or path animation	MonkeyJam iMotion	Stop-Motion Plus StopMotion Studio	PowerPoint animation Powtoon
	Create a tutorial video	Real time screen-capture (with/without audio)	iMovie, PowToon Explain Everything	ShowMe, Doceri Office Mix, Snip	iXplain, Screen Chomp Vittle LITE
Create numerical content	Create/capture relevant numeracy content	Calculators, charts charting, inking apps	Distance Measure Ruler, Protractor	FingerRuler Numbers, MS Excel	Calculator In-app inking
Create other content	Get extra content from subject-specific apps	E.g. use screen-capture to document activity in apps	TanZen HD free Area & perimeter	Bridge Builder LITE GeoMeasure	Google Earth Angles, Origami
Perform media transfers	Collect all the media into one presentation	Shared "cloud" space Network transfer app	iTunes, Google Drive School LMS, email	External drives/USB WebDAV	In-app exporting AirDrop
Get feedback, evaluate, improve on the original	Get feedback from teacher and peers	Apps with shared chat or workspace	SeeSaw, Evernote Email, MS Teams	OneNote Class Notebook CanvasLMS	GoogleDocs EtherPad LITE
Present and submit finished work	Publish work, share and celebrate	Tech required to present/share work	iBookshelf Air printer, AirDrop	Presentation apps Portfolios, Journals	Data projector, IWB
Reflect on outcomes	Record a personal task evaluation	Camera, microphone and/or text creation	Camera – using the video setting	iMovie, Photo Booth	AudioNote In-app recording tools

Source: Clarke, J. (2016), Apportunities to shine: Using mobile technologies in classrooms and other amazing places, p. 143.

households in Australia owned a mobile or smart phone during 2016–2017, with 66% of connected households owning a tablet. Ninety seven percent of households in Australia with children under the age of 15 reported having an Internet connection, although rural and remote households were less likely to be connected. These statistics are in line with international trends, where mobile technology ownership has continued to rise, and children are experiencing increased mobile device use in the home. For example, 98% of households in the USA, in 2017, where children in the zero to eight age range resided, had at least one mobile device (Rideout, 2017), and young children (zero to eight) were spending an average of 48 minutes a day on mobile devices. It is acknowledged that there are some countries in the world there is much less access – see Chapter 9, Supporting Children's Literacy Learning in Low- and Middle-income Countries Through M-learning, by Oakley and Imtinan (2018) in this volume.

In addition to increased access at home, the author's ongoing discussions with both schools and colleagues in other Independent jurisdictions suggest a rapidly increasing number of Independent sector primary schools in Australia offer 1:1 mobile availability (in various management configurations) from Year 2 upward, and an increasing proportion require, or provide, personally owned or leased devices from Year 4 onwards. Indeed, there is a growing trend internationally for students to be required take their own device from home into the school for learning purposes. Bring your own device models in Hong Kong (Song, 2014), the USA (Clark, 2013) and New Zealand (Falloon, 2015), and many other countries have been discussed in the literature.

6.2. Guiding Principles for Using Mobile Devices in Literacy Learning

While implementing changes in technology use over the last decade, the schools I have worked with have been following various guidelines, informed by research, in an attempt to leverage the best value for the investment made in technology. The recommendations and considerations generated from early research in Independent schools in Western Australia (Oakley, Pegrum, Faulkner & Striepe, 2012) has proven to represent sound advice. Three categories of recommendations – technical, pedagogical and organisational – emerged from this research. It is, however, beyond the scope of this chapter to discuss all of the recommendations.

From my perspective, some of the most interesting and innovative examples of mobile learning used in schools relate to four of Oakley et al.'s (2012) recommendations, which encourage teachers to: include apps that promote the creation of content and higher order thinking skills; take advantage of multimedia tools and multimodal texts; include access to online virtual spaces (extending the notion of 'the classroom' by accessing remote experts, excursions, collaborative documents and imaginary worlds), and; include physically mobile activities (e.g. forming different groups, finding quiet or motivating places to work, learning outside, moving around and taking photos, capturing interviews, using Quick Response (QR) codes in various spaces and following GPS trails).

Using mobile devices in such ways can enable what Puentedura referred to as the 'redefinition' of learning tasks (Puentedura, 2011), which involves designing technology-infused learning tasks that were previously inconceivable. It can also provide meaningful variety in the contextual use of mobile technologies. The examples of practice provided in this chapter highlight the potential for enhancing literacy across the curriculum using mobile devices such as tablets and mobile phones.

6.3. Some Key Tools to Support Rich Task Processes

A wide range of mobile devices and software (apps) are available to help students generate, represent, capture, organise and share their learning in rich interdisciplinary tasks or projects. For example, multimodal digital journals, portfolios and presentations can be developed. Mobile devices such as tablets and smartphones have camera, audio recording and annotation tools that are particularly useful and efficient for capturing processes and evidence of student learning. Apps for concept mapping, data charting, creating flowcharts, rubrics, timelines, info-graphics and graphic organisers can all help students collect, organise, write, read and communicate their learning (see Table 6.1 e.g. of suitable apps). As many educators realise, available apps vary enormously in quality and have different features. As a response to this, many primary schools tend to have a standard set of 'tried and trusted' apps installed on devices that can be used across year levels and subject areas, although it is acknowledged that there is always a need to be trying and evaluating new devices and software so that practices can be updated. Table 6.1 offers examples of a generic process that can be applied to any rich task and example apps that suit each stage of the process. The process starts with getting to know the project and ends with sharing or publication. It is apparent in the 'Kind of Task' column of Table 6.1 that most of the activities in the process involve various aspects of literacy – whether it be researching, note-taking, learning new vocabulary, planning and creating multimodal texts, or presenting work to peers.

Two recent examples of products constructed using mobile devices come from Year 3 and 4 classes, at different schools, with whom I worked. Both used the *Book Creator* (Red Jumper Ltd.) app to create a multimodal 'learning journal' (or 'digital portfolio') of work. A preloaded template of 10 pages or fewer was used, with set page headings and a sketched storyboard of what was to be done, along with a suggested app, was provided to students for each heading. The template was used to expedite the process and give clarity to a first-time experience with this type of activity, with a view to students designing their own journals in future iterations. Working in pairs, students populated the pages with the required content in any order they preferred. Content included photos of hand-done work, sentence writing, annotated diagrams and maps, recorded video, drawings, timelines, screenshots and word clouds.

The journal of one class was based on classroom history lessons and an excursion, where data were collected, observations made and photos taken at a museum. The journal of the other class was designed to trial the potential for documentation of science work, in this case the topic, Heat. In both cases, it was clear that most of the participating Year 3 and 4 students (with no prior experience) had no difficulties in reading and following the visual instructions, navigating the e-pub app, transferring content created in various apps to the e-pub app ('app smashing') or managing their activities. They were engaged and enthusiastic, enjoyed using the new medium, appreciated the independence and responsibility, and appeared to greatly enjoy the freedom of moving around and making their own choices. Through the use of multimodal journals/portfolios that are built using apps on mobile devices, opportunities for enhancements in the ways that teachers assess literacy processes and products, as well as other areas of learning, are noteworthy. Self-assessment among children is also supported. See Figure 6.1 for an example of a Year 3 science journal.

6.4. Mobile Devices, Spaces and Places

Much of the literature on mobile learning refers to the learning benefits associated with moving around, or getting out and about with mobile devices, and learning in meaningful or authentic contexts (Kearney, Schuck, Burden & Aubusson, 2012; Traxler, 2012). Mobile devices can be used to enhance and transform learning in various spaces within the school grounds, such as maths corners, science areas and labs, drama spaces, design workshops, sports fields, art and music studios and language learning centres, among others.

QR codes, scanned with mobile devices, are a popular way for primary school teachers to give students quick access to online texts and resources when they are out and about or working in various spaces around the school. Online resources may include websites, images, video clips, written texts or audio files, the consumption of which can promote literacy learning. In some cases, QR codes may link to websites or services where students need to create texts of various kinds. QR codes can also be used to facilitate information or data sharing, linking users to student-generated works (usually saved on a school website) or public URLs. In addition, they can be used for outdoor trails, games and puzzles, treasure hunts or to encourage community connections and participation. The codes are extremely easy to generate (see, e.g. https://www.qr-code-generator.com/), simple to use and can be made applicable to any learning area. When used outside the school, they can link real places with relevant information in various formats and modes, or perhaps just instructions for what to do at that location. However, devices need an Internet connection, so use is limited to the extent of the WiFi signal, unless devices have cellular connection (and many devices used in primary schools do not).

The next few pages of this chapter describe rich cross-curricular tasks and projects undertaken by several schools where the author played a key role in supporting the integration of mobile devices to augment or transform the learning activities. The examples are presented according to the age group of the students involved.

6.5. Using Augmented Reality to Learn about Animals: Year 2

At a college in the Swan Valley on the outskirts of Perth, an early career classroom teacher worked with an experienced Information and Communications Technology (ICT) mentor teacher to design a rich learning experience as the culmination of a term of classroom studies about animals (Science) and information report writing (English) in a Year 2 classroom. Mobile technologies such as iPods (video capture) and iPads were extensively used during this project.

Initially, students were explicitly taught two different note-taking methods, and how to write information reports. They practised note-taking skills as a class, while watching sample videos of teacher-selected zoo animals. Using iPads, they generated colour-coded mind maps from their notes, after a discussion about advantages of colour coding for categorisation. To do this, they employed the *SimpleMind* app by XPT Software and Consulting BV. There are similar mind mapping apps that could be used if preferred.

Using the visual prompts in their mind maps, students wrote their own practise information reports, with support from the teacher. Once the process was understood, they were given time to browse animal information and select an animal for their project. To facilitate this, the teachers had located age-appropriate websites and videos about zoo animals and organised these in the *Aurasma* (an augmented reality (AR) app) editor, a cloud-based video hosting service. Photos of the animals (acting as triggers) opened the websites containing information and animal videos. Students were taught how to use the *Aurasma* app on their device. The trigger images were spread around the room and students had 20 minutes to view as many videos of animals as they could, before choosing the animal they wished to fully research (Figure 6.2).

In the ensuing lessons, students used the *Aurasma* app to independently access and read/view the information from the website provided for their chosen animal. They recorded and organised their facts using *SimpleMind* and wrote an information report (by hand) about their zoo animal using their research. Here, a blend of digital and non-digital was successfully used to promote children's writing skills. During the zoo excursion, students read their information report aloud, while standing in front of their researched animal. This presentation was video recorded by a partner student, using the camera/video function on iPod touch devices. Once back at school, photos of students (triggers) were linked to their videoed presentations, through the *Aurasma* hosting platform, to share with parent and peer audiences. This was a successful way for them to 'publish' or share their texts.

Students had also been learning about different habitats, animals and shelters. From this knowledge, they then began designing an imaginary animal and repeated the same general writing and reporting process as previously. In Art

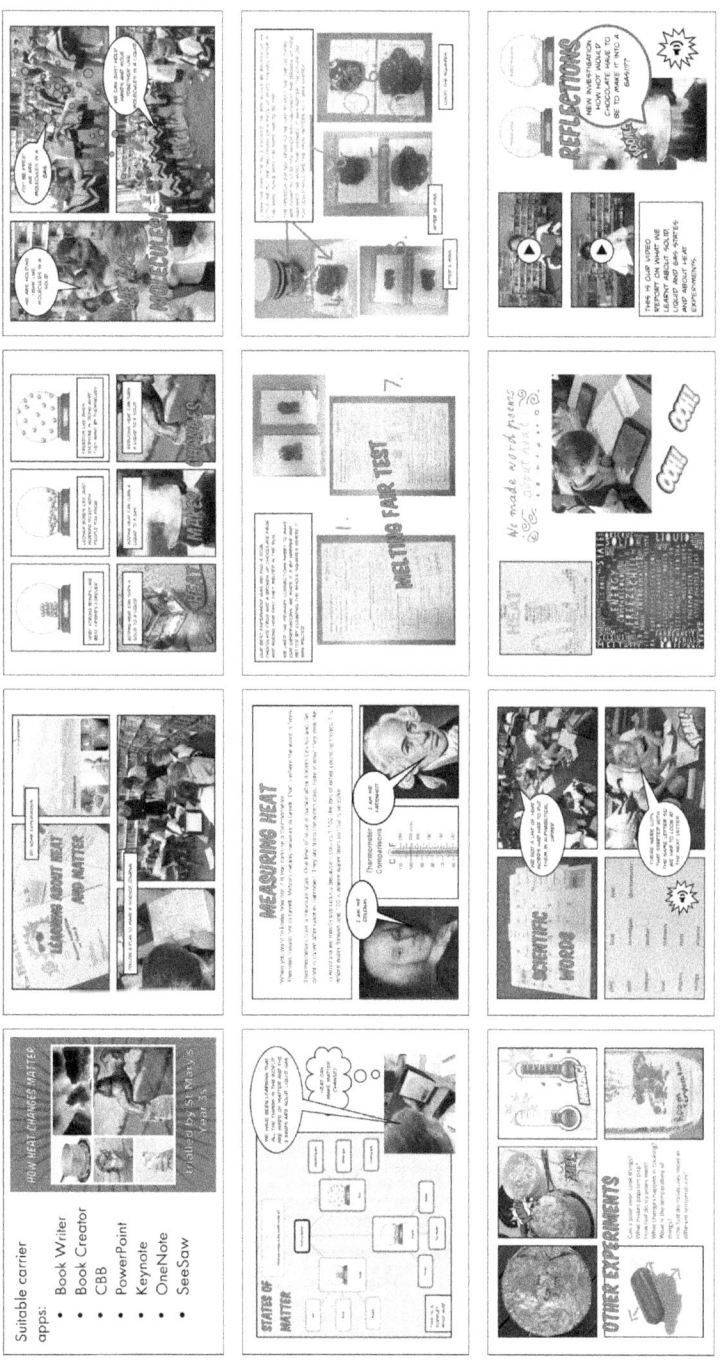

Figure 6.1: Year 3 Example of e-pub. Used as a Science Journal. *Source:* Clarke (2016), Apportunities to shine: Using mobile technologies in classrooms and other amazing places, p. 146.

classes, they drew, painted, sewed and stuffed a soft toy version of their imaginary animal. They then painted a background picture of the environment and made the animal's shelter out of craft materials. This new report was also presented, video-recorded on iPods and then linked to a 'trigger' picture of themselves, pinned to their diorama. Students used the *Aurasma* app on iPads to view each other's picture-triggered videos and provided feedback on each presentation using a paper-based template reflection sheet (*Two Stars and a Wish*). Again, this blend of the digital alongside traditional paper-based activities was in line with recommendations in Oakley et al.'s (2012) report, which was commissioned by AISWA. Parents were also invited into the classroom to view the children's videos.

Teachers and parents were impressed and enthusiastic about the level of skill and task management exhibited by the Year 2 students. The teacher stated that using the *Aurasma* app had significantly reduced the time usually taken for students to locate websites, leaving more time for research activities. Information was available for students to access independently and this allowed personalisation in terms of text choice, as well as access to facts online, task ownership, independence and working at an individual pace. The teacher reported that having the class so focused, engaged and working independently gave her, the teacher, more time to work with students who required one-on-one support. It was noted that the students' preferred method of notetaking was with the *SimpleMind* app, which enabled them to quickly and neatly categorise information when preparing their report writing. Additionally, the predictive text function and spelling auto-correct in the app assisted weaker spellers.

Student work was assessed by the teacher using checklists and rubrics. The assessable curriculum outcomes from the Australian Curriculum (Australian Curriculum Assessment and Reporting Authority, 2015) for the project were read, gather and record facts from websites in an organised manner (English); write an information report using sentences, an opening statement, a description (headings and paragraphs) and an evaluation (English); present orally, using clear speech, expression and at an audible volume (English); use technology systems to access websites and record videos and manage data, design and create a product using materials (Technologies). Students were able to achieve these literacy outcomes through carrying out authentic research tasks that involved them using their mobile devices and an AR app in a range of places, both inside and outside the school.

6.5.1. Telling Multimodal Tales of Lost Things in a Remote Aboriginal Community: Years 2 to 6

In a small, remote Kimberley Region community school, the teachers endeavour to ensure strong connection to the local indigenous language, land and culture. The predominant local languages in Aboriginal community are Gija and Kimberley Kriol. Proactive and participatory community members (Aboriginal Education Workers) formally support teachers to ensure that community and cultural connection is ongoing. They consistently model two-way (in English +

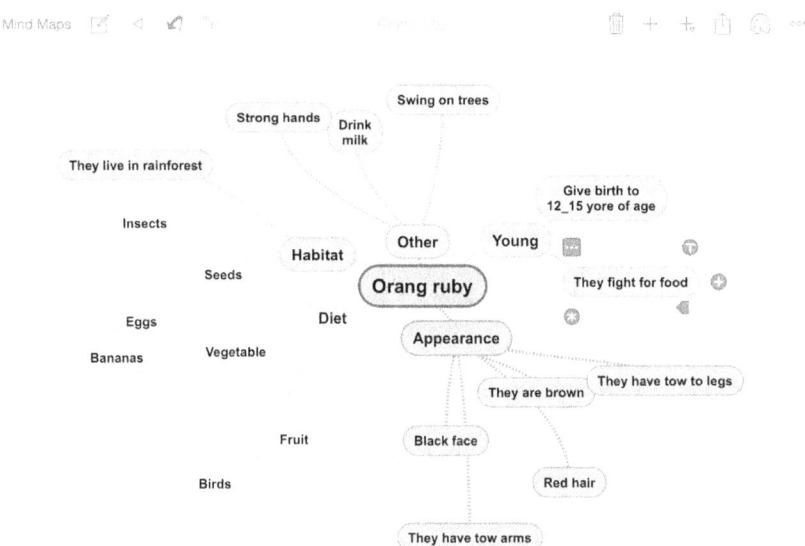

Figure 6.2: Year 2 Mindmap. *Source*: Clarke (2016), Apportunities to shine: Using mobile technologies in classrooms and other amazing places, p. 27.

local language) strategies (Malcolm, 1995), for example, by translating some popular children's picture books into bi-lingual multimodal texts for students to read and enjoy (for school use only). Students have also created talking, self-illustrated e-books in the three languages, giving them opportunities to write narratives based on local culture and share knowledge on important topics, such as fire. Students in this school frequently use digital devices both at desks and in a mobile, flexible way. They enjoy moving while working, learning outdoors and working in groups. The teachers at the school acknowledge that mobility is an important factor of engagement. One of the affordances of multimodality is the opportunity for second language learners to represent personal identity, or contribute their ideas, using more familiar and accessible communication strategies. Together with written words, multimodal representation can significantly enrich personal communication and digital devices increase the options and opportunities for doing so.

This project was designed to blend English (which has three strands in the Australian Curriculum – literacy, language and literature) with digital literacy and design technologies. Students from Year 2 to Year 6 read, viewed and discussed print and animated (video) versions of the picture book, *The Lost Thing* by Shaun Tan (2000). Both texts were used to explore aspects of the English curriculum, including story mapping, plot development, descriptive vocabulary and characterisation. The younger students drew (by hand) their own imaginary versions of a 'lost thing' that had arrived in their community and wrote sentences about its characteristics. They used tablets to photograph the drawings and also some places in the school grounds. Using the *Puppet Pals* (a 2D animation app by Polished Play LLC) app on their tablets, they cropped their pictures and used them as two-dimensional animated characters against photos of their local scenery, while speaking and recording a self-generated narrative. Even these younger students used the app without difficulty and most were not shy to narrate their story, and teachers reported that several students sang their animated story. Students were quite particular about finding 'just the right' background for their animations and most re-recorded their animated stories several times, without prompting, to improve them.

The *123D* (Autodesk Inc.) modelling app was used with the older students to create 3D models of their character. The students had not worked with 3D design before but managed to create a character, with varying degrees of detail. With assistance, the digital models were exported for 3D printing by the teacher. The intention was to use these for future oral language, narrative activities, stop-motion animation and/or board game design.

Teachers noted that levels of engagement were high, as was students' sense of ownership over their own creations (animations and 3D modelling). Plenty of productive talk resulted, including the use of newly introduced technical vocabulary. Students code-switched between English and their local language during this talk, productively using (speaking and singing in) both languages. The teachers suggested that an extension/enhancement activity would be to audio record in both languages or animate some cut-out words (vocabulary) to be part of the story. Through this activity, children practised their speaking and listening, a fundamental aspect of literacy.

6.5.2. Our Giant Fantastic Interactive Map: Blending Technology and Nature-based Learning: Years 3 to 4

This small Independent school in regional Western Australia promotes nature-based learning and community connection throughout all year levels. The purpose of the project being described in this chapter was to teach curriculum content, maintain a focus on student-centred learning, deepen the Year 3-4 students' understanding of local environment and Noongar culture, strengthen a sense of community and include the use of various technologies, both inside and outside the classroom (thus addressing curriculum expectations for ICT literacy). The students learnt about local animal life, ecosystems, history and culture, both inside and outside the classroom.

The shared class goal was for each student to study a local animal and its habitat (particularly cultural aspects of the habitat), write a science report on the animal, use the report as the basis of a video documentary, create a detailed and artistic still-life drawing of the animal (using taxidermy specimens from the local museum) and use these as *Aurasma* triggers for their documentaries, placing them on a giant student-generated map of the local area. Ultimately, QR codes were to be placed in wifi accessible outdoor areas to create an interactive 'local knowledge tour' using the student-generated content.

Students used tablets, laptops and digital cameras to collect, capture and edit their media. The teacher was inspired to adapt an existing idea into a more mobile AR activity to 'redefine' (Puentedura, 2011) her design of this classroom science report activity and investigate how m-learning could support and enhance a nature-based educational philosophy. She planned for her students to investigate local examples of science and history curriculum content, both in the classroom and in the outdoors environment, using tablets and digital cameras. Students were required to undertake active, collaborative tasks such as measuring distances and collecting numerical data outdoors, then scale the data and create a giant interactive map. The teacher aimed to involve parents and grandparents, who would bring their own device, bridging a generation gap and opening up conversations in a creative, authentic manner.

This Science, Technology, Engineering, Arts and Mathematics (STEAM) project had links across every subject area and general capability and it included the peer mentoring, buddy activities and community contribution important to the school. Technology (digital camera, tablet and laptop) facilitated differentiation for cognitive levels, intelligences, various learning styles, communication methods and inclusivity (specifically via spell check and a text-to-speech apps for certain students). The activity included features such as student-led learning, tackling real-world problems, team work, self-management, responsibility, independence, risk-taking and contextual situated learning.

Traditional literacy activities were incorporated in the project – reading for research and enjoyment, note-taking, learning and spelling new vocabulary, listening and comprehending during explicit instruction, explaining, describing, listing, investigating, considering the validity of information sources, writing and following instructions, creating multimedia presentations (print, video, images and audio) and scriptwriting. There was also an emphasis on visual texts – video, photos, diagrams and annotations, drawing, mapping, timelines and learning basic principles of good design. Students developed their skills using various mobile apps (similar to those in Table 6.1) as well as traditional learning materials. Individual choices were made about tools to complete activities, supporting the teaching/learning philosophy and a personalised approach. The emphasis of the inclusion of m-learning was to give the students flexibility to explore various simple ways to use technology tools for learning outdoors – a working model for colleagues of how natural and curriculum-mandated technological resources could be blended.

Activities involving collaboration included peer mentoring (social literacy and empathy), 'walking and talking' with purpose (while trail hiking), negotiating project management and establishing rules for shared responsibility regarding safety in the outdoors. Students engaged in cultural conversations with a Noongar Elder who assisted them in naming and identifying landmarks of historical and cultural significance. Numeracy content included collecting/recording data (measurements to create visual texts) and transposing/scaling up a small map to create their giant map (Figure 6.3).

Students took the responsibilities and the challenges inherent in this rich task seriously, motivated by the promise of creating an interactive product for their authentic audience and an enthusiasm for using technology. The teacher noted that the quality of the student work, and student participation was generally outstanding. Students had no problem taking responsibility for independent task management (especially using mobile devices outdoors and in groups) as this has always been part of the class culture, according to the teacher. The responses from students included: 'I love doing work outside because it doesn't feel like working but you learn a lot', and, 'You notice things you have never seen before because the teacher shows you how to look properly'.

6.5.3. Historical Discovery: A Contemporary Journey to Acknowledge the Past: Year 4

This project with Year 4 students was undertaken by an early career teacher in a Perth metropolitan school that favours inquiry-based approaches to learning. The school promotes a strong sense of identity, culture and participation in community. The goal was for students to create a QR code trail, incorporating research about school and community history that they had undertaken as a way of publishing and sharing their research. Using QR codes that they had generated using a QR generator, students were able to publish their historical information in the multimedia app format of their choice (although all chose webpages) and this would create the accessible content for the interactive QR code trail. The project incorporated note-taking, interviews, discussion and formal letter and instruction list writing. Students used *Popplet*, a brainstorming app (by Notion), *Puppet Pals* and *iMovie*, a video editing app (by Apple), *Scan QR Code and Barcode Reader* to read QR codes (QR Code City) and the device camera. They also carried out Internet research (on community history) using the iPad. Finally, they embedded their multimedia texts into student-designed webpages on the school's internal wiki site. The rich task was designed as an extended challenge for able students in 40 minute blocks over several weeks.

The students used a range of historical sources in their project, including: face-to-face interviews with community members; *Google Earth* (Google) satellite view 'historical imagery slider tool' to highlight past geographical locations of the school; the camera for capturing evidence from school archives; and the Internet for researching the history of prominent families in the community (matching the names on school buildings). By modelling each step of the process first, the teacher developed the project as a hands-on learning journey. This also provided an opportunity for her to consider and discuss any barriers to success and negotiate problem-solving strategies with the students. An example that arose was negotiating the use of shared devices. Another was meeting the needs of a large and varied viewing audience, including having the students' research work checked by the school principal (involvement of a significant other). The teacher also needed to negotiate/collaborate with other staff members who were sharing the devices, as well as the librarian/archivist and the IT manager. The class teacher sought and received contributions of information, anecdotes and assistance from parents and other community members to help students complete the research and noted that it ended up being a real community effort.

Once the research, scripting and multimedia text production parts of the project had been completed, the group collaborated to design posters containing

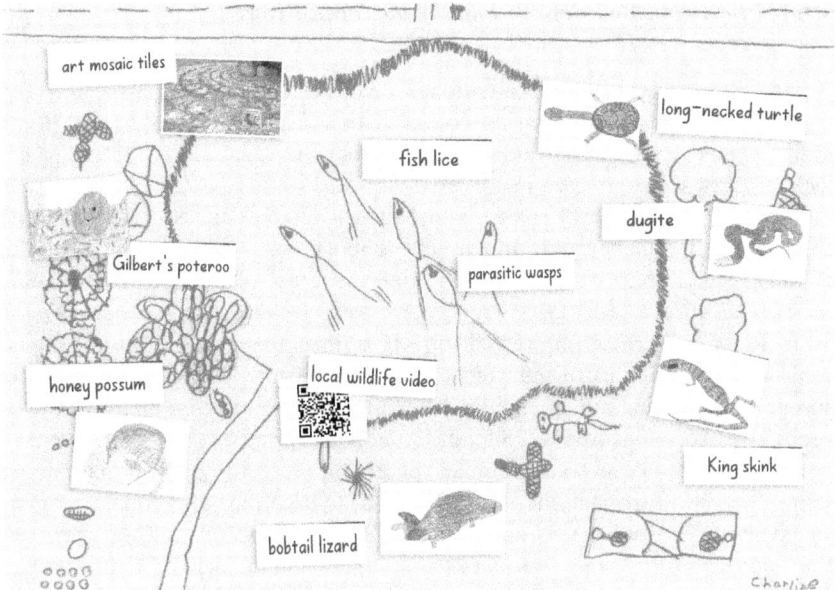

Figure 6.3: Interactive Map Creation, a Collaborative Activity for Year 3-4 Students. *Source*: Clarke (2016), Apportunities to shine: Using mobile technologies in classrooms and other amazing places, p. 37.

simple instructions on how to access the information they had linked to the QR codes. These instructions were disseminated at a school assembly, through the school newsletter and via student-generated posters located next to the QR codes that were displayed on project-related buildings throughout the school, so that audiences could find and access them.

The teacher was satisfied that her good preparation had paid dividends. To make the project work, she had needed to learn about QR codes. It had also been necessary to collaborate with technical support staff to have student websites hosted within the existing infrastructure. To make it manageable for the students, she had split the large project into small segments. Given that the project had a strong well-planned framework, she had been confident to transfer decision-making and responsibility to the students, facilitating and guiding where necessary, giving students a degree of agency. Engagement was sustained despite the project involving research (sometimes considered 'boring' by the age-group). The collaborative tasks meant that students were able to use their strengths in group tasks. A range of literacy and ICT skills were extensively used in context. Previous practise/play with the apps and device functions had allowed the students to concentrate on their goals rather than becoming anxious about or being distracted by new technology. Smaller skill building projects had been a useful place to start, such as creating a simple *Popplet* brainstorm about a classroom topic.

6.5.4 An Augmented Reality Trail by the Swan River: Years 6 to 10

A particular advantage of the situational use of QR codes, location-specific GPS triggers (e.g. using tools such as *FreshAiR* or *ARIS*) or image-triggers (using tools such as *Aurasma* by Aurasma Inc.) is that they can allow students to use their physical senses to learn in context.

Modelled on Dunleavy, Dede, and Mitchell (2009) studies of students and their use of an immersive AR app, middle school classes (ages 12–15), a handful of Independent sector schools in WA trialled the use of the *FreshAiR* (MoGo Mobile) location-aware (GPS trigger) AR app. I chose one location (by the Swan River in Perth) and created an AR trail in the *FreshAiR* editor cloud. Both natural and constructed points of interest in this location were plentiful and diverse, opening a huge number of possibilities for location pins (GPS markers). These locations were GPS 'pinned' and appropriate multimedia content or instructions (for taking water samples, photographs, recording information and so on) was linked through the *FreshAiR* editor to each pin. This content primarily involved the students reading, viewing and listening for various purposes. For each class, the trail was tweaked (pins/content hidden or made visible) according to the topic that best suited their studies. Classes chose options from history, art, science, sports, Indigenous culture, biology, geography, built environment and politics.

Students brought along their personal smartphones to follow the trail. Those without cellular connection or data download were responsible for gathering other data (such as photos, audio recordings or keeping notes) on their devices. Students proved to be capable of navigating the GPS points, working enthusiastically in groups and collaborating well. They accessed and engaged with a great deal of multimodal text (through devices) and behaved responsibly.

In terms of challenges, it was found that viewing screens in the Australian sun created difficulties, local noise made some audio hard to hear, inbuilt GPS in phones varied in accuracy and battery life was an issue. The content (number of locations and amount of information to consume at each location point) was found to be excessive for some students (risking cognitive overload) and more reflection time was needed ('stop, look and listen') so that students could really take advantage of what the environment and the linked information had to offer. Several classes have since successfully built their own trails.

The example earlier, which was carried out by slightly older students, has been included in this chapter because upper primary students (e.g. Year 6) would certainly have been capable of doing this activity. However, at the time of the trial in 2015, the number of primary aged students with cellular, data enabled smartphones were not sufficient to make the activity viable. The *FreshAiR* app now works on the iPad, which is very popular in primary schools, and portable WiFi has become more reliable. Furthermore, a greater number of Year 6 students now own smartphones with suitable features. It would be appropriate to trial this with primary classes in the future.

6.5.5. Taking a New Way Home: Testing a Pathway to Independence in Learning: Year 6

The purpose of this project with Year 6 students was to introduce them to a new method for engaging in reading/viewing, studying and practising grammar, as well as developing empathy and social conscience through critical examination of a picture book text. The development of a prototype e-pub template text (scaffolded for independent, self-paced learning) was a collaborative effort by AISWA English and ICT Literacy consultants. It was first tried in a Year 6 classroom in regional Carnarvon in Western Australia.

The picture book studied was *Way Home* by Hathorn and Rogers (1994), which is a story, written in blank verse, about a homeless boy who befriends a stray cat. The content was informed by the requirements of the Australian Curriculum: English syllabus. The overarching concepts of home, homelessness, community, comfort, friendship, familiarity and compassion were included. This was the pastoral context of the learning, addressing aspects of Humanities and Social Science (HASS), Health and Physical Education, Religious Education and community awareness in this school.

An e-book template scaffolded with page headings, activity instructions on each page (deleted once addressed), video links and language strand activities was preloaded onto each student's tablet within the *Creative Book Builder* app (Tiger Ng). At that time, students were not familiar with the *CBB* app or with the concept of 'app smashing' (combining a variety of apps to achieve a larger goal, see Table 6.1). They had limited experience with using the technology for activities other than Internet searches, taking photos and skill and drill type games. They were asked to try to complete the various activities with as little teacher input as possible to determine how well they could self-manage. Some of the activities included in the e-book were extensions of explicit whole class teaching and others were new.

The apps and activities were selected from the kinds listed in Table 6.1. The English concepts studied were text analysis, narrative development, contractions, syllables, figurative language, adjectives and adverbs, symbolism, quotation marks, vectors, persuasive text, parables as teaching texts, framing, visual literacy, code switching, note-taking, dot points, literacy with comic and documentary texts, sequencing, new vocabulary, sentence structures, capitalisation, reading numerical (statistical) texts, justification, explanation, speaking and oral presentation skills.

Ethical considerations around authorship, intellectual property and copyright needed to be an explicit part of whole class discussion. While students referred to a full class set of purchased copies of the print text, the activities required them to photograph pages and reproduce, annotate and remix the text in a digital format in their e-pubs. Although these would not be published in a public arena, the potential ethical and legal issues needed discussion.

Creative Book Builder was chosen as the main authoring app instead of other popular, more intuitive e-pub or e-portfolio apps (such as *Book Creator*, *Book Writer* or *OneNote*) because of the particular range of tools it offered. The idea was to ascertain how much difficulty students of this age (typically aged around

11) might have in reading and negotiating more complex menu systems and tool types. It was found that this perceived complexity posed no problem for the students, despite them being novices with this app. Peer collaboration sorted out any issues.

The teacher was particularly impressed by the students' commitment to this rich task. He suggested that the scaffolds and the 1:1 scenario supported a significant level of independence and ownership and maintained student interest by offering diverse ways of working, opportunities for peer collaboration and the use of engaging tools to complete fairly standard classroom tasks. The template e-pub (and hybrids that use other apps such as Microsoft's *OneNote*) has since been trialled in various classes from Years 6 to 12 in independent schools around Western Australia, and teachers of all year levels have commented on the increased and sustained engagement and particularly on the output exhibited by less academic students who may have shorter concentration spans. These teachers reflected that students responded well to their perceived learning freedom- to be allowed to consult with their classmates and complete learning tasks in a context-based interesting, practical, flexible, personally empowered more and less teacher-directed way. This feedback suggests that the teacher was successful in introducing a degree of personalisation, authenticity and collaboration (Kearney et al.,2012) into the learning tasks. This enriched their literacy learning more and allowed them to practise and develop the literacy skills described above in collaborative and authentic contexts than might otherwise have been possible.

6.6. Concluding Comments

When curriculum content, pedagogy and technology are deeply understood by the teacher and activities are well planned, even younger students find rich, complex tasks using mobile devices such as tablets surprisingly manageable. In the examples of practice presented in this chapter, the teachers effectively capitalised on the resources they had available – environmental, community and digital – and designed rich learning tasks that developed students' literacy skills and used mobile devices, particularly tablets, productively and purposefully within the context of various areas of the curriculum. Large, collaborative projects were broken into manageable chunks and planned thoroughly enough to avoid foreseeable problems, and teachers improvised where necessary to take advantage of incidental learning and manage unforeseen logistical issues. The obvious enthusiasm the teachers had for the projects (and topic area) was contagious.

Designing rich tasks is not easy. The risk of diminishing important subject-specific content by not providing necessary explicit teaching time should be acknowledged. The skill and time required on the part of the teacher to blend and build content into rich cohesive tasks that present open-ended challenges, authenticity and relevance and promote engagement and agency, is considerable. Deep knowledge of the curriculum and a range of tools (digital and non-digital), strategies and scaffolds are needed. The teacher must be able to plan for, and tease out, any formative and summative assessment and reporting requirements from the mix. Time for the activity has to be found and the abilities and interests of different students need to be considered. Resources need to be collected and managed. However, in return for the investment in time and effort in planning, the rewards can be significant.

From their research, Aubusson et al. (2014, p. 220) describe the 'intellectual strategies students acquire in the process' as a perceived and valuable outcome of rich projects involving technologies (in their case, Interactive Whiteboards). Results of their study suggest that teachers 'have strong alignments with rich task pedagogy' (p. 228) and are indeed willing to tackle logistical and attitudinal barriers about using technology, and put effort into planning rich tasks, when they expect the students will enjoy the work, be engaged and learn more than they would otherwise.

Mobile devices are "compact, go-anywhere, affordable multi-function tools with customised functionality, personal relevance, contextual learning opportunities, connectivity to people and information – plus the access to a full range of multimodal multimedia-rich texts for communication" (Clarke, 2016, p. 6). From my observations in classrooms and personal involvement with professional learning delivery and action research projects as a jurisdiction technologies consultant, I am convinced that the general level of teacher competence and confidence' with digital technologies (and specifically mobile devices in primary years) has significantly grown, particularly over the last five years. An emphasis on process and project management in two new Technologies subjects of the Australian Curriculum, as well as a surge of interest in integrated *STEM/ STEAM* content-related projects, augers well for appropriate, purposeful and practical application of literacy skills in a contextually relevant, technology-rich environment. As learning environments diversify and transitions between them become increasingly seamless, literacy and educational technology maintain their strong and critical synergy.

References

Aubusson, P., Burke, P., Schuck, S., Kearney, M., & Frischknecht, B. (2014). Teachers choosing rich tasks: The moderating impact of technology on student learning, enjoyment, and preparation. *Educational Researcher, 43*(5), 219–229. doi:10.3102/0013189X14537115

Australian Bureau of Statistics. (2018). *Household Use of Information Technology, Australia, 2016–17* (Cat. No. 8146). Retrieved from http://www.abs.gov.au/ausstats/abs@.nsf/mf/8146.0

Australian Curriculum Assessment and Reporting Authority [ACARA]. (2015). *Australian Curriculum: Foundation to year 10 curriculum V 8.1.* Sydney, NSW. Retrieved from https://www.australiancurriculum.edu.au/f-10-curriculum/

Beach, R. (2014). *Using apps for learning across the curriculum: A literacy-based framework and guide.* Florence: Taylor and Francis.

Clark, T. (2013). *Advantages of the BYOT Classroom.* [Web log post]. Retrieved from http://www.eschoolnews.com/2013/10/30/hallmarks-byot-classroom-202/

Clarke, J. (Ed.). (2016). *Apportunites to shine: Using mobile technologies in classrooms and other amazing places.* Perth: Association of Independent Schools of WA.

Dunleavy, M., Dede, C., & Mitchell, R. (2009). Affordances and limitations of immersive participatory augmented reality simulations for teaching and learning. *Journal of Science, Education and Technology, 18*, 7−22. doi:10.1007/s10956-008-9119-1

Falloon, G. (2015). What's the difference? Learning collaboratively using iPads in conventional classrooms. *Computers & Education, 84*, 62−77. doi:10.1016/j.compedu.2015.01.010

Fisher, D., & Frey, N. (2015). Revisiting content area literacy instruction. *Principal Leadership, 15*(6), 54−56.

Grabinger, S., Dunlap, J. C., & Duffield, J. A. (1997). Rich environments for active learning in action: Problem-based learning. *ALT-J, 5*(2), 5−17.doi:10.1080/0968776970050202

Hathorn, L., & Rogers, G. (1994). *Way home.* London: Random House.

Kearney, M., Schuck, S., Burden, K., & Aubusson, P. (2012). Viewing mobile learning from a pedagogical perspective. *Research in learning technology, 20*(1), 14406.

Malcolm, I. (1995). *Language and communication enhancement for two-way education: report.* Perth, Australia: Edith Cowan University. Retrieved from http://ro.ecu.edu.au/ecuworks/7174

Oakley, G., & Imtinan, U. (2018). Supporting children's literacy learning in low- and middle-income countries through m-learning. In G. Oakley (Ed.), *Mobile technologies and language and literacy: Innovative pedagogy in preschool and primary education.* Bingley: Emerald Publishing.

Oakley, G., Pegrum, M., Faulkner, R., & Striepe, M. (2012). *Exploring the pedagogical applications of mobile technologies for teaching literacy* (pp. 76−78). Graduate School of Education, University of Western Australia.. Retrieved from http://www.education.uwa.edu.au/__data/assets/pdf_file/0003/2195652/AISWA-Report-FINAL-Final-101012-2.pdf

Puentedura, R. (2011). *SAMR and TPCK in action.* Retrieved from http://www.hippasus.com/rrpweblog/archives/2011/10/28/SAMR_TPCK_In_Action.pdf

Rideout, V. (2017). *The common sense census: Media use by kids age zero to eight.* San Francisco, CA: Common Sense Media.

Scott, C.L. (2015). *The futures of learning 3: What kind of pedagogies for the 21st century?* [ERF Working Papers Series, No. 15]. UNESCO Education Research and Foresight, Paris. Retrieved from http://unesdoc.unesco.org/images/0024/002431/243126e.pdf

Song, Y. (2014). "Bring your own device (BYOD)" for seamless science inquiry in primary school. *Computers & Education, 74*, 50−60. doi:10.1016/j.compedu.2014.01.005

Tan, S. (2000). *The Lost thing.* Sydney: Lothian Books/Hachette Australia.

Traxler, J. (2012). Educators go over the garden wall. *Interactive Learning Environments, 20*(3), 199−201.

Chapter 7

Mobilising Critical Literacies: Text Production in Children's Hands

Lisa Kervin, Annette Woods, Barbara Comber and Aspa Baroutsis

Abstract

The structures, procedures and relationships within schools both constrain and enable the ways that children and teachers can engage with the everyday 'business' of literacy learning. In schools and classrooms, the resources available to children, the spaces in which they work and how adults interact with them are often decided upon by others, including their teachers. In this chapter, we focus specifically on access to mobile digital resources and important spaces in the school, arguing that opportunities for children to be critical consumers and producers of text can be provided when children are afforded some control of decisions about how, where and when people, materials, tools and texts are used. Drawing from data collected as part of a larger study of learning to write in the early years of schooling, at two different schools in different Australian states, we examine two cases of 'disruption' negotiated by children and their teachers. We explore the potential of mobile technologies in children's hands as key elements in changing the socio-spatial power relations around text production that usually hold in schools. These instances are explicit opportunities to study what is possible when young children and teachers work to change children's relationships to materials, spaces and people in productive and provocative ways. We analyse the digital texts produced and the work of teachers and children to foreground digital literacies as a way to influence what goes on in their schools.

Keywords: Critical literacy; text producers; mobile technologies; mobility; children; digital texts

7.1. Introduction

Children's bodies are regulated in schooling in predictable ways that subject them to constant surveillance. School timetables, classroom routines and the organisation of spaces through furniture placement, accessibility to texts, resources and other materials, mean that individuals can be located and monitored as a matter of routine. This surveillance works to do much more than just keep children safe and able to learn, as has been argued by education scholars, particularly those drawing on Foucauldian, poststructural and posthuman frames (see e.g. Comber, 2000; Woods & Henderson, 2008).

From a critical literacy standpoint, we explore how teachers and children might contest traditional roles, positions and placements as they engage in learning at school. Vasquez (2014) identified the typical discourses of control that exist in artefacts of schooling – such as curriculum and testing – and the need to deliberately disrupt these in everyday classroom life. We argue that digital and smart technologies provide particular mobility affordances while 'being' a student. This also means researchers need new ways to understand the structures, procedures and relationships within schools and how these may constrain and/or enable children and teachers as they engage in literacy learning. We focus specifically on access to mobile, digital resources but also focus on spaces, particularly on occasions when children and teachers use or access spaces differently. Our argument is that opportunities for children to be critical consumers and producers of text can be provided when children are afforded some control of decisions about how, where and when people, materials, tools and texts are used and move.

International studies indicate that the regulation of children's bodies is particularly significant (e.g. Dixon, 2011; Kamler, Maclean, Reid, & Simpson, 1994; Luke, 1992) with respect to early school literacy instruction (Dyson, 2016; Marsh, 2016). Children's posture, stillness and noise output are all subject to teacher attention (Comber, 2004). In addition, how children are understood to be literate, or not, often has implications for where they might be seated, who they might have access to and what resources they are encouraged or even mandated to use. This may not be surprising as we know that teachers are encouraged to group and differentiate instruction accordingly. When, how and with what tools children can communicate in schools is also highly regulated. Their own voices, writing and drawing implements, mobile phones and other digital technologies for producing texts are all subject to regulated access and typically under strict adult control (Kuby & Gutshall Rucker, 2016).

Critical literacy in early childhood classrooms can be understood as incorporating at least three major forms of practice – repositioning students as researchers of language, respecting minority language practices and problematising texts (Comber, 1994), which contest the usual regulation of young children in schools. In the cases which follow, we particularly see instances of children being repositioned as researchers of language and how this can work to alter school socio-material relations. Significantly, the children are not only repositioned in the investigatory aspects of critical literacy concerning language use, but also with this repositioning they have more license to participate in different spaces in the school. This combination of repositionings of young learners, materially, academically and by placing the means of multimodal text production into their hands, is potentially a major shift in the power economies of schooling. More recently, literacy researchers have recognised the need to study what is going on beyond literacy events and practices in order to more fully conceptualise diverse learner identities and trajectories. In this chapter, we explore how departures from the ordinary organisation of children's bodies, technologies and school spaces can productively shake up what constitutes early literacy development and force us to attend to difference, power and literate repertoires.

The communities in which we research, in a range of poor and working class Australian locations, are a constant reminder that access to technologies is not equitable. Many households do not have computers, iPads, tablets or computer games. Access to technology through smart phones — which we know has made technology cheaper and more accessible now than in previous decades — has provided some alleviation to this equity gap. However, while we recognise that the affordability of information and communication technologies through smartphones and other devices is resulting in more young children having increasing access to a range of technologies to play, communicate and produce multimodal texts of various kinds (Danby, Davidson, Theobald, Houen, & Thorpe, 2017; Kervin, 2016; Wohlwend, 2008), access to quality in technologies and digital texts is still not equitable. In the long term, schools play an increasingly important role in providing access to technologies for children in poorer communities. And yet for many reasons, including the inability of education systems to provide open free access to online technologies in schools and top-down imperative to push back to the basics, schools have generally been slow to change their practices with regard to students accessing a range of technologies for a range of purposes. Despite this, there are early childhood educators who are willing to experiment with a range of technologies where children come to understand the potential power of text as multimodal producers in school contexts (Baroutsis and Towers, 2017; Comber, Woods, & Grant, 2017; Kervin, Comber, & Woods, 2017; Kuby & Gutshall Rucker, 2016). In this chapter, we draw from the innovative practices of teacher-researchers with whom we are collaborating on a three-year study of the ways in which children are learning to produce texts.

7.2. Looking for Departures

Our approach has been to foreground the materiality of learning to write, but to also be conscious of social and spatial issues related to children as learners, and to learning. So we have been open to learning new things about who, where, what, with what and with whom children are involved as they become writers. Through this line of thought, the social and material are in a relationship — they are constitutive of everyday life in what Barad (2007) has called *intra-action*. Fenwick (2016) reminds us that it is not enough to focus on just the social elements of engaging in everyday practices such as learning to write — rather the social and the material – the human and non-human – are entangled in ways that defy their separation. A sociomaterial approach is cognizant that 'things' or 'stuff' are not just used by humans, rather they must be explored as 'effects of heterogeneous relations' (Fenwick & Edwards, 2011, p. 2).

Kuby, Rucker, and Kirchhofer (2015) describe their grappling with the process of using posthuman theory and notions of sociomateriality to analyse data collected in early childhood literacy classrooms in order to find enabling approaches to consider space and materiality of how children learn to write. They settle on an approach to analysis, by focusing on three aspects: 'departures from the expected, the notion of becoming, and intra-activity' (p. 403). Taking forward some of their thinking here, we aim to take a sociomaterial approach to understanding the opportunities that are opened when teachers and children intentionally shift authority and control of literacy learning towards children, and when children use learning spaces differently.

We use two examples to represent what can happen when there is a departure from the norm. Many years of experience in schools observing and participating in literacy lessons has provided us with intricate understandings of the macro, meso and micro ways of teaching and learning literacy. So each of these examples demonstrates teachers and children practicing 'learning to write' in ways that were unexpected. The children experienced space differently and indeed experienced or filled different spaces. As children moved fluidly within and between spaces, there were unexpected decisions made by children on what to focus on, specifically, what elements to include in the texts they produced.

We were also interested in what these instances of critical literacy pedagogy enabled for the young children involved in terms of the literacy learners they were and were to become. By this, we mean that we were able to focus on the new ways of being that the children involved took on. The notion of *becoming* allowed us to observe how the children involved took up and engaged with materials, how they used the time provided to them to take charge and how they moved through spaces to get their work done (Kuby et al., 2015). Finally, as with Kuby and her colleagues, we have allowed the idea of intra-action to shift our minds to thinking not about children as learners, nor about mobile technologies as tools to support this learning – but instead to consider the in-between entanglements of human child with material resources. This has enabled a focus on the child and technology, moving through physical and virtual spaces, to produce texts. Taking these theoretical ideas forward, we move in the next section to detail two recent examples of young children where technology is used to mobilise critical literacy in their schools.

7.3. Two Examples of Children, Mobility and Technology for Literacy Learning

The data discussed in this paper were collected as part of a larger federally funded, Australian study where teachers, researchers and children have worked together to understand how the teaching of writing is enacted across schools at this time. The project Learning to Write in the Early Years (LWEYs)[1] was conducted in two state-funded primary schools in communities of high poverty. Our overall objective was to consider with teachers and children what learning to write in contemporary political, policy and education contexts could be. Our emphasis was to investigate high quality, high equity literacy education and how this might be achieved for all children in schools and classrooms. We have worked with teachers to consider learning to write as a collaborative, collective practice and as a multimodal task where the aim should always be text production and meaning making. The study was conducted in three parts: a school audit where we collected data and reported findings to each individual school; design-based experiments where teachers and researchers worked together to renew and reform the teaching of writing in their classrooms; and case studies of children as they engage in learning to write in their classrooms and schools. In this chapter, we draw on data collected as part of two design-based experiments, conducted by teachers in two schools. Design-based classroom experiments enable a better understanding of the learning environment as teachers identify and plan a pedagogical intervention to better support learning (Cobb, Confrey, diSessa, Lehrer, & Schauble, 2003). Design-based experiments are framed by the notion that 'systematic and disciplined inquiry into real problems in authentic classrooms is vital to developing workable solutions to support teachers if they are to implement instructional practices that benefit children' (Bradley & Reinking, 2011, p. 305). Importantly, when researchers and teachers work collaboratively on authentic classroom inquiries, they 'close the gap between research and practice' as well as provide teacher professional learning that works towards improving 'teachers' instructional practice and transforming classroom environment' (Bradley & Reinking, 2011, p. 309).

Both of the schools featured in this chapter are located in Australian communities of high poverty. The first is part of the suburban sprawl of a state capital city. The community has high levels of unemployment and under-employment. The school is surrounded by other schools, but numbers are steadily increasing. There are currently just over 500 students from Foundation year to Year 6, 10–12% of whom identify as Aboriginal and/or Torres Strait Islander people. More than 50% of attending students have a language background other than English with many receiving English as Additional Language/Dialect (EALD) Support, and the school publicly positions itself as multicultural and catering for the needs of diverse cultural groups harmoniously. The second school is smaller, with 200 students, and approximately 12–15% of those students identifying as Aboriginal and/or Torres Strait Islander people. The number of children

---

[1]The *Learning to Write in the Early Years* project team includes Annette Woods, Barbara Comber, Lisa Kervin and Aspa Baroutsis. We acknowledge the Australian Research Council for funding through its Discovery Program (DP150101240). We wish to thank the leaders, teachers, children, their families and communities who are our research partners and acknowledge their time effort and intellectual input into our work.

accessing support for English language is approximately 10% of the student cohort. The neighbourhood, once prosperous, has been hit by unemployment and transience with local industry closure. Student numbers at the school are decreasing, and the school finds itself competing with other schools in the area for student numbers. Despite these statistics of disadvantage, both schools have had success and the teachers have continued to focus on pedagogy and curriculum reform over many years and they were eager to participate in the LWEYs project as part of this ongoing work. As with most schools such as these, staff focus has been directed towards improving student outcomes on national tests, with some evidence of improvement at both schools over the past few years.

In the sections that follow, we present details of our work with two teachers and several cohorts of children. The first case details children becoming writers in a writing Club, an elective activity for children from Year 3 and Year 5, which was conducted in lunchtime through to the end of the school day, once a fortnight for each of the year levels. The second case details children operating within a classroom unit of study to forge an opportunity to take a mobile device to the office to document the activities of office staff. Pseudonyms are used for all participants in our presentation of these cases. As we examine each case, we ask the following question: *What happens when children leave their classrooms and are allowed some choice about how bodies, materials and tools move and are used, and how texts are produced and consumed?* We are interested particularly in how children represent these experiences using digital or multimodal texts, and the place of digital technologies in how children engage with representing their worlds.

7.4. Example 1: Writer's Club

This case details engagement of a teacher leader – Pam (pseudonym) – whose role at the school was to lead classroom teachers in curriculum and pedagogy reform. Part of the leadership team at the school, she also had responsibility for improving outcomes in literacy and numeracy, especially as measured by national literacy and numeracy tests.[2] As such, one component of her role included working with groups of children or individual children, usually with a specific focus on literacy and numeracy. The school, and specifically Pam, had recently started to look closely at a more diverse range of data related to children's literacy outcomes and as a result there was a push to provide access to time to work with Pam to a broader range of children. As such, in a departure from normal practice, from how things had occurred in the past, the idea for the *Writers' Club* for writers in Years 3 and 5 was initiated.

---

[2]In Australia, in 2018, all children in Years 3, 5, 7 and 9 sit national tests in literacy and numeracy. The National Assessment Program in Literacy and Numeracy (NAPLAN) involves all Australian children being tested across five domains – reading, writing, spelling, punctuation and grammar and numeracy – in tests held each May.

Writers' Club was an outside classroom literacy learning space where children attended on a fortnightly basis – Year 3 children one week, Year 5 children the next. Pam and the classroom teachers discussed who should be invited, identifying those children who had potential to be strong writers. The teachers recommended some children, and Pam identified others from assessment data – but each child invited to join was determined through a process of negotiation between Pam and classroom teachers before an invitation was issued. The selected children were provided with the choice to attend or not – the sessions went over a lunch time as well as afternoon class time so the children had to be willing to be involved during their free time. All the children who received an invitation agreed to become members. One additional Year 4 child came to the Club uninvited, and managed to negotiate her inclusion with Pam, such was her enthusiasm for writing.

There was a general level of excitement during each Club session, lots of talking, lots of writing, and lots of laughter. All Club members were provided with a folder and writing materials. They were told why they had been selected, and their responsibilities were identified – including the responsibility of care for the new Club folders. The purpose of the Club was expressed as having two dimensions. First, to support members to become better writers and second, for the members to become leaders of writing in their classrooms. The first weeks of *Writers' Club* engaged the first purpose. Children wrote in their folders, they were involved in mini lessons about sizzling starts for writing. They settled into a practice of writing a newsletter entry to tell their parents, teachers and friends about what they were doing in the Club. This activity was usually completed by a small group with the researcher. In the first few weeks, all Club members participated in an external writing competition and almost all received the wonderful news that their texts would be published in a yearbook. The children wrote as much between Club sessions as they did during the sessions, and often came to Club to have the adults who attended read their written texts.

The Club struggled to find a home – a space that could be usefully used for purpose. They began in Pam's Office, but often struggled to find places to sit, to work together or with adults or to see computers or texts being modelled. The small space seemed to amplify noise. They moved to another classroom which housed a variety of intervention programmes and staff. This space worked well during the lunch time, but interfered with other activities during the afternoon class time. So they returned to the rather cramped office space, making do with sharing chairs or finding floor space to write and talk. Pam and the children talked about this use of space and what would work best – the decision to return to the Office was made collectively. The children were part of the decision-making process about where to meet. This issue alerts us to the politics of space within schools; it is not simple for teachers and students to find places to write together at times which have not been time-tabled, such is the specific designation of people, technologies, furniture and resources. This challenge makes us attend to the sociomateriality of everyday literate practices in schools. Disruption to the usual routines produces more work for Pam, as she advocates for the children to actively support their peers in writing.

The children had access to additional materials and had some control over how they worked and where; interactions between children and adults were informal although focused on the task at hand − writing and producing texts. However, for the most part, the *Writers' Club* engaged children in writing as they might in many classrooms where independent writing or process writing is the approach taken. What we are interested in for this chapter is when Pam and the children shifted the purpose Club membership from *being a writer* to *being an advocate − a supporter of others and their writing*.

This move was deliberate on the part of Pam and it marked several other shifts in the material, spatial and relational practices of what 'being' a Club member involved. After being told of the shift, the children were asked what their first move might be. An active discussion ensued − resulting in a decision that they should produce messages and texts that would encourage other children to write. They then asked the adults in the room to help with how this could be accomplished, with each of us suggesting something where we had some expertise to offer. The choice towards microphotography was no doubt driven by the promise of access to digital tools. The children were handed iPads and left the Office space to find inspiration. After a short tutorial from one of the researchers on different techniques and effects possible, the children ran, holding iPads close to their chests, stopping to look closely and then capture surprising images. They often returned to one of the adults to show the effects they had produced, suggesting how they might use the photo. They discussed locks and unlocking writing and ideas, looking into other worlds as they took close shots of drains and metal fencing, looked up and down with their camera's capturing the different perspectives and engaged human bodies with materials and texts already available such as murals on walls, fences and trees and plants. Some focused their ideas on particular groups of students who they perceived might need more support, for example some girls found the word 'boy' wherever possible and photographed many different versions − this they explained would mean they could create a stimulus specifically for the boys in their class who they said were having trouble learning to write. The point is, that removed from the constraints of a classroom space, these children and their iPads captured and recorded different perspectives of the place they called school. Children had become other than students, they decided where to go and what to do − their roles had shifted and they were in charge of making some decisions. They looked through the digital technology and recorded different versions of the world − the in-between, as human and non-human worked together to produce different views and perspectives.

On returning to the Office, the children worked with Pam and each other on desktop and laptop computers, with paper and pencils to produce their posters and stimulus posters. Words, images and effects coming together to make meanings that had not existed before this process, that neither resided with the children, the adults or the technologies or tools. The texts produced were the result of what Lenz Taguchi (2010) discusses as the intra-active relationship between human, non-human, materials and we would add spaces.

Eventually the posters were produced and laminated for use around the school grounds and in classrooms. But the children continued to take their role as writing advocates to mean they could continue to drive the process of supporting others to want to write. With a great deal of support from Pam, the children produced writing tubs for each class, seeming to understand the privilege of access to materials to produce texts. The Club members were involved in naming these packs – *Motivation to Write* tubs – and several children presented their imminent arrival in 'a classroom near you' on the school parade. The impact of these activities on the school more broadly remains to be seen – but regardless it is worth noting how young children can be involved in their own and others' learning and the potential of allowing children to move, to engage space and materials and to take authoritative roles where decisions are made collectively and materials and people come together.

7.5. Example 2: Children Using Mobile Technologies to Become Researchers and Producers

While in the previous example we see the school leader's office was used as a meeting room for the Club, some school spaces are reserved for the important adults who 'run' the school as an institution – particularly the leadership team and the administrative staff. For instance, the principal's and assistant principals' office, as well as the spaces behind the counter in the foyer staffed by administrative colleagues, are almost always reserved for adults. Children usually only enter such spaces when something is amiss (illness or inappropriate behaviour) or being privileged to take a message from a teacher or to be rewarded for something exceptional.

This next example comes from a Year 1/2 composite class. The teacher – Simon (pseudonym) – was in his third year of teaching (his second year at this school) and the children were aged between six and eight years and in their second or third years of school. This classroom was in the block furthest from the office area; the office area and the classroom were connected by a winding pathway past another three classroom blocks and more than 50 steps to access the tiered buildings on quite a steep block of land. Neither area was visible to the other.

In this example, Simon encouraged the children to become researchers and digital text producers. During a unit of study on 'communication', the children engaged with a photo study of historical communication forms and examined different strategies for communication (including telephones and telegrams through to computer-based technologies). The unit of work then addressed communication strategies in different locations within their school. Initial discussions were focused on typical interaction patterns between the teacher and children in the classroom, before considering what communication strategies were like in different locations in the school (such as the school canteen, during assemblies, at the recent school disco and eventually the office building). After whole class discussion, Simon invited the children to capture their insights into communication strategies within the school; the children worked in pairs to write, draw or create multimodal digital representations of their understandings.

In this example, two children (Sam and Catherine, pseudonyms) chose the office as a location, sought permission from their teacher to access the space, and then directed and captured photographs on a class iPad as they talked with their participants (two office staff – the office manager and office assistant) for 19 minutes about how they communicate with others. As Sam and Catherine asked questions of their participants in the office space, they made decisions about what images to capture on the iPad. They directed the office staff to pose for photographs as they highlighted their use of communication tools within the office space. Using the technique of a Digital Story (Kervin & Mantei, 2016), the children used the still images they captured and narrated these into a cohesive account of communication in their selected space. They reviewed and sequenced their images as they decided what to record for their oral narration. Further, as they edited images and audio together on the iPad, they also composed written annotations to further emphasise their meaning.

In this one minute and five seconds Digital Story, these two seven-year-old children collaborated to capture their experience of interviewing the office manager and office assistant in the School Office within their school. In this example, we see the potential of positioning students as researchers of everyday places and practices. We also see what can happen when the means of production are in children's hands. Table 7.1 provides an overview of the time sequence within the Digital Story and the oral narration, written annotation and description of the image that accompanied each section.

Through the authority of this literacy activity, the children were able to visit a space they were typically not allowed to go – the school office. Here, we see a shift in the equilibrium of the power relations, between child in the role of 'the student' and the adult in the role of 'the office staff'. Further, they not only visited but also asked questions and documented their experience through planning and capturing photographs where they were able to manipulate the adults who inhabited the space (through their staging of photographs and providing written annotations to capture their intention in creating the image and their own interpretations). The mobile device they took with them positioned these children as researchers and thereby made it allowable for them to ask the office staff to pose for photographs and provide information, and simultaneously enabling these children to document their learning experiences. The children were in control of the experience. We see adult bodies directed by the young text producers. This example disrupts established adult child-relationships in this office space as the human participants and the non-human (communication resources) are entangled in ways that are directed by the young children to facilitate their literacy learning.

Mobilising Critical Literacies 129

Table 7.1. Overview of Time, Oral Narration, Written Annotation and Image within the Digital Story.

Time Sequence	Oral Narration	Written Annotation	Image Description
00:00–00:10	Sam: Hi I'm Sam Catherine: And I'm Catherine Sam: We went to the office to see ways we can communicate	Sam and Catherine investigate How to Communicate in the Office	Photograph of Sam and Catherine in front of a brick wall near the office block
00:11–00:17	Catherine: When people come to our school, they go to the desk to ask questions	Ask and answer questions	Photograph of smiling office manager standing behind from counter
00:18–00:24	Sam: When the office wants to send out information, they use a letter	Send letters	Close photograph of the office manager's hands holding an envelope and note slip, both featuring the school emblem and contact details
00:25–00:39	Catherine: Sometimes the office asks parents questions. Sometimes parents ask the offices questions	Talk on the phone	Photograph of the office assistant holding the phone to her ear, smiling at the camera
00:40–00:49	Sam: Sometimes the school emails the parents and sometimes the parents email the school	Use the computer	Photograph of the office assistant pretending to work on the desktop computer, side view to the camera
00:50–00:56	Catherine: If there's a message the whole school needs to hear, they do it on the loudspeaker	Talking into the loudspeaker	Photograph of the office assistant pretending to speak into the microphone on top of a filing cabinet, side view to the camera
00:57	Sam: The people in the office are very, very busy Catherine: and have to communicate with heaps of people	The end	Blurred photograph of office assistant standing behind the front counter

7.6. Discussion

These two cases demonstrate children reinterpreting school spaces through their creation of digital texts. In both cases, the children, as co-researchers, were engaged in meaningful and sustained literacy learning as they moved across school spaces not always available to students for literacy learning work. These critical literacy practices pose implications for all educators as to how literacy and critical literacy can be taught to young children when they are afforded some control of decisions about how, where and when people, materials, tools and texts are used. In particular, these cases encourage us as educators to examine how children might be readers, writers and analysts and in so being, how they might resist traditional roles, positions and placements in their literacy learning. Further, we think there is more to be done to consider how mobile technologies might support children to produce texts that challenge understandings of learning spaces. Rather than early literacy constituting training in the management of students' bodies and their quiet confinement to limited places and activities, early *critical literacy* could be re-imagined as active, collaborative, mobile and public.

These cases demonstrate teaching and learning approaches to critical literacy that position the children as researchers, producers and teachers. In each case, they were learning literacy in spaces outside the traditional classroom and were given opportunities to challenge and shift the relationships between themselves, materials and adult experts. The children assumed tech-savvy roles (Vasquez & Felderman, 2013) as they used technology to become leaders, photographers, interviewers and authors. In each instance, the children were asked to problematise and challenge who, how, where, when, with what and with whom things like producing text get done in schools.

Mobile technologies in children's hands potentially shift the socio-spatial power relations around text production that usually hold in schools. In these cases, the children used technology to create artefacts that reflected their mindsets, identities and literate practices (Kuby & Gutshall Rucker, 2016; Vasquez & Felderman, 2013). In those moments, supported by teacher-researcher advocates, the children took control of the technology to reshape their response to curriculum. Their activation of their 'technoliteracies' (Marsh, 2002) enabled them to produce texts to support their learning and rearticulation/redefinition of the types of learning that occurs within school spaces. These instances indicate what can be possible when young children and teachers work in different relationships with materials, spaces and other people in productive and provocative ways. Children's capacities to co-produce multimodal texts of various kinds are contingent upon the extent to which the school opens its spaces and resources, both material and human, to afford children ongoing access in order to meet genuine demands of learning together. We recognise that such innovation requires long-term hard work and commitment on the part of classroom teachers and school leaders, and this is all the more pressing at a time when minimalist approaches to early literacy instruction are constantly portrayed in the media and frequently by political leaders as a solution to low levels of performance on literacy standardised tests. Children as co-researchers with their teachers enable spaces and literacy opportunities to be transformed. Further, with the incorporation of mobile technologies, we argue critical literacies have the potential to become truly mobilised as children actively participate with the 'business' of literacy learning.

References

Barad, K. (2007). *Meeting the universe half way: Quantum physics and the entanglement of matter and meaning*. Durham: Duke University Press.

Baroutsis, A., & Towers, C. (2017). Makerspaces: Inspiring writing in young children. *Practical Literacy: The Early and Primary Years, 22*(3), 32–34.

Bradley, B. A., & Reinking, D. (2011). Enhancing research and practice in early childhood through formative and design experiments. *Early Child Development and Care, 181*(3), 305–319.

Cobb, P., Confrey, J., diSessa, A., Lehrer, R., & Schauble, L. (2003). Design experiments in educational research. *Educational Researcher, 32*(1), 9–13.

Comber, B. (1994). Critical literacy: An introduction to Australian debates and perspectives. *Journal of Curriculum Studies, 26*(6), 655–668.

Comber, B. (2000). What really counts in early literacy lessons. *Language Arts, 78*(1), 39–49.

Comber, B. (2004). Three little boys and their literacy trajectories. *The Australian Journal of Language and Literacy, 27*(2), 114–127.

Comber, B., Woods, A., & Grant, H. (2017). Literacy and imagination: Finding space in a crowded curriculum. *The Reading Teacher, 71*(1), 115–120. doi:10.1002/trtr.1539

Danby, S., Davidson, C., Theobald, M., Houen, & Thorpe, K. (2017). Pretend play and technology: Young children making sense of their everyday social worlds. In S. Lynch, D. Pike, & C. à Beckett (Eds.), *Multidisciplinary perspectives on play from birth and beyond* (pp. 231–245). Singapore: Springer Singapore, Singapore.

Dixon, K. (2011). *Literacy, power, and the schooled body: Learning in time and space*. New York, NY: Routledge.

Dyson, A. H. (Ed.). (2016). *Child cultures, schooling and literacy: Global perspectives on children composing their lives*. New York, NY: Routledge.

Fenwick, T. (2016). Social media, professionalism and higher education: A sociomaterial consideration. *Studies in Higher Education, 41*(4), 664–677.

Fenwick, T., & Edwards, R. (2011). Considering materiality in educational policy: Messy objects and multiple reals. *Educational Theory, 61*(6), 709–726.

Kamler, B., Maclean, R., Reid, J.-A., & Simpson, A. (1994). *Shaping up nicely: The formation of schoolgirls and schoolboys in the first month of school*. Canberra, AUS, Australian Government Printing Service.

Kervin, L. (2016). Powerful and playful literacy learning with digital technologies. *Australian Journal of Language and Literacy, 39*(1), 64–73.

Kervin, L., Comber, B., & Woods, A. (2017). Toward a sociomaterial understanding of writing experiences incorporating digital technology in an early childhood classroom. *Literacy Research: Theory, Method, and Practice, 66*, 183–197. doi:10.1177/2381336917718522

Kervin, L., & Mantei, J. (2016). Digital storytelling: Capturing children's participation in preschool activities. *Issues in Educational Research*, *26*(2), 225–240.

Kuby, C., & Gutshall Rucker, T. (2016). *Go be a writer! Expanding the curricular boundaries of literacy learning with children*. New York, NY: Teachers College Press.

Kuby, C., Rucker, T., & Kirchhofer, J. (2015). 'Go be a writer': Intra-activity with materials, time and space in literacy learning. *Journal of Early Childhood Literacy*, *15*(3), 394–419.

Lenz Taguchi, H. (2010). *Going beyond the theory/practice divide in Early childhood education: Introducing an intra-active pedagogy*. London: Routledge.

Luke, A. (1992). The body literate: Discourse and inscription in early literacy training. *Linguistics and Education*, *4*(1), 107–129. doi:10.1016/0898-5898(92)90021-N

Marsh, J. (2002). Colloquium: Electronic toys: Why should we be concerned? A response to Levin and Rosenquest. *Contemporary Issues in Early Childhood*, *3*(1), 132–137.

Marsh, J. (2016). Gareth: The reluctant writer. In A. Dyson (Ed.), *Child cultures, schooling, and literacy: Global perspectives on composing unique lives* (pp. 17–27). New York, NY: Routledge.

Vasquez, V. M. (2014). *Negotiating critical literacies with young children* (10th Anniversary Ed.). New York, NY: Routledge.

Vasquez, V. M., & Felderman, C. B. (2013). *Technology and critical literacy in early childhood*. New York, NY: Routledge.

Wohlwend, K. (2008). Play as a literacy of possibilities: Expanding meaning in practices, materials and spaces. *Language Arts*, *86*(2), 127–136.

Woods, A., & Henderson, R. (2008). The early intervention solution: Enabling or constraining literacy learning. *Journal of Early Childhood Literacy*, *8*(3), 268–276.

Chapter 8

Personalised Learning with Digital Technologies at Home and School: Where is Children's Agency?

Natalia Kucirkova

Abstract

This chapter explores children's agency in using mobile technologies at home and in school. Supporting children's agency has been offered as a rationale for adopting personalised education worldwide. Children's agency is also drawn upon as a justification for children's use of personal mobile devices. This chapter considers children's agency in light of the personalised education in one UK primary school and the children's use of mobile technologies at school and at home. The findings are based on eight days of observations of classroom practice and interviews with six case study children in the Year 6 classroom. In sessions that were supported with mobile technologies, children's learning was personalised to each child, but constrained by the amount of time that the activity lasted and that the technology was available for. Based on children's accounts, their use of mobile technologies at home was constrained by their parents' restrictions and monitoring practices. The chapter discusses the reality of children's agency in light of adults' mediation and children's actual experiences of personalised learning.

Keywords: Personalised learning; mobile technologies; children's agency; personalised pluralisation; literacy; tablets

8.1. Introduction

Most primary school teachers know that effective education needs to be personalised to individual children and, at the same time, connected to the wider socio-cultural community in which children grow up. When educational researchers study this complex process of effective pedagogies, they need to analyse the intersection between individualised approaches and community-oriented approaches to learning. Such an approach is described as a fine balancing act between individualisation and standardisation (Garrick, Pendergast, & Geelan, 2017), or what we termed personalised pluralisation (Kucirkova & Littleton, 2017). In Kucirkova and Littleton (2017), we argued that personalised pluralisation is the most effective model for deploying mobile technologies in UK primary schools, but the model's application needs to be context-sensitive.

In this chapter, I focus on the context of one classroom in a primary school in the UK to outline what personalised learning might look like; that is, what learning opportunities it might engender and what pedagogical practices it might entail. I build on some empirical observations from six 10-year-old children's interactions with technologies in the classroom, and their accounts of technology experiences at home, to explore the notion of agency in personalised learning. The ultimate aim of this chapter is to share some innovative practices and guide an effective deployment of digital technologies that would honour children's agency and connect their home and school learning experiences.

8.2. Digital Technologies: Key Considerations

Technologies have always been an integral part of classrooms, but while their purpose of use has little changed over the years, their forms have changed significantly. For example, the purpose of using a ballpoint pen or an iPad pen stylus is the same: to capture a verbal or mental thought. However, the final product and the process leading to its development are in the twenty-first century by and large digital. Many educational researchers therefore make the distinction between old and new technologies or digital and non-digital technologies. For instance, Mercer, Hennessy, and Warwick (2010) describe how interactive whiteboards (digital technologies) relate to flipcharts and dry-wipe boards (non-digital technologies) but fulfil the same aim of collaborative learning.

There are some common factors that influence children's learning, and these factors interact with personalised and pluralised educational approaches. Even though children's use of technology is often studied in terms of access to technology or the technology's availability in a given setting, educationalists need to study more nuanced issues concerning the actual use of technologies, not just whether children own or access them. A useful way of framing these considerations is to think about the various 'Cs' of technology use. The Cs relate to the content, context and individual child (Guernsey, 2012), or what Blum-Ross and Livingstone (2016, p. 4) described as focus on the 'screen context (where, when and how digital media are accessed), content (what is being watched or used), and connections (whether and how relationships are facilitated or impeded)'. I have argued (see Kucirkova, 2015) that the Cs of children's technology use (context, content, individual child and their combinations or compounds) are conveniently related to another set of Cs, namely the Cs in children's skills, as listed by Golinkoff and Hirsh-Pasek (2016): critical thinking, creative innovation, collaboration, communication and content. The Cs are thus a simple but powerful frame to consider the added value of technologies to children's learning.

The first C – context – encourages us to consider the influence of a specific context on the usefulness of a given technology. For example, in developing countries, where there is often lack of basic sanitation and safe water, it seems to be a misguided attempt to send iPads to schools. Yet, the techno-driven (rather than vision-driven) agenda behind many technology-donating projects, such as, for example, One Laptop per Child, seems to be little informed by the local context (e.g. Kraemer, Dedrick, & Sharma, 2009).

The second C – content – reminds us that the usefulness of a technology very much depends on the content delivered or enabled by this technology. There needs to be a match between the content and the task at hand. Even if two children sit in the same classroom with the same tablet in their hands, they could be having very different learning experiences. For example, one child might be playing Minecraft, while the other child might be watching inappropriate YouTube cartoons.

The third C is a reminder of the influence of individual characteristics of children, including their needs, talents and preferences. Despite this seemingly obvious fact, young children's use of technologies is often associated with the popular rhetoric of 'digital natives' (Prensky, 2001). The term 'digital natives' implies that children are one homogeneous group and are born into the world knowing how technology works. However, as I have discussed at length (Kucirkova, 2018), even though many children, especially those born in Western countries, grow up in environments that are saturated with technologies, the children are not born as digitally proficient. Any assumption of homogeneity among young children needs balancing, and in the case of the digital natives, it is important to recognise and research the complex circumstances in which individual children interact with technologies.

In this chapter, and in my work more generally, I aim to identify and explain the nuances and complexities in children's use of technology in relation to personalised pluralisation and the many 'Cs' of technologies related to children's learning. This approach necessitates time and space for discussion, so I limit myself to a specific argument in this chapter. I consider the pedagogy and practices within a specific context (a Year 6 classroom in an English primary school), with a particular type of technology (mobile technologies) and a specific type of learning and pedagogical approach (personalised learning). Before I outline the context of the study in more detail, I define what I mean by mobile technologies and personalised learning.

8.3. What Are Mobile Technologies?

As the name reveals, mobile technologies are mobile; that is, they can be transported from one location to another one. The mobility is facilitated with their light weight, a long battery life and suitable size. Mobile technologies have been on the market throughout the twenty-first century in the form of netbooks and laptops, but it wasn't until early 2010s that tablets, iPads, smartphones and iPhones began to replace older mobile devices. In this chapter, I focus on this second generation of mobile technologies, often subsumed under the umbrella term of digital or new technologies. iPads and tablets are particularly popular among pre and primary school-aged children (Ofcom, 2015, 2016), with thousands of software programs (apps) developed for this age group (Vaala, Ly, & Levine, 2015). The quality of apps is variable, with many self-proclaimed educational apps not meeting researcher-developed quality criteria (see Papadakis, Kalogiannakis, & Zaranis, 2018). This chapter doesn't focus on any particular apps, but on a particular way in which apps might be used in the classroom. It focuses on personalised learning, to complement the multiple uses of mobile technologies among young children discussed in this book.

8.4. What Is Personalised Learning?

Personalised learning is a key theme in innovative educational approaches (Sharples et al., 2015) and it is also one of the five key ways in which mobile technologies have been claimed to transform education (Traxler, 2009). There are several practices that can be subsumed under personalised education. For instance, the 2015 'Innovating Pedagogy' report details five 'personalisation' themes that have emerged over the last four years: personal inquiry learning, dynamic assessment, adaptive teaching, analytics of emotions and stealth assessment (Sharples et al., 2015). In higher education, personalised learning relates to self-paced and self-selected learning paths that students can choose from (Garrick et al., 2017). Whether these learning paths are truly personalised or simply the same content offered to learners in a different sequence (a question raised by Neil Selwyn, 2016, in his book 'Is Technology Good for Education?') is to be debated. What is clear is that the prevalence of personalised learning opportunities has risen with the advent of mobile technologies.

Educators use mobile technologies in a variety of ways, for example to document and evaluate children's progress with multimedia (video, audio and picture-based) evidence of activities or to enhance their existing activities with additional resources (e.g. by using a counting app to enrich a Maths lesson). Mobile technologies are, with their small screen, portability and user-friendly interface, designed for individual use and offer apps that can be used to personalise the learning experience. In addition, personal mobile technologies come with algorithms that are capable of measuring students' engagement with particular content and tailor subsequent content based on the students' performance. These characteristics mean that mobile technologies can be used for learning analytics, which is a particularly popular aspect of personalised learning in the twenty-first century.

More specifically, learning analytics can model learner characteristics and provide subsequent recommendations, as if they were the students' personal tutor (Johnson, Adams Becker, Estrada, & Freeman, 2015). With increasingly more children to teach and fewer graduates interested in the teaching profession in Europe and the UK (see e.g. Bélanger & Broeks, 2016), learning analytics are becoming integrated in many educational institutions worldwide. Learning analytics are also a key component of new textbooks developed to motivate students to learn, such as for example the McGraw Hill's LearnSmart system, that allows teachers to tailor digital textbooks according to individual students or classrooms they teach in.

Thus, personalised learning can take many forms, some of which are determined by the child/learner and some of which are provided by the adult to the child. In considering these different forms, it is useful to ask whether personalised education is offered as a programmatic/prescriptive or participatory approach.

8.5. Programmatic versus Participatory Personalised Learning

The participation/prescription axes allow for bringing together the 'Cs' of technology use and its learning impact and thus weave in the perennial questions of media use. Programmatic personalised learning occurs when learners are provided with personalised content automatically, with little agency and choice given to the learners. For example, personalised books are personalised according to a reader's preferences and characteristics (e.g. in the *Lost My Name* book by Wonderbly, the main story character in a book carries the child's name). Personalised reading systems are often based on programmatic, dynamic and on-demand personalisation (e.g. the iRead by UCL Knowledge Lab ecosystem of personalised reading apps provides children with reading content relevant for their reading level). These products are personalised based on children's data that are either collected automatically or supplied by the children's carers to the providers.

At the other end of the spectrum lies participatory personalised learning where learners can participate in the design of education tailored to their own needs and preferences. An example of participatory personalised learning is the study by Van Dijk and colleagues with Dutch children in a science museum. van Dijk, Lingnau, and Kockelkorn (2012) asked a group of children to use a tabletop to select the exhibition areas they liked most. Children were divided into two groups and were asked to select the content on their own. In one group, the children were given the option to follow their own (personalised) route through the museum, and in the second group, the children followed a route that didn't contain their favourite objects. Although the children in the two different groups did not notice a difference, there was a difference in their understanding measured at the end of the activity. The children who could choose their preferred subjects scored higher on the tests evaluating their understanding. Given the design of the study, van Dijk and colleagues argue that this was because children in this group had greater interest in the topics encountered during the tour. The study thus provides tentative results for concluding that when children are given the choice and can individualise their learning path, it can have a positive learning effect.

I am interested in participatory personalised learning that honours the child's own choices and that considers children's agency. To understand how agency relates to personalised learning and how it differs from related terms, such as autonomy or volition, I use the 5As of personalisation framework. This framework was developed in my previous work (Kucirkova, 2017), in which I reviewed a broad range of literature on personalised reading. It consists of five research variables or psychological phenomena: attachment, autonomy, authorship, authenticity and aesthetics. The 5As are all related to each other and can be represented as a set of five interlinked Venn diagrams. The autonomy and aesthetic dimensions are most closely related to agency in the context of using mobile technologies for digital reading. In this chapter, I focus the attention on agency as a core variable in children's personalised learning with mobile technologies (Figure 8.1).

8.6. Children's Agency in Personalised Learning

Broadly speaking, children's agency refers to the extent to which children's engagement is determined by them rather than anyone else. Supporting children's agency is a key rationale and justification for adopting personalised education as opposed to standardised education. There are different definitions of agency depending on the disciplinary perspective adopted. Agency is defined differently in business administration and economics (Kunz & Pfaff, 2002) than in sociology, for example (Shapiro, 2005). In the sociology literature, agency has been conceptualised in terms of socially just pedagogies and learner agency

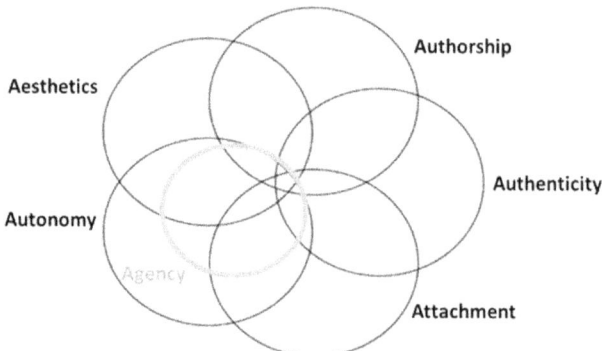

Figure 8.1. The '5As' of Personalisation: Five Variables with Agency at the Core.

facilitated by adults (e.g. Lupton & Hempel-Jorgensen, 2012). Hempel-Jorgensen (2015, p. 6) alludes to the transformative learning power of children's agency in the context of socially just pedagogies. For learning to occur, children need to be given opportunities to question, analyse and re-imagine their own learning environments. In specific activities such as, for example, book reading, agency has been defined as a 'compulsive reiterative role-playing in which individuals attempt to find themselves by going outside the self' (Travis, 1998, p. 6). In the NP3 project, from which I draw in this chapter, agency was defined as 'evidence of choice or involvement in decision making' (Twining et al., 2017, p. 49). In the project, agency was considered as a key component of an innovative pedagogy framework, in which active knowledge construction was characterised by learners' agentive engagement with technologies in their immediate and wider socio-cultural environment.

8.7. Adults' Mediation of Children's Technology: Classroom and Home

Children's agency can be constrained or enhanced by the adults around them. From a broader theoretical perspective, adults' mediation of agency and children's technology use relates to their rights and democracy principles. Applying Bernstein's (1971) framework for 'conditions for democracy', Leaton-Gray (2017) discusses the so-far little explored relationship between technology and time in education. She outlines how time and access to technology can provide deep insights into the nature of children's learning with technologies. Notably, she makes a distinction between personal and social agency and argues that access to resources is only one way of understanding actual technology use and children's personal agency. Drawing on Bernstein's (1971) pedagogic rights framework, Leaton-Gray argues:

> Even if routine and reliable access to high-level technology is technically possible, it may be that some groups of pupils are unable to afford it or do not wish to engage with it for their own reasons. Under such conditions it is not enough to see the role of educational technology relating exclusively to issues of individual agency. This represents a wider problem to do with the fair and effective distribution of resources across society, including within areas and amongst groups where it is not financially profitable for businesses to invest substantial resources (…). (p. 67)

There is a rich set of literature on how parents' attitudes towards technology influence children's use of technologies at home (Kucirkova & Littleton, 2016) but also children's understanding of what technology is for. For example, Eisen and Lillard (2017) examined in an experimental design whether children see the functionality and purpose of touchscreen devices differently from traditional media like televisions (TVs) and computers. They showed children photographs of a book, an iPad, a flat screen TV, an iPhone, a PC laptop computer and a wireless home telephone and asked them to comment on their functionalities. The researchers found that parents' perceptions can influence children's understanding of technology functionalities. For the 14 four-year-olds, 14 five-year-olds and 15 six-year-olds who took part in their study, touchscreens were perceived to be for play while computers for work. There was a significant age difference, with older children recognising multifunctionality of mobile devices more than the young children, whose experiences are informed more by home than school use. In Gillen and Kucirkova (2018), we discuss how the home-school difference in using technologies might influence children's perceptions.

This chapter aims to contribute to this body of work and answer a set of questions related to personalised learning with a focus on children's agency. I ask, first more broadly: How do teachers make use of mobile technologies in the school? The second and third research questions are more specific: What does agency look like in the context of a primary school classroom where children use mobile technologies? What are children's experiences and perceptions of the ways mobile technologies have had an impact on their agency?

8.8. Methods

8.8.1. Study Context: The NP3 Project

The data discussed in this chapter are part of the New Purposes – New Practices – New Pedagogy Project, NP3 Project for short. The NP3 project was funded by the Society for Educational Sciences in the UK and was led by Professor Peter Twining in 2015–2017, together with colleagues from the Open University and Lancaster University. The project aimed to explore the digital practices that children engage with outside school and the extent to which these are recognised and valued inside the school settings they attend. The main concern of the research project was to establish the institutional factors that impact on schools' responses to pupils' digital competences and digital practices outside school. The project involved intense data collection in 13 schools across the UK, with over 100 children and more than 60 teachers participating in the study. A number of publications and reports resulted from the project, all of which are available on the project website: http://www.np3.org.uk. In this chapter, I focus on data that I collected while working as a consultant on this project. The data were all collected in one school and I only focus on one classroom to maintain the integrity of the argument.

8.8.2. The School

This school, called Northgate Primary for anonymisation purposes, is a small Community Foundation school in an urban/suburban area of Northern England. The school is smaller than the average-sized primary school in the

UK, with 189 children attending the school overall. The majority of children are White British, although there are some children with English as a Second Language. The school caters for children from nursery to Year 6, that is, children aged between 3 and 11 years. The school has a higher than average number of children on Free School Meals (measure of socio-economic deprivation in the UK) and with Special Educational Needs. A small proportion of children come from relatively affluent households. The school uses national research from major funding agencies to inform their strategic decisions and has received a number of prestigious awards, recognising the school's innovative practices in the area of art, engagement with local community and use of technologies.

I visited the school in autumn 2016 and in this chapter summarise findings based on overall eight days of observations of classroom practice and interviews with six 'log children' in the Year 6 classroom.

8.8.3. Study Participants

There were 43 'log children' in the NP3 project, who were selected by their teachers to provide additional evidence of how the children engage with technologies at home. The researchers collected more detailed information about these children and the log children were also provided with digital cameras and encouraged to take pictures of any technology they have at home. At the school visit, the researcher interviewed each log child and asked him/her to describe what the pictures represented. In the Northgate school, six log children were interviewed. The children were aged between 10 and 11 years and there were two girls and four boys in the group. I draw on the transcribed interview data with these children to present evidence on children's use of technologies at home.

8.8.4. Data Collection and Analysis

During my visits to the Northgate school, I took video recordings of all observed lessons as well as audio recordings of interviewed teachers, school senior leadership team and the six log children. I took field notes to capture moments that may have not been captured digitally. I also took several still photographs to describe the specific technologies children used or the physical layout of the classrooms and artefacts produced by the children. The audio and video data were entered into the Maxqda data analysis tool and transcribed by the research team. For the analytical purposes in this chapter, I only focus on the fieldnotes, video and audio transcripts salient for personalised learning. I analysed these data thematically; that is, I collated similar examples of audio/video and observational data that clustered around the same theme. I illustrate the themes with selected audio excerpts and descriptions, chosen for their representativeness of children's agency and for their correspondence with some of the major findings that emerged from the other schools visited by the NP3 research team.

8.9. Findings

I begin by describing the school's context and deployment of technologies more generally, followed by a close zoom on the agentic opportunities.

8.9.1. Digital Technologies and School Ethos

In comparison to other typical primary schools in the UK, the Northgate Primary had an atypically high amount and wide range of technologies available for the children. In each classroom, there were eight iPads and an interactive whiteboard. Each classroom had the possibility to use a bank of notebooks, coding Bee-Bots, stopwatches, visualisers or digital cameras. In the preschool classroom, children had also access to a wall-mounted large touchscreen and a music system with loudspeakers. It was clear from the interviews with the teachers and senior leadership team that they were keen to make the best use of the technology resources. In particular, the teachers planned daily activities with attention to the different technologies they had at their disposal and often discussed the ways in which specific technologies might support children's specific skills. There was also evidence that conscious effort was made by the school to ensure that all children could access the technologies. For instance, there were several booster seats and comfortable cushions available for each classroom to enable children to sit comfortably regardless of their size or height. In addition to technology support, children were offered one-to-one support by a Teaching Assistant when they struggled with a certain programme or app. The school had a floating ICT coordinator, who regularly responded to children's and teachers' queries and troubleshoots ICT-related problems. Teachers regularly set up homework that included a digital component, such as for example encouraging children to complete a part of an online activity at home or to produce a PowerPoint slide show to summarise children's understanding of a topic. Children who did not have technologies at home were encouraged to use the laptops and PCs available in the school.

The senior leadership team had detailed knowledge about new technology developments and told me about their strategic investment in new devices. For example, during one of the interviews, the Deputy Head mentioned she would like to use part of the ICT budget to purchase new visualisers to show children artefacts in 3D. The teachers I spoke to engaged in regular coding-related activities in all year groups, but especially in Year 6. Additional activities were offered to children outside the school hours, such as the Coding Club on Monday or a course in touch-typing skills. The school used technology to communicate with parents and share children's achievements via social media. The school had its own Twitter account and a blog page, with regular contributions from children in Year 6. This whole-school approach to active and constructive use of technologies corresponded to some agentic engagements with technology by the individual children.

8.9.2. *Personalised Learning with Digital Technologies*

The interviews with the deputy head teacher and members of the teaching team contained several examples of the school's aim to nurture each child's unique profile – a hallmark feature of personalised education.

Deputy Head:

> So in school our approach is not just you come in, you sit down and you learn. It's are you ready to learn? You know, are you okay? Are you in the right frame of mind? Do you need to take ten minutes in the reading area to just relax and read a book? And then I'll come over to you, when you are ready. And one of our main things is that our school's strap-line is that every child is unique. And it, it isn't a cliché really. It really is true.

Teacher in preschool:

> I mean, normally we take inspiration from the children's interest first, so we have got an awful lot of boys in school which is why we've got the cars, the electronic cars and why, you know, we've been reading about owls, so we've been finding out about they eat, so we've been cooking worms for snacks. So, trying to inspire the boys' inspiration really and imagination. Take it from the children all the time, what are their interests, what do they enjoy doing? And try and work on that. And what are their gaps in learning really as well.

8.10. Children's Agency in Technology Use

8.10.1. *Active and Self-paced Learning*

To identify and analyse children's agency in technology use, I focus on a specific lesson that I observed in the Year 6 classroom. This was a mathematics lesson and focused on practising fractions in five different activities that were supported with five different resources at five tables. At Table 1, children could write their reasoning directly on the table surface and wipe it off if they made a mistake. At Table 2, children worked in pairs with domino pieces and a stopwatch to measure the time it took them to solve each domino challenge. At Table 3, the children solved various maths scenarios individually and wrote their responses in pencil on a worksheet. At Table 4, the children used iPads with a preloaded maths app. Table 5 was dedicated to the use of netbooks, which were preloaded with the school's online maths learning software. Each activity was thus supported with a set of different resources, related to the practice of different maths tasks and skills. Each activity included a competition element and a different support mechanism (human- or technology-mediated). It thus provided opportunities for children to gauge their knowledge against their peers (Table 1 and Table 2), a software program (Table 4 and Table 5) or their own knowledge without any support (Table 3 and the worksheet). Such a pedagogical set-up reflects the pluralisation values of diversity and collaboration.

In terms of personalisation and markers of agency, the individual activities were set up by the teacher, and children did not have a choice in deciding which activity they wanted to take part in. The teacher carefully measured the time to ensure that all children spent an equal amount of time at each table. However, children were given ample opportunities to analyse a set of mathematical problems and discover the answers by themselves. Each child had access to one resource (digital or non-digital) at a time and apart from Table 2, which was set up for work in pairs, children could self-pace their own progress. The learning was thus personalised to each student, within the constraints of a typical classroom setting characterised by groups of children and restricted time for each activity.

8.10.2. Self-directed Learning

Children's agency did not happen automatically; rather, there was a set of rules and behaviours embedded in the classroom culture that facilitated children's agentic engagement. For instance, children's independent use of notebooks and iPads was facilitated by a rotating group of students and digital ambassadors, who helped as and when needed. In addition to the classroom rules, I noted instances of agentic use of technologies at the school level. These were partly included in my observations as well as in the interviews with the senior leadership team. For instance, the school actively promoted children's use of the school's social media account, which was an email service similar to a synchronous chat with which children could send short messages to each other as well as their teachers. At the end of the lesson, the teachers encouraged the children to edit their individual profiles on the school secure internal web server to suit their aesthetic preferences and share them with their classmates. The children were provided with log-in details and were repeatedly reminded to keep their passwords safe so that they could access their online profiles anytime they wished.

8.10.3. Awareness Enabling Choice

These technology-related activities mirrored children's agentic engagement in other school activities. For instance, the school had a Pupils School Council, a group of pupils elected by their fellow pupils to represent their opinions. For Golden Time activities (activities at the end of the school day), children could choose their own activities, with any resources available in the classroom. Children were very aware of the opportunities given to them and there was a noticeable sense of pride in their verbal descriptions of the school's policies.

Individual interviews with the case study children also indicated that there have been frequent conversations with the ICT coordinator about e-safety. For example, all children were familiar with restrictions for Facebook or Instagram use. This extract is from a focus group interview with Year 6 pupils, in which we discussed the school's learning platform and communication server:

I: Okay, do you have passwords for other computers and other devices that you are using?

R: Yes, I have a lot of passwords.

I: A lot of passwords.

R: Yes, because in school, it isn't just you put a password onto your computer and you can log onto everything, because you have this, our own platform called Learn Anywhere and it's like you can talk to your friends from school and have picture and things.

R1: Messages and things.

R2: It's basically like mini like child friendly Facebook.

R: Like child's WhatsApp?

R2: Like say if you went on Facebook there's random people, you can only find your friends on it.

R1: And you can't get any other school's people on it, it's only your school and it's safe and if someone like messages you [inaudible 05:56] Miss Z [school's ICT coordinator] to help.

R2: You can say if you press it, someone has not sent you a very nice picture or email it flags it straight up to Miss Z and it sends her an email and she finds out what's going on.

R: Even if you don't flag it up, or an inappropriate word in it then it automatically it flags straight up to Miss Z.

R1: Even if you don't.

8.10.4. Restrictions of Agency

The interviews with the log children also revealed an opposite trend in relation to agency and technology use. There seemed to be significant restrictions concerning children's use of technologies at home. The restrictions were content-, time- and device-related. For example, Child6 revealed that at home she only has access to apps that are free.

Ch6: Yeah, I type it into other the apple app store or Kindle's games store. And then I get the app, if I find anything suitable.

R: What if it's a paid game?

Ch6: If it's a paid game, then I just don't get it.

(Continued)

R: Okay, so you only get the free games?
Ch6: Yeah. Pretty much.

Child2 revealed that she can't go online because she doesn't have full Internet access at home.

R: Do you ever go online, do you look for ideas there or not really?
Ch2: Not really. Because I don't have full Internet access. I can't really, but.
R: Would you like to have Internet access?
Ch2: Yeah.
R: Or you prefer not to have it?
Ch2: I would like to have it.
R: You would like to have it.
Ch2: Because, yeah, I like looking at like pictures and like looking up stuff.

Child3 recounted how she enjoyed playing a game with a social component where players need to follow other players. However, she was not allowed to use the follow feature when playing the game at home.

R: Oh, so what would you say is your favourite game?
Ch3: Well, I've, I think my favourite game is one where you've got like this, it's a bit American, but it's like you've got this mall, and you've got to look like, collect all the money from it and build stuff and, and you can have several floors, and you can visit other people's malls and follow people, except we don't follow people because it's a bit dangerous.

As children talked about these restrictions, they articulated the reasons for not being allowed to use particular programmes or features. It was apparent that the rules and restrictions were imposed by their parents and that often there did not seem to be a consistent or logical rationale. For example, Child4 was told he could not access the YouTube channel but he was allowed to use free Google search, as shown in this extract:

R: Okay, okay. Do you ever go on YouTube to look for different things as well or…?
Ch4: Sometimes, but my dad doesn't really like me using YouTube because obviously there could be somebody using it that are very inappropriate.
R: Right, right, so Google is okay but not YouTube?
Ch4: Yeah.

There were restrictions related to devices too. For instance, Child1 made it clear that she was given a smartphone because her parents wanted her to use the smartphone. There was little enthusiasm apparent on the child's part for using the phone for her own purposes.

Ch1: My mum got me I think mainly because she just wouldn't want me not to, because she really doesn't even like being away from me for the weekend so, she asks for a certain number of texts. I don't know why, she just does. She probably bought it so I can text her.

The fact that smartphones are used by children to comply with their parents' monitoring preferences was also evident in Child5's response. It was striking to note that the child has developed different communication strategies for different family members.

R: So is it a smartphone, that you can access different things with it?
Ch5: It's an iPhone that I use. I like take it the school as because I walk to and from school so like I use it to tell my parents like when I'm at school and when I'm leaving the house and when I'm back home and things.
R: Do you call them or do you text them?
Ch5: Sometimes I'll ring and sometimes I'll just send a message because I have a group with both my parents on.
R: Okay.
Ch5: So like I can send them text messages so they both see.
R: So is it through WhatsApp or …?
Ch5: Through iMessage.

Drawing on the interviews with the children, it was clear that they make distinct choices based on the technologies they have at home and they have at school. Moreover, when given the choice, they were discerning about which resource to use for which purpose, as illustrated in this extract about the Child5's preference for digital books.

R: So, do you listen to your music before you go to bed or …?
Ch5: Yeah, I normally go sit in bed for a bit, listen to music and then I'll put, switch everything off and then read for a bit, and then go to bed.
Ch5: Do you read on your iPad? Or do you read?
Ch5: Real books.
R: Real books?
Ch5: Yeah.
R: Why is that?

(*Continued*)

Ch5: I think it's more, I just like reading actual books instead of using devices for reading. I think it's a bit better.

(...)

Or my mum will use her Kindle.

R: But you ... for reading you prefer the real books?

Ch5: Yeah, I prefer real books otherwise it's just, I don't know why but I just like it.

R: That's interesting. I mean you are reading a real book now, right, so. Is it because you can feel the book or ...?

Ch5: Yeah, I like being able to actually look at the front cover and everything, and read the blurb, whereas if you have it on a Kindle you can't really read the blurb or anything, its straight into the book. I just...

R: Yeah, that's a good point.

Ch5: I got a Kindle once, but I didn't really like it as much as reading real books, so I just went to back to reading books. I just prefer it.

8.11. Discussion

The rules around technology use for young children are decided by their teachers and parents, who can either enable or restrict children's agency and personalised learning. For the children in the Northgate school, there was a disconnect in children's accounts in relation to what they could do with mobile technologies at school or at home. In the school, the children had a set of options and they all had equal opportunity to try one of the options, such as one of the five activities mediated by technologies in the maths lesson. The children could not choose which particular app or device to access on the device, but when personalising their online avatars, they could choose any picture they wanted and message their friends any content they wished, as long as it complied with the school's rules. Each child needed to comply with the same set of rules but, within them, they were free to personalise their own learning. Such an approach is in alignment with the personalised pluralisation agenda. Yet, when using the technologies at home, the rules were decided by the individual parents and they varied from family to family. Many of the rules were content-related, restricting personalisation. The purpose of using technology at school was to enrich children's learning or communication with each other. The purpose of using technology at home was more diverse and often oriented towards adults', rather than the children's, interests. While in the school there was an adult physically present all the time, at home, adults were present at distance, via the technology used by the child.

The first three themes of the analysis – Active and Self-Paced learning; Self-Directed Learning and Awareness Enabling Choice – were all related to children's use of technologies in the school. There was evidence of personalised learning happening in the maths lesson that I observed. There was a restricted time for each activity within the maths lesson but each child had equal opportunity to achieve as much as they could within this restricted timeframe. This is different from classrooms led by standardised curriculum based on large groups where highest achieving students need to wait for the low achievers who struggle.

In contrast, the theme Restrictions of Agency came up strongly when children described their use of technologies at home. It might be that children were more negative about their experiences at home because the interviews took place in the school, thus giving them some distance from home, possibly facilitating more open and critical answers. Yet, all log children were interviewed one-to-one with the researcher, without the teacher's presence. In addition, the interviews were facilitated with pictures of technology used by home, which were taken by the children themselves and featured a range of technologies available to them at home. It is possible that children expect to be agentive at home and therefore note when they are prevented from being so more than they do when in school. Overall, however, the many restrictions listed by children in relation to their use of technologies at home seemed to indicate that the school supports more agentic engagement than children's parents at home. This is not a typical finding; indeed, in another school that participated in the NP3 study, the opposite was the case. In the Northgate school, children's volitional, independent and autonomous use of technology was noticeable in children's learning activities, as well as their attitudes towards technology use in the school.

This finding conveniently skirts the question of what does personalised learning look like and what its impact on children's experiences might be. To answer this question, we need to go beyond the immediately obvious markers such as access or availability of technology. The 'Cs' framework reminds us that the context, content and the individual children's experiences matter. For the Northgate children, the access and availability of technology were not an issue neither at home nor at school. It was the opportunities mediated by the teachers and parents that influenced children's agentic use of the technology available to them.

8.11.1. Supporting Children's Agentic Use of Technologies

When we consider Northgate children's perceptions about the usefulness of digital versus print books, it seems that they were discerning about the purpose and added value of specific technologies. To develop this level of understanding, however, they needed to be old enough to explore and understand the features of the technologies. Different contexts of technology use (e.g. reading digital books) provide different learning opportunities. For Child5, there was a clear difference between reading on Kindle or on paper. Research with simple digital books (e-books) shows that children use them to read for information, escape, review of knowledge and study (Schcolnik, 2001). Individuals differ in how they process information from texts to derive meaning from them (Linderholm & van den Broek, 2002), and some text genres might be more associated with one reading purpose than others (Best, Rowe, Ozuru, & McNamara, 2005). However, there is an almost universal agreement in the reading literature that books are important for children's learning and the role of digital books in children's reading diet must be better understood (e.g. Kucirkova, Snow, Grover & McBride, 2017). Granting children more agency in choosing the appropriate reading format, as evidenced at home for Child5, would be more in alignment with the participatory model of personalised learning.

8.11.2. Asking the Right Questions

From Bernstein (1971) and Leaton-Gray's (2017) perspectives, the time children spend using technology at home counts as part of their learning but their personal agency becomes constrained if, as it was the case with the Northgate children, technology is allowed only for monitoring or playing free and limited-feature apps. In their recent book, Leaton-Gray and Phippen (2017) discuss how adults' understanding of children's risk undermines, if not erodes, children's rights and free identities. The potential for home-school connected learning afforded by mobile technologies was not realised for the Year 6 children. Interestingly, as we discuss in Gillen and Kucirkova (2018), for the early years classrooms, there were noticeable trajectories in children's technology use and signs of flow between home and school. It is essential that researchers search for detailed counter-examples, such as the ones presented here, to think more deeply about children's actual experiences with digital technologies at home and in school.

8.12. Conclusion

Personalised learning with digital technologies appears in several guises and this chapter has illustrated primary school children's (non)agentic engagement with mobile technologies in the classroom and at home. With mobile technologies such as tablets and smartphones, children's learning engagement could travel between home and school — so long as the adults who mediate the technology use in these spaces create opportunities rather than barriers for children's agency. Although on the surface level, children might have access to many devices, it is the agency they are afforded in their use that influences their learning experiences. I therefore conclude that the potential of mobile technologies to support personalised pluralisation can be realised, but only if we address the attitudes of all adults mediating children's learning in schools and at home.

References

Bélanger, J., & Broeks, M. (2016). *Attracting and retaining teachers in Cambridgeshire: Working conditions and teachers flows from a school workforce census data perspective*. RAND Europe. Retrieved from http://www.rand.org/randeurope/

Bernstein, B. (1971). *Class, codes and control: Volume 1 theoretical studies towards a sociology of language*. London: Routledge and Kegan Paul.

Best, R. M., Rowe, M., Ozuru, Y., & McNamara, D. S. (2005). Deep-level comprehension of science texts: The role of the reader and the text. *Topics in Language Disorders, 25*(1), 65−83.

Blum-Ross, A., & Livingstone, S. (2016). *Families and screen time: Current advice and emerging research. Media Policy Brief 17*. London: Media Policy Project, London School of Economics and Political Science. Retrieved from http://eprints.lse.ac.uk/66927/1/Policy%20Brief%2017-%20Families%20%20Screen%20Time.pdf

Eisen, S., & Lillard, A. S. (2017). Young children's thinking about touchscreens versus other media in the US. *Journal of Children and Media, 11*(2), 167−179.

Garrick, B., Pendergast, D., & Geelan, D. (2017). Personalised or programmed? Current practices of university systems. In B. Garrick, D. Pendergast, & D. Geelan (Eds.), *Theorising personalised education* (pp. 83−93). Singapore: Springer.

Gillen, J., & Kucirkova, N. (2018). Rivers that flow both ways: Creative ways of using digital technologies to connect children's school and home lives. *British Journal of Educational Technology* (in print).

Golinkoff, R. M., & Hirsh-Pasek, K. (2016). *Becoming brilliant: What science tells us about raising successful children*. Washington, DC: American Psychological Association.

Guernsey, L. (2012). *Screen time: How electronic media from baby videos to educational software affects your young child*. New York/London: Hachette USA/UK.

Hempel-Jorgensen, A. (2015). Learner agency and social justice: What can creative pedagogy contribute to socially just pedagogies? *Pedagogy, Culture & Society, 23*(4), 531−554.

Johnson, L., Adams Becker, S., Estrada, V., & Freeman, A. (2015). *The NMC Horizon Report: 2015 Museum Edition*. Austin, TX: New Media Consortium.

Kraemer, K. L., Dedrick, J., & Sharma, P. (2009). One laptop per child: Vision vs. reality. *Communications of the ACM, 52*(6), 66−73.

Kucirkova, N. (2015). *The Cs in children's screen time: Some food for thought*, Huffington Post. Retrieved from http://www.huffingtonpost.co.uk/dr-natalia-kucirkova/the-cs-in-childrens-screen-time_b_8034994.html

Kucirkova, N. (2017). *Digital personalization in early childhood: Impact on childhood*. London: Bloomsbury.

Kucirkova, N. (2018). (submitted) Against the myth of digital childhoods. In H. Montgomery & M. Robb (Eds.), *Children and young people's worlds*. London: Open University Press.

Kucirkova, N., & Littleton, K. (2016). *The digital reading habits of children: A national survey of parents' perceptions of and practices in relation to children's reading for pleasure with print and digital books*. London: Book Trust.

Kucirkova, N., & Littleton, K. (2017). Developing personalised education for personal mobile technologies with the pluralisation agenda. *Oxford Review of Education, 43*(3), 276−288. doi:10.1080/03054985.2017.1305046

Kucirkova, N., Snow, C. E., Grøver, V., & McBride, C. (Eds.). (2017). *The Routledge international handbook of early literacy education: A contemporary guide to literacy teaching and interventions in a global context*. New York, NY: Routledge.

Kunz, A. H., & Pfaff, D. (2002). Agency theory, performance evaluation, and the hypothetical construct of intrinsic motivation. *Accounting, Organizations and Society*, *27*(3), 275–295.

Leaton Gray, S. (2017). The social construction of time in contemporary education: Implications for technology, equality and Bernstein's 'conditions for democracy'. *British Journal of Sociology of Education*, *38*(1), 60–71.

Leaton Gray, S., & Phippen, A. (2017). *Invisibly blighted: The digital erosion of childhood*. London: UCL IOE.

Linderholm, T., & van den Broek, P. (2002). The effects of reading purpose and working memory capacity on the processing of expository text. *Journal of Educational Psychology*, *94*, 778–784.

Lupton, R., & Hempel-Jorgensen, A. (2012). The importance of teaching: Pedagogical constraints and possibilities in working-class schools. *Journal of education policy*, *27*(5), 601–620.

Mercer, N., Hennessy, S., & Warwick, P. (2010). Using interactive whiteboards to orchestrate classroom dialogue. *Technology, Pedagogy and Education*, *19*(2), 195–209.

Ofcom. (2015). *Children and parents: Media use and attitudes report*. Retrieved from https://www.ofcom.org.uk/research-and-data/media-literacy-research/childrens/children-parents-nov-15

Ofcom. (2016). *Children and parents: Media use and attitudes report*. Retrieved from https://www.ofcom.org.uk/research-and-data/media-literacy-research/childrens/children-parents-nov16

Papadakis, S., Kalogiannakis, M., & Zaranis, N. (2018). Educational apps from the Android Google Play for Greek preschoolers: A systematic review. *Computers & Education*, *116*, 139–160.

Prensky, M. (2001). Digital natives, digital immigrants part 1. *On the Horizon*, *9*(5), 1–6.

Schcolnik, M. (2001). *A study of reading with dedicated e-readers* (pp. 1–145). Fort Lauderdale, FL: Nova Southeastern University.

Selwyn, N. (2016). *Is technology good for education?* New York, NY: John Wiley & Sons.

Shapiro, S. P. (2005). Agency theory. *Annual Review of Sociology*, *31*, 263–284.

Sharples, M., Adams, A., Alozie, N., Ferguson, R., FitzGerald, E., Gaved, M., ... Yarnall, L. (2015). *Innovating pedagogy 2015: Open University innovation report 4*. Milton Keynes: The Open University.

Travis, M. A. (1998). *Reading cultures: The construction of readers in the twentieth century*. Carbondale, IL: SIU Press.

Traxler, J. (2009). Learning in a mobile age. *International Journal of Mobile and Blended Learning*, *1*(1), 1–12.

Twining, P., Browne, N., Murphy, P., Hempel-Jorgensen, A., Harrison, S., & Parmar, N. (2017). *NP3 – New purposes, new practices, new pedagogy: Meta-analysis report*. London: Society for Educational Studies. Retrieved from http://www.np3.org.uk. Accessed on November 13, 2017.

Vaala, S., Ly, A., & Levine, M. H. (2015). Getting a read on the app stores: A market scan and analysis of children's literacy apps. Full Report. In *Joan Ganz Cooney*

Center at Sesame Workshop. New York, NY: Joan Ganz Cooney Center at Sesame Workshop.

van Dijk, E. M., Lingnau, A., & Kockelkorn, H. (2012, October). Measuring enjoyment of an interactive museum experience. In *Proceedings of the 14th ACM international conference on multimodal interaction* (pp. 249–256). New York: ACM.

Chapter 9

Supporting Children's Literacy Learning in Low- and Middle-income Countries Through M-learning

Grace Oakley and Umera Imtinan

Abstract

In this chapter, we discuss initiatives that aim to improve children's literacy in low- and middle-income (LMI) countries through m-learning. These projects, predominantly introduced by governments and international aid organisations, often involve the provision of e-books and apps including game-based apps, to be used either inside or outside school. In some cases, lesson plans and content for teachers in poorly resourced schools are also delivered via mobile devices. After a general overview, we briefly describe a selection of projects with reference to m-learning and literacy theory and research. It is indicated in this chapter that the use of mobile devices to improve literacy opportunities for children in LMI countries has a great deal of potential but that, in many cases, there are limitations in pedagogical design and implementation practices, not to mention restricted views of what literacy is and might be for children in these locations.

Keywords: M-learning; literacy; developing countries; low-income countries; apps; mobile learning

9.1. Introduction

Globally, there are deep inequalities in children's access to quality literacy education. A vast number of children and adults around the world have low levels of literacy, with a disproportionate amount of these being female. According to the United Nations World Women's report (2015), 781 million adults over the age of 15 were estimated to be 'illiterate', or not be able to read and write at a basic level, with two thirds of these people being women. In many countries around the world, there are numerous children with limited access to schooling and literacy resources. Many of these children have no access to formal schooling while numerous others attend school but the quality and/or quantity of schooling is inadequate and they learn very little literacy through attending (World Bank, 2018). It has been estimated that approximately 250 million children around the world are not achieving basic skills in literacy (UNESCO, 2016). Wagner (2014) has pointed out that in some countries, a high proportion of children still cannot read a single word after being enrolled in school for two or three years. There are several explanations for this troubling situation. In many countries such as Nigeria and Pakistan, there are severe shortages of teachers (UNESCO, 2017). Where there are teachers, they may not be well educated in the content and pedagogy necessary for teaching (UNESCO, 2017). They may work in poor conditions with substandard resources and extremely large class sizes. In many cases, teachers cannot rely on support from families and communities, who may live in poverty or conflict and themselves have very low literacy levels, as well as having limited access to books and other reading and writing materials. For a variety of reasons, school attendance rates are often low, and numerous children stop attending school after only a few years (Wagner, 2017).

Furthermore, in many parts of the world, children speak a local language at home which may not necessarily have a written form or may not have much written material available. Consequently, a great number of children start school with limited concepts about print and 'funds of knowledge' (Moll, Amanti, Niff, & Gonzales, 1992) in written literacy practices. These children are often expected to learn to read and write in a language other than, or in addition to, their mother tongue (UNESCO, 2011; Wagner, 2017), which makes becoming literate in school-based literacies even more challenging.

Mobile learning or m-learning has the potential to address some of these challenges, and what has been referred to as a Mobile Learning for Development (ML4D) agenda, which has Mobile for Reading (M4R) and Mobile for Literacy (M4L) sub-domains (Wagner, 2014), has emerged. The aim here is to work towards remedying inequalities in literacy learning opportunities for people in low- and middle-income (LMI) countries such as Ghana, India, Ethiopia and Pakistan, particularly for groups such as women and girls, refugees and culturally marginalised groups, as well as children with disabilities including auditory and visual impairments. Governments and non-governmental organisations (NGOs), along with commercial entities, have entered into partnerships in an effort to find effective, scalable and sustainable solutions to the educational issues that occur in these complex geo-political settings through the implementation of m-learning projects (Wagner, 2014). Pegrum (2014) discusses how m-learning is used to further these social justice agendas.

In this chapter, several of these projects, of which there are many, are briefly discussed with reference to literacy and m-learning theory and research. It is clear that projects targeting children's literacy learning do not always harness the full potential of m-learning or align with contemporary theory and research on what constitutes literacy and how children best learn literacy. Importantly, projects do not always take into account local contextual features or recruit and foster local expertise (Nag, Snowling, & Asfaha, 2016). There are significant tensions and challenges that need to be overcome in order for m-learning to make a real difference to the literacy achievement of children in LMI countries. Having said this, there are many pockets of success that can be seen as encouraging.

While this chapter mainly focuses on projects put into place by organisations that have international aid and social justice agendas, the impact of more organic and informal uses of mobile devices for literacy learning — those initiated and practised on the ground by individuals and communities without the formal input of organisations — should not be underestimated. It could, in fact, be argued that in many respects, these kinds of practices, involving informal learning (Cross, 2007), have the potential to be more nimble, authentic, culturally appropriate and fit-for-purpose than many of the well-intentioned interventions and projects put into place by organisations. Research on how individuals, families and communities in developing countries use mobile devices in ways that promote children's literacy is limited, however.

It is acknowledged here that the use of existing literacy learning theory and m-learning theory, which has largely been developed by researchers in Western and developed countries, and often with reference to the English language, may not be entirely fitting for linguistically, culturally, economically and politically diverse situations around the world. There is a danger of imposing Western perspectives and priorities onto complex international conditions. Traxler (2017) has also pointed out that terms such as 'developing countries' are themselves imbued with Western ideologies. These cautions should be kept in mind by readers of this chapter.

9.2. Teaching and Learning Literacy

As outlined in earlier chapters of this book, there are many definitions of literacy, some of which are considerably more expansive than others. Literacy is dynamic — arguably more so than ever before — and defining it is no simple matter (de Silva, Feez, & Thickstun, 2015). Many contemporary definitions assert that literacy involves being able to understand and create a range of texts, including multimodal and digital texts, for a variety of purposes and with critical awareness (Fellowes & Oakley, 2014). Mills (2016) has noted that there are many theoretical lenses, which lead researchers to consider socio-cultural literacies, critical literacies, multimodal literacies, socio-spacial literacies, socio-material literacies and sensory literacies. Children who have access to digital technologies — even young children — also need to learn how to safely and appropriately engage in digital literacies (Dudeney, Hockly, & Pegrum, 2013; Sefton-Green, Marsh, Erstad, & Flewitt, 2016), which are intertwined with other kinds of literacies. The term 'mobile literacies' has also been used

(Frawley & Dyson, 2014; Pegrum, 2016), but this is not fully theorised as yet. It goes without saying that literacy is so much more than decoding words and oral reading at a particular pace.

As millions of children around the world cannot decode or recognise any words at all, even after being in school for several years (Wagner, 2014), it may seem overambitious to broaden the scope of M4L to better include the kinds of literacies mentioned above, moving beyond the narrow frame that currently seems to drive the majority of literacy projects in LMI countries. The dominant, narrow frame has possibly been brought about by the influence of psycholinguistic research on international literacy policy (Nag et al., 2016). Rather than being overambitious, a stronger focus on a multiplicity of literacies may be a key to success; we argue that there is a need for children in LMI countries to acquire as broad a literacy repertoire as possible within school, which will better equip them to become lifelong learners who have the skills, confidence, motivation and critical awareness to continue their literacy learning outside the context of formal schooling. A statement supporting the idea that there are multiple literacies, and that it is unhelpful to think in terms of a literate/illiterate dichotomy, came from UNESCO (2008, p. 17) some time ago: "Rather than assuming a divide between literate and illiterate, researchers propose a continuum, with differing levels and uses of literacy according to context. Thus, there is no single notion of literacy as a skill which people possess or not, but multiple literacies".

As well as definitional issues, there are ongoing debates about pedagogical approaches in literacy education and it is certainly beyond the scope of this short chapter to discuss them all. Some approaches emphasise decoding/encoding at the word level before moving on to teaching broader text comprehension and construction (bottom up approaches); others foreground text comprehension and construction and teach word level concepts within this context (top down approaches); others attempt to balance these two approaches (Fellowes & Oakley, 2014). In recent years, there have been claims that synthetic phonics, which involves teaching the sounds associated with letters and how to blend them together to sound out words, is the best route to literacy (Rose, 2006); however, this contention has been vigorously critiqued (Wyse & Styles, 2007). It may be the case that approaches based on synthetic phonics work better in languages with transparent orthographies, such as Finnish and many other languages other than English, like Bantu (Ojanen et al., 2015).

Literacy researchers have also revealed the importance of play, dialogue, quality children's literature, the role of the family and community, content area reading, socio-linguistic background (Saracho, 2017), physical environment (Roskos & Neuman, 2011) and many other factors. Teaching and learning literacy is complex and there is no 'one best way'. Skilled and knowledgeable teachers, who recognise and respond to contextual factors and student needs, are crucial. However, the fact remains that many teachers in LMI countries are *not* sufficiently skilled and knowledgeable (Ojanen et al., 2015), or simply not available to students. It is in this space that mobile technologies may have the most powerful impact.

9.3. The Technology and the Potential

Access to mobile devices is increasing globally and it is likely that the majority of the world's people will have access to information, communication and learning resources via mobile devices in the not too distant future. There was a global mobile Internet penetration rate of 44% in 2015, and an expected penetration rate of 60% by 2020 (GSMA, 2016). Since 2013, more people have been accessing the Internet via mobile devices than through computers (GSMA, 2016) – a trend that has been fuelled by the fact that mobile devices have been becoming more and more affordable and rapidly improved in terms of the affordances they offer, with such features as the touch screen, camera, GPS, bluetooth, gyroscope, accelerometer and NFC sensor being commonplace. Better and cheaper mobile broadband network coverage has played a role in this. There has also been a 'connected device explosion' (GSMA, 2016, p. 9), with more and more device types including mobile phones, tablets, computers, wearables and other 'things' (as part of the so-called 'Internet of things' or IoT) such as household utilities, toys and robots being connected to the Internet and to each other. These factors, combined with easier access to cloud platforms and the use of data analytics to determine patterns of use and provide customised products and learning experiences, have great implications for the future of mobile literacy learning in developed and less developed countries alike. It is acknowledged, however, that in lower income countries, particularly in rural areas, devices with less sophisticated features and less Internet connectivity are more prevalent and this can present significant challenges to effective learning design (Zualkernan, 2015). In many countries, a large proportion of people do not as yet have access to the more expensive smartphones and tablets, but may own a 'feature phone' or a 'basic' mobile phone, which will have less sophisticated features and, thus, affordances. According to the Pew Research Center (2016), many countries in Africa, as well as some Asian countries, have low smartphone ownership rates. For example, only 4% of people in Ethiopia owned a smartphone in 2016, with 11% people in Tanzania, and 28% in Nigeria owning one. In Asia, only 11% of people in Pakistan owned a smartphone, 17% in India and 21% in Indonesia. In these countries, family members often share phones – this may increase access but often women and girls have the least access. Also, sharing a phone decreases personalisation. However, some of these countries (such as Indonesia, India and Pakistan) are expected to experience a steep growth in smartphone ownership in the future (Pew Research Centre, 2016) and will therefore be potential candidates to benefit from the affordances of these devices to promote literacy learning.

9.4. M-learning Theory

It is beyond the scope of this chapter to discuss m-learning theory in depth, so we are including only a few key concepts that seem most relevant to the discussion. Please refer to the introductory chapter of this book (Oakley, 2018) for fuller coverage.

Traxler (2013a) has asserted that m-learning has the potential to transform learning by enabling contingent learning and teaching; situated learning; authentic learning; context aware learning; augmented reality (AR) mobile learning; personalised learning; game-based learning and assessment techniques that harness the affordances of connected mobile devices. These types of learning are discussed elsewhere in this book and are not repeated here due to space limitations. A framework that encapsulates and extends much of what Traxler proposes is the iPAC framework, which is based on the Mobile Pedagogical Framework (Burden & Kearney, 2017; Kearney, Schuck, Burden, & Aubusson, 2012). The iPAC framework presents three main constructs, namely, personalisation, authenticity and collaboration, which are further broken down into customisation and agency (under the personalisation construct); task, tool and setting (under authenticity); and conversation and data sharing (under collaboration). See http://www.mobilelearningtoolkit.com/ipac-framework.html for further detail.

Another framework for thinking about m-learning and how it might be transformative is Wong and Looi's (2011) 10 dimensions of Mobile Seamless Learning (MSL). The 10 dimensions, which have been slightly modified since 2011, are summarised here. The framework highlights that mobile technologies can be used to unite or bridge people, places, timeframes, learning activities and resources, as well as knowledge sources and ways of thinking, that might previously have been separate and distant from each other. The dimensions include formal and informal learning; personalised and social learning; time; location; the ubiquitous access to knowledge; the physical and the digital; the use of multiple device types; multiple learning tasks; synthesis of knowledge from different sources and disciplines; and the use of multiple pedagogical approaches (Wong & Looi, 2011, p. 2367). These theories will be referred to where appropriate in the remainder of this chapter.

9.5. Mobile Resources for Literacy Learning

UNESCO (2014) has suggested that mobile phones have resulted in a 'revolution' in reading in developing countries, with children and adults being able to access a wide variety of texts and stories on their mobile phones in locations where, previously, books were scarce or absent. There has also been an increase in the availability of texts in local languages, which sometimes but not always reflect local cultures. For example, *Worldreader* provides more than 42,000 books in 43 languages in digital format (www.worldreader.org). An app can be downloaded to facilitate reading of the digital texts, which is available for feature phones as well as smartphones. Similarly, the *African Storybook* project has over 800 free attractively illustrated digital storybooks available in over 100 languages (see http://africanstorybook.org/). An organisation called Book Dash (http://bookdash.org/) gathers together authors and illustrators who voluntarily produce books for such programmes within very short timeframes, with the books being published under creative commons (CC-BY 4.0) license so that they can be freely translated to other languages and distributed. The books are sometimes distributed in hard copy or physical form as well as/instead of digitally, to better serve the schools and children in question and to provide a balance in the ecology of resources available.

It is not only written text that can be accessed via mobile devices, but multimodal texts may be accessible too (depending on the type of device). An advantage of this is that audio and visual elements can help children comprehend and learn from texts (Takacs, Swart, & Bus, 2015). The flip side is that multimodal literacies are complex and need to be taught (Walsh, 2010), and evidence that this is being taught in schools in LMI countries is lacking. In many cases, mobile devices offer text-to-speech (TTS) and speech-to-text (STT) tools that can help readers and writers with lower literacy levels comprehend and compose texts (Takacs et al., 2015). People with visual and auditory impairments may also find these technologies useful. Not all languages are supported as yet, however.

As well as facilitating access to Internet-based texts and e-books, smart mobile devices can provide access to apps that are dedicated to teaching various aspects of literacy, such as reading, handwriting, spelling, grammar or vocabulary. In recent years, many free apps in a range of languages (including local languages) have been developed to assist people around the world to learn literacy (Wagner, 2014). Mobile devices can also provide access to a range of resources to help children become literate in English, which is often seen as a lingua franca (Seidlhofer, 2005) that can provide access to a host of opportunities and interactions in a context of increasing globalisation. There are many free of charge English learning apps available for mobile devices, including those provided for children by the British Council (see https://learnenglishkids.britishcouncil.org/en/apps).

Many apps incorporate game elements such as challenges, rules and rewards and reiteration which may be motivational to learners and help them learn (Butler, 2017). However, a lot of game-based apps available are of fairly low quality and do not appear to adhere to principles of game-based learning such as those proposed by Gee (2007) and others. Many such apps reflect information transmission and behaviourist pedagogies (Murray & Olcese, 2011; Pegrum, Oakley, & Faulkner, 2013) and particular conceptions of literacy (often narrow and traditional), targeting decoding and word identification. Further, a large proportion of educational apps focus on consumption rather than production of knowledge, content and texts (Pegrum et al., 2013), and do not tap into the range of possibilities afforded by mobile technologies and multiple literacy theories. Creative/productive apps designed for writing and sharing digital stories can allow more transformative practice (Oakley, 2017) but there is little evidence of how these are being used in LMI countries, although one project called *1001 Stories* in Uganda and India encouraged children to use mobile devices to write digital texts in local languages in order to foster their creative storytelling. Some of these stories were selected to be uploaded for sharing (paid). This project was not evaluated (Wagner, 2014), however, so its impact has not been ascertained.

Mobile devices can also, of course, facilitate access to social media, which may enhance motivation to engage in literacy practices for authentic and social purposes; it would be true to say that these dynamic literacy practices are being embraced by people from many walks of life in many countries. In developing countries, social media is extremely popular among adults who have access (Pew Research Center, 2016), and this is something that young children will witness and possibly engage in as home literacy practice. It should be noted that the rise of social media means that children also need to learn social media literacy (Livingstone, 2014), which involves digital safety and responsible use of technology, but this is not part of the narrower definitions of literacy often used when issues of literacy learning in LMI countries are being addressed. There is a need for people accessing texts via social media to be proficient in critical literacy, whereby they analyse texts (Luke & Freebody, 1999) in terms of the agendas of the authors and the language devices used.

Cutting edge AR tools can be used in literacy teaching and learning (Clarke, 2013). AR involves the superimposition of a digital layer over the real world when viewed through a mobile device, creating a mixed reality of the physical and the digital. Physical classroom materials such as jigsaw puzzles and word cards (Yilmaz, 2016) as well as books and other reading materials can easily be augmented by linking them to digital resources such as websites, video clips, images or audio files. AR can be used in creative ways to enhance texts by linking them to additional content that can change, clarify or enhance meaning or provide additional information or support (Oakley, 2014, 2017), However, to use mobile AR, it is generally necessary to have a fast and stable connection to the Internet, which is still not available in many rural areas in LMI countries. As yet, there appears to be no research evidence of AR being used in literacy education in LMI countries.

9.6. Projects, Successes and Challenges

As already mentioned, there have been many m-learning projects designed to help children in LMI countries learn and engage in literacy. Unfortunately, not all of those introduced have been well conceived or stringently evaluated, and their impact is unclear (Acedo, 2014; Langer, Winters, & Stewart, 2014). Furthermore, they have not generally been evaluated in terms of how they align with literacy and m-learning theory. In many cases, there is a focus on lower order skills such as decoding and word identification with less attention given to comprehension, writing or the conceptions of literacy outlined by Mills (2016). In terms of m-learning theory, projects vary in the extent to which they make use of the affordances of mobile devices. The majority of them probably do not measure up when evaluated using the m-learning frameworks offered by researchers such as Traxler (2013a), Wong and Looi (2011) and Kearney et al. (2012).

9.7. Focus on Adult and Community Literacy

Before discussing projects aimed directly at children's learning, it is important to acknowledge that those aimed at promoting adult literacy also have great potential to assist in raising children's literacy levels; it is well known that when parents and communities participate in their children's literacy learning, for example by reading to them and modelling reading practices, there are many benefits (Barratt-Pugh & Allen, 2011; OECD, 2012; UNESCO Institute for Lifelong Learning, 2017; Vally, Murray, Tomlinson, & Cooper, 2015). Nonetheless, it is acknowledged that more research evidence is needed on the impact of home reading practices on the literacy achievement of children in LMI countries (Kim, Boyle, Zuilkowski, & Nakamura, 2016).

An example of a project aiming to improve adult literacy that may have potential to improve children's literacy is one supported by the international non-profit organisations, ProLiteracy (https://proliteracy.org/) and Worldreader. In this project, e-readers were rolled out to help women in rural Kenya learn to read (Diecuch, 2017). Here, digital e-readers were made available to women so that they could be empowered through improved literacy. The e-readers had approximately 100 e-books preinstalled on them to overcome poor or non-existent Internet connections. The e-books constituted a range of genres and were made available in local languages as well as English. Solar powered charging stations were provided to enable the recharging of the devices in areas with no or unreliable electricity provision. The women gathered in schools to read the texts, providing a social and support network as well as digital reading materials. Women participating in such programmes, by improving their own literacy and confidence, are in a better position to model literacy practices and to actively assist their children in learning. Because the women were not able to read at a time and place of their choosing, and there was no online social learning and so on, many of the advantages of m-learning suggested by m-learning theorists were not apparent in this project. However, the women were able to choose the texts they wanted to read, which represents a small degree of personalisation. There was some authenticity too as the women were reading real texts for real purposes.

Tens of thousands of people in LMI countries have installed the Worldreader Mobile (WRM) app on their phone, and are able to access reading materials through this app. *Reading in a Mobile Era: A Study of Mobile Reading in Developing Countries* (UNESCO, 2014) reported on a survey that was completed by over 4,000 people in seven countries (Ethiopia, Ghana, India, Kenya, Nigeria, Pakistan and Zimbabwe) to find out who reads on mobile phones and why; if and how mobile reading changes reading habits and attitudes towards reading; what people read and want to read on their mobile phones; what the central barriers are to mobile reading; and what factors predict people's intentions to read and keep reading on mobile phones (UNESCO, 2014, p. 17). An invitation to participate in the survey, written in English, was sent out via the WRM app. Because it was sent out through the app, a representative sample of the general population of the countries surveyed was obviously not reached.

A total of 62% of the survey respondents indicated that they read more after gaining access to the WRM app, and 33% reported that they read to children from their mobile phones, which has the potential to make a difference in contexts where books are in short supply. A further 34% said they would read to their children if more books and stories for children were available on their mobile. Interestingly, a higher proportion of men than women reported that they read to children from their mobile phones. This may be because they tended to have more access. Also, school teachers (who constituted 18% of the sample) reported that they were reading aloud stories from their mobile phones to students in class to counter a shortage of texts. Survey responses were cross-checked against usage statistics of the WRM app, which measured such behaviours as amount of time spent reading the digital texts and what was accessed. In this project, readers were able to choose what, when and where to read – the digital books could be downloaded from Worldreader and read at the user's convenience – but other possibilities afforded by mobile devices were not harnessed. For example, there was no online collaboration or chatting about the books.

The *Reading in a Mobile Era* report (UNESCO, 2014) points out that there are still significant issues of gender inequality when it comes to accessing mobile phones, with women in sub-Saharan Africa being 23% less likely than men to own a mobile phone, and the gap is even wider when it comes to connectivity with data. As women are still the primary carers of children in many countries, this restricted access could impact on their ability to improve their own literacy and to read texts to children in their early years, denying them the opportunity to engender a love of reading, exposure to book language and exposure to a wider vocabulary and knowledge about the world than might otherwise be the case. There are other apps and games aimed at improving adult literacy, but it is beyond the scope of this chapter to discuss them.

9.8. Projects Focusing on Children's Literacy

9.8.1. Digital Text Provision

A home-based programme aimed at helping adults support children's literacy learning was called *MobiLiteracy Uganda* (MLit-U). This provided parents and caregivers with literacy activities to carry out at home on a daily basis with their children. The activities were delivered in the form of audio SMS and presented letters and sounds, along with a word starting with the letter being taught. In addition, one story a week was provided via the mobile. An evaluation of the pilot showed that participating children learned slightly more than a control group but less than those using a paper and pencil version of the programme (Pouezevara, 2015). No reasons for the paper version being superior in this regard were given, but some parents experienced problems with the technology, which may have been a factor.

A school-based project that appears to have been useful was the *Ghana iREAD 2* project, which ran from 2013 to 2014, following from iREAD 1 in

2011–2012 (Worldreader, 2014). The implementation of iREAD 2 was a response to the fact that at least half of Ghana's Grade 2 children could not read a single word, and a dire shortage of reading materials available in primary schools in Ghana. The iREAD 2 project involved students from Grades 1, 2 and 3 in under-resourced schools being given access to e-readers. The e-readers, which had 240 titles installed on them, were loaned to all students, teachers and school heads at each of four participating schools. Most of the e-books installed on the e-readers were authored by African people, with a large proportion (57%) being authored by people from Ghana and Kenya. Books were in the local language, Akuapem Twi, and in English. Most of the texts (79%) were storybooks, while 18% were non-fiction textbooks and the rest were reference books. As well as the provision of e-readers, a phonics programme was put into place to help the children decode. Staff at the school were given professional development in managing iREAD 2 and out of school reading activities were also put into place to encourage reading (Worldreader, 2014). A Worldreader team undertook an internal evaluation of iREAD 2. Using the Ghana Early Grade Reading Assessment (EGRA) to measure student reading achievement, a sample of 720 of the children who had participated was found to outperform children from other schools who had not participated in iREAD 2. An evaluation showed that only 35.4% of non-participants in iREAD 2 could read at least one word in Akuapem Twi, whereas 89.3% of those in iREAD 2 were able to do this. Only 49.3% of Grades 1 to 3 students who were non-participants could read at least one word in English, compared to 88.4% of children who had participated in iREAD 2 (Worldreader, 2014). Also, gains in fluency and comprehension (as measured by the EGRA) were recorded. A sample of children ($n = 117$) participated in a survey on reading habits and it was found that there was a relationship between the amount that was read by the child (in the previous 24 hours), being able to name a favourite book and the final EGRA score.

There are some limitations in the evaluation of iREAD 2. Because the e-readers were part of an integrated programme that included phonics instruction, the effect of the use of the mobile devices and the digital texts were not isolated. Also, the EGRA, although widely used in LMI countries, can be critiqued for its underlying simple model of reading (Hoffman, 2012) and, perhaps, limited appropriateness for younger children (along with many other formal, standardised tests). The test has known limitations and specific purposes, which are not always fully understood by those employing it (Dubeck & Gove, 2015). Furthermore, EGRA includes a non-word component, something that has been criticised by many literacy researchers as being an inappropriate assessment for young children, who may not understand the concept of nonsense words or non-words (Clark, 2013).

A disadvantage of iREAD 2 was that 20% of the e-readers were damaged or broken, affecting the project's sustainability. It is noted that more durable e-reader devices have since been developed (Worldreader, 2014). In terms of harnessing the affordances of mobile devices, iREAD 2 did not allow children options regarding the time and place of reading, as they were not permitted to take the e-readers off school grounds for security reasons. In terms of personalisation, there were choices in terms of books to be read.

The *African Storybook* project (http://africanstorybook.org/) is another e-book project, and *Storyweaver* in India (https://storyweaver.org.in/) is similar, with stories in a range of languages such as Hindi, Bengali, Punjabi, Gujarati, English and others being provided. It is beyond the scope of this chapter to describe all of these programmes – suffice to say that there are many efforts globally to provide appropriate and affordable (often free of charge) digital texts to disadvantaged groups through mobile devices. It is acknowledged that the mere provision of stories and reading materials will not in itself lead to increased literacy rates.

9.8.2. Apps and Games for Children

Examples of projects that have involved game-based apps include the *Mobile and Immersive Learning for Literacy in Emerging Economies (MILLEE)* project, which involved the use of games on cellphones that targeted English as a Second Language (ESL) for out-of-school children in rural and slum areas in India (Kam, 2013); the *Total Reading Approach for Children Plus (TRAC+)* in Cambodia, which involves the use of a game-based phonics app, Aan Khmer (Read Khmer), as part of a wider reading intervention for children in the early grades of school (Oakley, Pegrum, Kheang, & Seng, 2017, 2018); *GraphoGame* (see http://info.grapholearn.com/), which has been successfully used in schools in Zambia in a local language, ciNyanja (Jere-Folotiya, 2017; Jere-Folotiya et al., 2014; Ojanen et al., 2015); and *Antura and the Letters* and *Feed the Monster*, two games that aim to assist children who have been affected by the Syrian crisis (All Children Reading, 2017). In the paragraphs below, we discuss some of these projects in more depth.

MILLEE involved the use of immersive language learning games (largely out of school) that targeted children's reading, listening, sentence construction and spelling in English. The design of the games was informed by a study of traditional village games (Kam, 2013). The MILLEE project was subject to ongoing evaluation and modification over several years and it was found that the games did lead to learning gains (Kam, 2013), although it was difficult to design games that were meaningful to children in rural contexts. Kam has suggested that it may not be realistic to look for 'one size fits all' solutions for multiple contexts and that the local culture must be taken into account in designing mobile games, and this includes gender roles in the community concerned. Another insight from MILLEE is that children with higher baseline knowledge seemed to get more out of the games, again suggesting that customisation according to student characteristics is important.

The *Total Reading Approach for Children TRAC+* project in Cambodia involves the use of an app called Aan Khmer to help children in Grades 1 to 3 improve knowledge of the alphabet and correspondences between sounds and symbols in the Khmer language, and to improve vocabulary and fluency (World Vision International, 2016). The identification of high frequency words is also targeted through the provision of matching games and digital flashcards. At the end of each lesson, a short narrated story is presented. Children have peer tutors from Grade 4 and above to help them use the app, as well as literacy coaches, who are teachers, retired teachers or school librarians. A study carried out by Oakley et al. (2017) found that there were some aspects of the design and implementation of the m-learning aspect of the TRAC+ project that appeared to inhibit its effectiveness. Use of the app was found to make only a small difference to the students' learning, as measured by the Cambodian EGRA, and Grade 1 children did not appear to benefit. Although qualitative data (e.g. interviews with literacy coaches, teachers, librarians, peer tutors and school directors) indicated that most of the people involved in TRAC+ thought that the app was useful, they also reported challenges. In most cases, children were not getting much time 'on task' with the app. Further, they were not necessarily doing the targeted activities on the app that they had been directed to do. Despite training and mentoring, peer tutors were not experts at guiding the younger children in using the app. Also, classroom teachers were not always very involved in what their students were doing with the app and were therefore unable to meaningfully integrate the use of the app with classroom teaching and other literacy activities. Practical issues around charging and storing the tablets were also experienced, in common with many other m-learning projects in LMI countries. In terms of the design of the Aan Khmer app, there were some limitations. For example, it was possible for children to proceed through the app by merely guessing the answers. As in many other apps, there was an emphasis on reading without any writing. As reading and writing are closely inter-related, teaching that integrates these two aspects of literacy are beneficial for young children (Tierney & Shanahan, 1991).

Although the Aan Khmer app has some game-based features, these are limited. Kam (2009) has pointed out that if games are to be used, they should be at the right level of challenge and should be meaningful for children; ideally, they need to reflect cultural ways of doing things. They should also be enjoyable. The Aan Khmer app was developed from a preexisting template used in multiple countries and was thus not designed specifically with the Cambodian culture in mind (Oakley et al., 2017).

GraphoGame is a phonics game that has been used successfully in Finland for children with literacy difficulties and modified for use in several African countries (Ojanen et al., 2015). The game uses synthetic and analytic instructional approaches to teaching phonics. Because the game is adaptive, an optimal level of challenge is provided. Frequent positive feedback is also a feature of the game. The game has also been used in Zambia, where the local language (ciNyanja) has a transparent orthography which was deemed to render the phonics-based app appropriate. Another rationale for using the game in Zambia was that the teachers did not have a solid knowledge of letter-sound correspondences in the language, so it was hoped that they could learn from the game alongside their students (Ojanen et al., 2015). Students used the games in two school terms for a mean amount of time of 94 minutes a term, with access being over three to five days during each of the two terms. Actual length of time playing the game was seven to nine minutes per session, with a break of one to nine minutes before resuming play. Although the teachers had little or no teacher training or experience in teaching with ICT or mobile devices, it was found that the game led to significant improvement in students' decoding skills when compared to a control group. When teachers played the game, this also had a positive effect on students' results (Jere-Folotiya et al., 2014). In the case of GraphoGame in the Zambian context, it appears that children were able to understand and play the game even though it had been imported from another culture, which seems counter to Kam's recommendations about the need to build on local games culture.

The Arabic literacy learning games, *Antura and the Letters* and *Feed the Monster*, aim to assist children who have been affected by the Syrian conflict. The games were developed through the EduApp4Syria competition (All Children Reading, 2017). See https://allchildrenreading.org/eduapp4syria-competition-launches-unique-literacy-learning-apps-can-reach-millions-war-affected-syrian-children/ for more information. The games, which can be downloaded as apps or played on Windows computers, have an inviting interface and were designed so that children can learn from them independently as many children affected by the Syrian conflict are out of school or struggling in new schools (All Children Reading, 2017). The games, which are compatible with older Android devices and have low data requirements, incorporate principles of game-based learning such as characters, journeys, game environments (places in the game), rewards, problem solving as well as ongoing assessments. However, they do not include social elements like competition and cooperation with others as they are designed to be played offline. The efficacy of the games has not yet been evaluated.

9.8.3. *Mobile Lessons and Content for Teachers and Students*

This section outlines two projects that aim to support teachers and students through the provision of lesson materials via mobile phones. *MeraSABAQ* is a project in Pakistan (see http://sabaq.edu.pk), where there are wide inequalities and millions of children are out of school. The purpose of the project is to provide learning content to primary school aged children in socially disadvantaged areas. Children access the content in school, as well as outside school in informal learning centres (ILMIdeas2, 2016). MeraSABAQ uses a custom-designed Android tablet for learning, which has preinstalled learning content that is suitable for the children of various age and year levels, based on the Pakistani national curriculum for primary education. Content is offered in multiple interactive formats, including video lessons, games, interactive flipbooks and practice exercises, and is available in multiple languages including Urdu, Sindhi and English. Since its inception in early 2016, the project has reached 4,000 students in and out of schools in two main states of Pakistan Sindh and Punjab. According to an independent study, results of the programme have so far been promising (Multinet, 2017). The project aims to reach one million socially and financially disadvantaged primary school aged children in the Sindh and Punjab provinces by 2020 and also aims to train teachers and develop m-learning content for the entire primary level national curriculum of Pakistan (ILMIdeas2, 2016). Although children cannot access the content any place and any time, due to having to go to centres or school to access it, the use of mobile devices allows access to content they would not otherwise receive.

A similar project was implemented in India, where there is unequal access to education (Wennersten, Quraishy, & Velamuri, 2015). The *BridgeIT India* project is a m-learning programme for low socio-economic areas in Andhra Pradesh and Tamil Nadu that cost less than 2 USD per child per year. The project ran from 2012 to 2013 in government schools and involved teachers and students using mobile-based learning content. BridgeIT has also been implemented in other countries such as Bangladesh, Chile, Colombia, Haiti, Indonesia, the Philippines, Nigeria, South Africa and Tanzania (Wagner, 2014). The project in India was piloted in 34 schools in the 2 participating states. Mobile-based video learning content based on the Indian national curriculum across all areas of the curriculum, including Mathematics, Science and English, was provided for students in Grades 5 and 6 students. Based on the success of the pilot, the project was expanded to 4,000 students from 86 schools in both states. Around 400 video-based lessons, mapped to the syllabus, were available for learners and teachers to access. A study indicated that students involved in the programme outperformed their non-participating peers by an average of 10% in English and more than 15% in Science. Children in Andhra Pradesh achieved better results than those in Tamil Nadu – this was attributed to the teachers' qualifications and the prior knowledge of the students. Participating teachers reported increased student engagement and an improvement in their own pedagogical, content and technological knowledge through their involvement in the programme (Wennersten et al., 2015).

9.9. Concluding Remarks

The use of mobile technologies has been embraced as a means of improving literacy outcomes for children and adults in LMI countries, but there is still much to learn about what works in each context and what the wider implications of M4L projects might be. In this chapter, we have attempted to highlight some of the potential benefits as well as limitations of these efforts.

One of the main tensions is the need to balance scalability and cost effectiveness against local culture and needs. Several projects seem to have been vexed by not working as expected due to local factors, such as the rural children in the MILLEE project (Kam, 2013) not understanding the game elements imported from Western games. With reference to this issue, Traxler (2013b, p. 134) has suggested: 'In essence, disadvantaged and distant communities need the educational version of mass customisation as the antidote to educational mass production, in order to access appropriate and sustainable m-learning'.

Another challenge is teacher professional development. Where children are using mobile devices in schools, there is a need for teachers to be educated in how to use them (UNESCO, 2017), how to design learning activities that make use of their affordances and how to integrate them into coherent and comprehensive teaching programmes. In a meta-analysis of the effect of using technology to teach literacy, Cheung and Slavin (2012) found that there was a larger effect size when comprehensive models of literacy instruction were used; that is, those that used technology *with* non-technology learning activities were superior. It is thus important that teachers have adequate content knowledge, pedagogical knowledge, technological knowledge and that they know how to bring these knowledge sources together to design effective learning experiences (Koehler, Mishra, & Cain, 2013) using a range of resources and approaches. Without this capacity, teachers may also find it difficult to incorporate newer technologies such as AR and VR when it becomes available to them. M-learning itself can be used in improving teacher professional development (Aubusson, Schuck, & Burden, 2009).

Another issue for consideration is the extent to which mobile-based literacy learning can and *should* replace face-to-face and traditional means of teaching and learning for children. Currently, using mobile technologies as a substitute for teachers may be an imperative in some parts of the world but it is conceivable that jurisdictions may decide to scale up the use of m-learning as an alternative to investing in schools and quality teachers, and this may not be the best path to take for a host of philosophical and social reasons – it may lead to unintended consequences. Indeed, Traxler (2013b) has warned about unintended consequences of m-learning in distant communities, such as the interfering with of the 'ecological balance' (Traxler, 2013b, p. 135) of local languages, cultures and ways of learning.

In terms of the content in apps for literacy learning, there is often an over-emphasis on lower order literacy skills such as letter sound correspondences and word identification, based on behaviourist or drill and skill pedagogies. There is also an over-emphasis on reading as opposed to writing. It may be fruitful to broaden the focus of M4L to the full range of literacies mentioned by Mills (2016) and others, to better equip students to participate in literacy practices and further learning independently, responsibly, and with a critical stance. Achieving only basic literacy while having mobile access to a plethora of texts and messages, many of which are inaccurate or malevolent, may be a dangerous thing.

Although educational researchers still have many questions to answer (and ask) about how the use mobile technologies can improve the literacies of children in LMI countries and heighten their participation, there is evidence that mobile technologies can help overcome barriers associated with a lack of human and material resources and geographical distance. However, because there are still inequities in access to mobile technologies, these could flow through to ongoing or deepening inequities in access to quality literacy education for the most marginalised groups such as girls, the disabled and those living in severe poverty.

References

Acedo, C. (2014). Mobile learning for literacy, teacher training and curriculum development. *Prospects, 44*(1), 1−4.

All Children Reading. (2017). *EduApp4Syria competition launches unique literacy learning apps that can reach millions of war-affected Syrian children*. Retrieved from https://allchildrenreading.org/eduapp4syria-competition-launches-unique-literacy-learning-apps-can-reach-millions-war-affected-syrian-children/. Accessed on August 8, 2018.

Aubusson, P., Schuck, S., & Burden, K. (2009). Mobile learning for teacher professional learning: benefits, obstacles and issues. *ALT-J, 17*(3), 233−247.

Barratt-Pugh, C., & Allen, N. (2011). Making a difference: Findings from better beginnings a family literacy intervention programme. *The Australian Library Journal, 60*(3), 195−204.

Burden, K. J., & Kearney, M. (2017). Investigating and critiquing teacher educators' mobile learning practices. *Interactive Technology and Smart Education, 14*(2), 110−125.

Butler, Y. G. (2017). Motivational elements of digital instructional games: A study of young L2 learners' game designs. *Language Teaching Research, 21*(6), 1−4.

Cheung, A. C. K., & Slavin, R. E. (2012). How features of educational technology applications affect student reading outcomes: A meta-analysis. *Educational Research Review, 7*(3), 198−215.

Clark, M. (2013). The phonics check for year 1 children in England: Unresolved issues of its value and validity after two years. *Education Journal, 177*, 13−15. Retrieved from http://www.tactyc.org.uk/pdfs/Margaret%20Clark.pdf

Clarke, J. (2013). Augmented reality, multimodal literacy and mobile technology: An experiment in teacher engagement. Paper presented at the 12th World Conference on Mobile and Contextual Learning (mLearn 2013), Doha, Qatar. Retrieved from http://www.qscience.com/doi/abs/10.5339/qproc.2013.mlearn.28

Cross, J. A. (2007). *Informal learning: Rediscovering the natural pathways that inspire innovation and performance*. San Francisco, CA: Pfeiffer.

de Silva, J. H., Feez, S., & Thickstun, W. R. (2015). *Exploring literacies: Theory, research and practice*. London: Palgrove Macmillan.

Dlecuch, M. (2017). *Empowering women through digital literacy. Paper presented at Mobiles for Education Alliance Symposium: Future proofing technology for education in international development*, Washington DC, October 5−6, 2017.

Dubeck, M. M., & Gove, A. (2015). The early grade reading assessment (EGRA): Its theoretical foundation, purpose, and limitations. *International Journal of Educational Development, 40*(Supplement C), 315−322.

Dudeney, G., Hockly, N., & Pegrum, M. (2013). *Digital literacies*. Harlow: Pearson.

Fellowes, J., & Oakley, G. (2014). *Language, literacy and early childhood education*. Melbourne: Oxford University Press.

Frawley, J. K., & Dyson, L. E. (2014). Mobile literacies. In M. Kalz, Y. Bayyurt, & M. Specht (Eds.), *Mobile as a mainstream − Towards future challenges in mobile learning*. mLearn 2014. Communications in Computer and Information Science (479, pp. 377−390). Cham: Springer.

Gee, J. P. (2007). *What video games have to teach us about learning and literacy*. (Rev. and updated ed.). New York, NY: Palgrave MacMillan.

GSMA. (2016). *Global mobile trends*. Retrieved from https://www.gsmaintelligence.com/research/?file=357f1541c77358e61787fac35259dc92&download. Accessed on September 30, 2017.

Hoffman, J. (2012). Standpoints: Why EGRA—A clone of DIBELS—Will fail to improve literacy in Africa. *Research in the Teaching of English*, 46(4), 340−357.

ILMIdeas2. (2016). *meraSABAQ makes learning fun*. Retrieved from http://www.ilmideas2.pk/merasabaq-makes-learning-fun/. Accessed on September 30, 2017.

Jere-Folotiya, J. (2017). GraphoGame Teacher Training Service (GG-TTS). *Paper presented at Mobiles for Education Alliance symposium: Future proofing technology for education in international development*. Washington DC, October 5-6, 2017.

Jere-Folotiya, J., Chansa-Kabali, T., Munachaka, J. C., Sampa, F., Yalukanda, C., Westerholm, J., … Lyytinen, H. (2014). The effect of using a mobile literacy game to improve literacy levels of grade one students in Zambian schools. *Educational Technology Research and Development*, 62(4), 417−436.

Kam, M. (2009). *Designing digital games for rural children: A study of traditional village games in India*. Retrieved from http://www.cs.cmu.edu/~mattkam/publications/CHI2009.pdf. Accessed on August 30, 2018.

Kam, M. (2013). Mobile learning games for low-income children in India. In Z. L. Berge & L. Y. Muilenburg (Eds.), *Handbook of mobile learning* (pp. 617−627). New York, NY: Routledge.

Kearney, M., Schuck, S., Burden, K., & Aubusson, P. (2012). Viewing mobile learning from a pedagogical perspective. *Research in Learning Technology*, 20(1), 1−17.

Kim, Y.-S. G., Boyle, H. N., Zuilkowski, S. S., & Nakamura, P. (2016). *Landscape report on early grade literacy*. Washington, DC: USAID.

Koehler, M. J., Mishra, P., & Cain, W. (2013). What Is technological pedagogical content knowledge (TPACK)? *Journal of Education*, 193(3), 13−19.

Langer, L., Winters, N., & Stewart, R. (2014). Mobile learning for development: Ready to randomise? In M. Kalz, Y. Bayyurt, & M. Specht (Eds.), *Mobile as a mainstream − Towards future challenges in mobile learning: 13th World Conference on Mobile and Contextual Learning, mLearn 2014, Istanbul, Turkey, November 3−5, 2014, Proceedings* (pp. 156−167). Cham: Springer.

Livingstone, S. (2014). Developing social media literacy: How children learn to interpret risky opportunities on social network sites. *Communications*, 39(3), 283−303.

Luke, A., & Freebody, P. (1999). A map of possible practices: Further notes on the four resources model. *Practically Primary*, 4(2), 5−8.

Mills, K. A. (2016). *Literacy theories for a digital age: Social, critical, multimodal, spatial, material and sensory lenses*. Bristol: Multilingual Matters.

Moll, L., Amanti, C., Niff, D., & Gonzales, N. (1992). Funds of knowledge for teaching: Using a qualitative approach to connect homes and classrooms. *Theory into Practice*, 31(2), 132−141.

Multinet. (2017). *ILM ideas2 programs Draft Final Report v.2*. Unpublished source. May 24, 2017.

Murray, O. T., & Olcese, N. R. (2011). Teaching and learning with iPads, ready or not? *TechTrends*, 55(6), 42−48.

Nag, S., Snowling, M. J., & Asfaha, Y. M. (2016). Classroom literacy practices in low- and middle-income countries: An interpretative synthesis of ethnographic studies. *Oxford Review of Education, 42*(1), 36−54. doi:10.1080/03054985.2015.1135115

Oakley, G. (2014). Teaching using augmented reality. *CS4HS Conference 2014.* 6−7 November Perth.

Oakley, G. (2017). Engaging students in inclusive literacy learning with technology. In M. Milton (Ed.), *Inclusive principles and practices in literacy education* (pp. 159−176). Bingley: Emerald Publishing.

Oakley, G. (2018). Mobile technologies in language and literacy practice and learning in preschool and primary school children. In G. Oakley (Ed.), *Mobile technologies and language and literacy: Innovative pedagogy in preschool and primary education* (pp. 1−14). Bingley: Emerald Publishing.

Oakley, G., Pegrum, M., Kheang, T., & Seng, K. (2017). *M-learning in TRAC+ to enhance the literacy of early grade students in Cambodia.* Mobiles for Education Alliance symposium: Future proofing technology for education in international development. Washington DC, October 5−6, 2017.

Oakley, G., Pegrum, M., Khaeng, T., & Seng, K. (2018). *An evaluation of the integration of m-learning in Total Reading Approach for Children Plus: Enhancing literacy of early grade students in Cambodia.* Washington, DC: World Vision and Foundation for Information Technology Education and Development.

OECD. (2012). *Let's read them a story! The parent factor in education.* PISA, OECD Publishing. Retrieved from http://dx.doi.org/10.1787/9789264176232-en. Accessed on August 30, 2018.

Ojanen, E., Ronimus, M., Ahonen, T., Chansa-Kabali, T., February, P., Jere-Folotiya, J., & Lyytinen, H. (2015). GraphoGame − a catalyst for multi-level promotion of literacy in diverse contexts. *Frontiers in Psychology, 6*(671).

Pegrum, M. (2014). *Mobile learning: Languages, literacies and cultures.* Basingstoke: Palgrave Macmillan.

Pegrum, M. (2016). Languages and literacies for digital lives. In E. Martin-Monje, I. Eloza, & B. García Riaza (Eds.), *Technology-enhanced language learning for specialized domains: Practical applications and mobility* (pp. 9−22). London: Routledge.

Pegrum, M., Oakley, G., & Faulkner, R. (2013). Schools going mobile: A study of the adoption of mobile handheld technologies in Western Australian independent schools. *Australasian Journal of Educational Technology, 29*(1), 66−81.

Pew Research Center. (2016). *Smartphone ownership and internet usage continues to climb in emerging economies.* Retrieved from www.pewglobal.org/2016/02/22/smartphone-ownership-and-internet-usage-continues-to-climb-in-emerging-economies/. Accessed on August 30, 2018.

Pouezevara, S. (2015). MobiLiteracy Uganda: Using mobile phones to engage mothers in improving early reading achievement in their families. Paper presented at the UNESCO Mobile Learning Week Symposium: Leveraging technology to empower women and girls, Paris.

Rose, J. (2006). *Independent review of the teaching of early reading.* Nottingham: DfES Publications.

Roskos, K., & Neuman, S. B. (2011). The classroom environment: First, last, and always. *The Reading Teacher, 65*(2), 110−114.

Saracho, O. N. (2017). Literacy and language: New developments in research, theory and practice. *Early Child Development and Care, 187*(3−4), 299−304.

Sefton-Green, J., Marsh, J., Erstad, O., & Flewitt, R. (2016). *Establishing a research agenda for the digital literacy practices of young children: A White Paper for COST Action IS1410*. Retrieved from http://digilitey.eu. Accessed on August 28, 2018.

Seidlhofer, B. (2005). English as a lingua franca. *ELT Journal, 59*(4), 339–341.

Takacs, Z. K., Swart, E. K., & Bus, A. G. (2015). Benefits and pitfalls of multimedia and interactive features in technology-enhanced storybooks: A meta-analysis. *Review of Educational Research, 85*(4), 698–739.

Tierney, R. J., & Shanahan, T. (1991). Research on the reading-writing relationship: Interactions, transactions, and outcomes. In R. Barr, M. L. Kamil, P. Mosenthal, & P. D. Pearson (Eds.), *Handbook of reading research* (2, pp. 246–280). New York, NY: Longman.

Traxler, J. (2013a). Mobile learning: Shaping the frontiers of learning technologies in global context. In R. Huang, J. M. Spector, & Kinshuk (Eds.), *Reshaping learning: The frontiers of learning technologies in a global context* (pp. 415–438). New York, NY: Springer.

Traxler, J. (2013b). Mobile learning across developing and developed worlds: Tackling distance, digital divides, disadvantages, disenfranchisement. In Z. L. Berge & L. Y. Muilenburg (Eds.), *Handbook of Mobile Learning* (pp. 129–141). New York, NY: Routledge.

Traxler, J. M. (2017). Learning with mobiles in developing countries: Technology, language, and literacy. *International Journal of Mobile and Blended Learning (IJMBL), 9*(2), 1–15.

UNESCO. (2008). *The global literacy challenge: A profile of youth and adult literacy at the mid-point of the United Nations Literacy Decade 2003-2012*. Retrieved from http://unesdoc.unesco.org/images/0016/001631/163170e.pdf. Accessed on August 17, 2017.

UNESCO. (2011). Enhancing learning of children from diverse language backgrounds. Retrieved from http://unesdoc.unesco.org/images/0021/002122/212270e.pdf. Accessed on August 17, 2018.

UNESCO. (2014). *Reading in the mobile era: A study of mobile learning in developing countries*. Retrieved from http://unesdoc.unesco.org/images/0022/002274/227436e.pdf. Accessed on August 27, 2017.

UNESCO. (2016). *Global education monitoring report 2016*. Retrieved from http://unesdoc.unesco.org/images/0024/002457/245752e.pdf. Accessed on August 30, 2017.

UNESCO. (2017). Supporting teachers with mobile technology: Lessons drawn from UNESCO projects in Mexico, Nigeria, Pakistan and Senegal. Retrieved from http://unesdoc.unesco.org/images/0025/002515/251511e.pdf. Accessed on August 27, 2017.

UNESCO Institute for Lifelong Learning. (2017). *Fostering a culture of reading and writing: Examples of dynamic literate environments*. Hamburg: UNESCO Institute of Lifelong Learning. Retrieved from http://unesdoc.unesco.org/images/0025/002579/257933e.pdf. Accessed on July 15, 2018.

United Nations. (2015). *World's women*. Retrieved from https://unstats.un.org/unsd/gender/worldswomen.html. Accessed on July 20, 2017.

Vally, Z., Murray, L., Tomlinson, M., & Cooper, P. J. (2015). The impact of dialogic book-sharing training on infant language and attention: a randomized controlled trial in a deprived South African community. *Journal of Child Psychology and Psychiatry*, *6*(8), 865–873. Accessed on August 30, 2018.

Wagner, D. (2014). *Mobiles for reading: A landscape review*. Retrieved from http://literacy.org/sites/literacy.org/files/publications/wagner_mobiles4reading_usaid_june_14.pdf. Accessed on August 30, 2018.

Wagner, D. (2017). Children's reading in low-income countries. *The Reading Teacher*, *71*(2), 127–133.

Walsh, M. (2010). Multimodal literacy: What does it mean for classroom practice? *Australian Journal of Language and Literacy*, *33*(3), 211–239.

Wennersten, M., Quraishy, Z. B., & Velamuri, M. (2015). Improving student learning via mobile phone video content: Evidence from the BridgeIT India project. *International Review of Education*, *61*(4), 503–528.

Wong, L.-H., & Looi, C.-K. (2011). What seams do we remove in mobile-assisted seamless learning? A critical review of the literature. *Computers & Education*, *57*(4), 2364–2381.

World Bank. (2018). *Learning to realise education's promise*. Washington, DC: International Bank for Reconstruction and Development/ The World Bank. Retrieved from http://www.worldbank.org/en/publication/wdr2018

World Vision International. (2016). *Project overview: Total Reading Approach for Children (TRAC+) Project*. Retrieved from http://dl4d.org/wp-content/uploads/2016/03/TRAC-Appendix-A.-TRAC-Project-Overview.pdf. Accessed on August 30, 2018.

Worldreader. (2014). *Ghana iREAD study: Final evaluation*. Retrieved from https://comms.worldreader.org/wp-content/uploads/2015/01/iREAD-final_web2.pdf?x80235. Accessed on July 15, 2017.

Wyse, D., & Styles, M. (2007). Synthetic phonics and the teaching of reading: the debate surrounding England's 'Rose Report'. *Literacy*, *41*(1), 35–42.

Yilmaz, R. M. (2016). Educational magic toys developed with augmented reality technology for early childhood education. *Computers in Human Behavior*, *54*, 240–248.

Zualkernan, I. A. (2015). Personalised learning for the developing world. In B. Gros, Kinshuk, & M. Maina (Eds.), *The future of ubiquitous learning: Learning designs for emerging pedagogies* (pp. 241–258). Berlin: Springer-Verlag Berlin Heidelberg.

Index

Aan Khmer app, 167
Aboriginal community, 108
ABS. *See* Australian Bureau of Statistics (ABS)
Active learning, 143–144
Adult literacy, 163–164
Adults' mediation of children's technology, 139–140
African Storybook project, 160, 166
Alborough, Jez, 44
Alpha, 53
Alpha 1 app, 60–61
Animalia app, 39, 44
Antura and the Letters, 166, 168
'App smashing', 104
AR. *See* Augmented reality (AR)
Artefacts, 76
Arts (K-6), 29–45
Atchley, Dana, 68–69
Audio recorder, 4
Augmented reality (AR)
 to learn animals at zoo, 106–113
 trail by the Swan river, 115–116
Augmented Reality apps, 4
Aurasma app, 106–108
Australian National Curriculum, 33
Authenticity, 6–7
Authentic learning, 6

Balloon power, 41
Base, Graeme, 39, 44
Bilingual children, 41, 42

Blabey, Aaron, 36
Blend English, 109
Blending technology, 110–112
Blue-Bot robotic toy, 53
 moving from symbol cards, 57
 programming language, 55
 TacTile Reader, 57
Blue Hat app, 44
Bluetooth, 4
Book Creator app, 22, 34, 104
Boynton, Sandra, 45
BridgeIT India project, 169
Browne, Anthony, 36
Burningham, John, 36

Camera, 4
Campbell, Rod, 44
Cellular connections, 4
Centre for Digital Storytelling, 68–69
ChatterPix, 22
Childhood education and care (ECEC) services, 55
ciNyanja, 167
Class
 art, 106–108
 discussions, 78
Classroom, 139–140
 design-based, 123
 examples of reading and writing multimodally with, 91–94
 participation in arts inside and outside, 42–45
Club session, 125
Code Karts app, 53

Coding
    introducing young children to, 55–56
    as literacy in early years, 53–54
    as literacy with mobile device, 60–62
'Cognitive space', 6
Collaboration, 6–7
Collaged faces, 37
Community literacy, 163–164
Composing, 92–93
Concept mapping, 104
Connecting literacy, 31–33
Constructivist approaches, 34
Context aware learning, 6
Contextualising play, 18–19
Contingent learning, 5–6
Creating flowcharts, 104
Creative Book Builder app, 115
Creativity, 31
Critical literacy, 120
Cubetto robots, 53, 58–60

123D modelling app, 110
Data charting, 104
Data collection/analysis, 141
David Wiesner, 36
Dear Zoo app, 44
Departures, 121–122
Design-based classroom experiments, 123
Design thinking, 71, 77–79
Develop dramatic play, 39–40
Developing language, 38–39
Developing literacy, resources for, 42–45
Development of rich task, 101–103
Digital age, dynamic literacy practices in, 15–26
Digital documentation, 20
Digital format, 36

Digitally enriched imaginative play, 16
Digital resources
    constraints of, 90–91
Digital storytelling, 68–69, 70
    approach, 75–76
Digital technology, 20, 120, 134–135, 142
    classroom examples of reading and writing multimodally with, 91–94
    personalised learning with, 143
Digital text provision, 164–166
Digitisation, 21
Discipline-specific literacy, 100
Dodd, Lynley, 39, 44
Don't Let the Pigeon Run this App app, 45
Drama, 31
Drawing app, 31, 36, 92–93
Duck in the Truck, 44
Dynamic literacy, 16, 18–20
    in early childhood education, 20–25
    in early years pedagogy, 21–24
    practices in digital age, 15–26
    space, 17

EAL/D. *See* English as Additional Language/Dialect (EAL/D)
Early childhood
    classrooms, critical literacy in, 120
    education, 21
    dynamic literacy in, 20–25
Early Years Learning Framework, 33
Early years pedagogy, dynamic literacy in, 21–24
e-book, 91–92, 115, 161, 163

ECEC services. *See* Childhood education and care (ECEC) services
Edmodo, 76
EduApp4Syria competition, 168
Educational story booklet, 58–59
Educators, 87, 136
Encompassing formal/informal learning, 8
Encompassing multiple pedagogical/learning activity models, 8
Encompassing personalised/social learning, 8
Encompassing physical/digital worlds, 8
English as Additional Language/Dialect (EAL/D), 123
English as a Second Language (ESL), 166
e-portfolio app, 115–116
e-pub app, 104
e-readers, 165
ESL. *See* English as a Second Language (ESL)
Explain Everything app, 36, 41, 43
Exploring arts, 30–33
Exploring skills for reading, 85

Faces iMake, 36
Falconer, Ian, 36, 44
Feed the Monster, 166, 168
Floyd, 36
Formative assessment approach, 76
Foster imagination, 18
French, Jackie, 36
FreshAiR, 114
Friendly-looking robot, 58
FutureSchools@Singapore program, 69–70

Game-based phonics app, 166

Games, 94
Gates, Bill, 53
Giant fantastic interactive map, 110–112
Giuseppe Arcimboldo, 36
Goodnight Safari app, 40, 45
Google Classroom, 76
Google Earth (Google), 112
Google Hangout, 74
Governments and non-governmental organisations (NGOs), 156
GPS (Global Positioning System), 4
Graphic organisers, 104
GraphoGame, 167
Gravett, Emily, 36

Hairy Maclairy, 39
Hairy Maclary from Donaldson's Dairy app, 44
The Heart and the Bottle app, 44
HI. *See* High transactional distance individualised m-learning (HI)
High transactional distance individualised m-learning (HI), 6
High transactional distance socialised m-learning (HS), 6
Holy Roman Emperor Rudolf II, 36
HS. *See* High transactional distance socialised m-learning (HS)
Hybrid literacy practices, 16

ICT. *See* Information and communication technology (ICT)
I Imagine app, 38, 39, 44

Illustrations, 54
Imaginative play, 16–18, 18–20
Individualisation, 134
Infographics, 104
Information and communication technology (ICT), 2, 68, 106
Innovative Pedagogy in Preschool and Primary Education, 1
Instagram, 87
Instruction
  approach, 89
  considerations and reflection, 91
  contribution to, 90
  goal, 88–89
Internet, 87
Internet-based texts, 161
'Internet of things' (IoT), 159
IoT. *See* 'Internet of things' (IoT)
iPAC framework, 7
iPads, 8, 106
iREAD 2 project, 165

Jeffers, Oliver, 36, 44

Kibo robot, 53, 58–60
Kidz Story, 44
Kimberley Region community school, 108
Kirk, David, 45
Knowledge synthesis, 8

Lambert, Joe, 68–69
Language development, 30–33
Learning
  active, 143–144
  environments, 20
  literacy, 18–20, 38–42, 157–158
  nature-based, 110–112
  personalised, 136–137
  play-based, 54
  self-directed, 144
  self-paced, 143–144
  teaching activities, 72
  testing pathway to independence in, 115–116
Learning to Write in the Early Years (LWEYs), 123
LI. *See* Low transactional distance individualised m-learning (LI)
Linoit, 75
Literacy, 3–4
  adult and community, 163–164
  emerging conceptions of, 83–85
  introducing coding as, early years, 53–54
  introducing robots to teach, 56–57
  learning, 18–20, 38–42, 157–158
  mobile resources for, 160–162
  technology for, 122–124
  starting with child and introducing, 55–56
LMI countries. *See* Low- and middle-income (LMI) countries
Lola's alphabet train app, 43
The Lost Thing, 109
Low- and middle-income (LMI) countries, 156
Lower primary, implementing digital storytelling at, 73–74
Low transactional distance individualised m-learning (LI), 6

Low transactional distance socialised m-learning (LS), 6
LS. *See* Low transactional distance socialised m-learning (LS)
LWEYs. *See* Learning to Write in the Early Years (LWEYs)

Markers of agency, 144
Maxqda data analysis tool, 141
MeraSABAQ, 168
Microsoft Photo Story 3 software application, 75
Microsoft PowerPoint, 75, 77, 78
Middle primary, making thinking visible at, 74
MILLEE project. *See* Mobile and Immersive Learning for Literacy in Emerging Economies (MILLEE) project
Miss Spider's Tea Party app, 45
Mobile
  devices, 2, 105–106
    coding as literacy with, 60–62
    in literacy learning, 103–104
    planning instruction with, 87–91
    writing multimodal texts with, 85
  learning, 29–45
    definitions and theory, 5–8
    and literacy learning in children, 2–3
    mobile devices, pervasiveness of, 2
    theory, 159–160
    toolkit website, 7
    lessons and content for teachers and students, 168–169
    resources for literacy learning, 160–162
    technology, 21, 33–38, 136, 159
      defining, 4–5
      to develop dramatic play, 39–40
      to support engagement with learning, 40–42
    tools for literacy learning, 99–103
Mobile and Immersive Learning for Literacy in Emerging Economies (MILLEE) project, 166
Mobile Pedagogical Framework (MPF), 6
Mobile Seamless Learning (MSL), 8, 160
MobiLiteracy Uganda, 164
MoMA. *See* Museum of Modern Art (MoMA)
Mother tongue language teachers, 75
Motivation to Write tubs, 127
MPF. *See* Mobile Pedagogical Framework (MPF)
MSL. *See* Mobile seamless learning (MSL)
Multiliteracies, 20
Multimodal text, 32, 85
  environment, 20
  planning instruction with, 87–91
Multiple device types, 8
Multitude of different forms of expression, 21
Museum of Modern Art (MoMA), 37
My Story, 34, 40
Myths, 22

Namatjira app, 42, 43
Narrative play, 18
Nature-based learning, 110–112
Neomad app, 42, 43
NGOs. *See* Governments and non-governmental organisations (NGOs)
NP3 project, 140

Olivia Acts Out app, 44
Online
 blogs, 74
 graphic organisers, 75
 social learning platform, 76
Oral storytelling, 84

Padlet, 75
Paper-based template reflection sheet, 108
Personalisation, 6–7, 144
Personalised learning, 6, 136–137
 children agency in, 138–139
 with digital technology, 143
 programmatic *versus* participatory, 137–138
Personalised pluralisation, 134
Photography, 19–20
Photostory, 3, 78
Play-based learning, 54, 55
Playschool Art Maker app, 40, 43
Playschool Play Time app, 39, 44
PopOut! The Tale of Peter Rabbit app, 45
Popplet, 75
Popplet app, 41, 44
Potter, Beatrix, 45
Presentation app, 36
Print-based texts, 92
Promo toys, 58
Psychological distance, 6
Puppet Pals app, 39, 40, 41, 44, 109
Puppets drama, 31–32

QR codes, 105

Reading in a Mobile Era, 163–164
Ready-made content, 24
Remote aboriginal community, 108–110
Research
 design, 70–71
 framework, 71–72
Restrictions of agency, 145–148
Rich cross-curricular learning activities, 99–100
Rich task
 development of, 101–103
 process, 104–105
Riddle, Tohby, 36
The Road Map for Arts Education, 30
Robots, 56–57
Rogers, Libby Hathornand, 115
The Room app, 44
Rubrics, 104

SAMR model. *See* Substitution, Augmentation, Modification and Redefinition (SAMR) model
School, 140–141
 based project, 164–165
 ethos, 142
ScratchJr app, 53
Scratch programming, 76
Seamless
 learning, 7
 switching between multiple learning tasks, 8
Self-directed learning, 144
Self-paced learning, 143–144
The Shape Game, 36
SimpleMind app, 106, 108
Situated learning, 5

Sketches app, 36, 44
Smartphones, 4, 19, 161
Smart technology, 20, 120
Smith, Craig, 45
Social learning, 6
  platforms, 76
Socio-cultural models, 32
Socio-cultural practices, 29
Sock Puppets app, 32, 44
Speech-to-text (STT) tools, 161
Standardisation, 134
Story Dice app, 44
Storytelling, 18, 41
  in school, design and developments of, 72–74
Storyweaver app, 166
STT tools. *See* Speech-to-text (STT) tools
Stuck, 36
Study participants, 141
Substitution, Augmentation, Modification and Redefinition (SAMR) model, 71, 77–79
Support rich task process, 104–105

Tablet computers, 4
TacTile Reader, 57
TD theory. *See* Transactional distance (TD) theory
Teacher professional learning, 8–9
Teaching, 157–158
  coding, 55
  learning activities, 72, 77–79
Technology Integration Planning Cycle (TIPC), 88
Telling multimodal tales of lost things, 108–110
Text-to-speech (TTS) tools, 161
ThingLink, 22, 24
Think & Learn Code-apillar app, 53

1001 Stories, 161
Timelines, 104
TIPC. *See* Technology Integration Planning Cycle (TIPC)
Toontastic app, 44
Total Reading Approach for Children Plus (TRAC+), 166–167
TRAC+. *See* Total Reading Approach for Children Plus (TRAC+)
Traditional alphabetic text, 85
Traditional literacy activities, 111
Transactional distance (TD) theory, 6
Transparent orthography, 167
TTS tools. *See* Text-to-speech (TTS) tools
Twitter, 87
2-in-1 devices, 4
Typology of play, 18

Ubiquitous
  knowledge access, 8
  learning, 8
Upper primary level, 76

Video viewing/production, 93
'Viral learning', 9
Visual art, 31
  app, 37
Visual image, 39
Voices in the Park, 36

The Waterhole app, 45
Way Home, 115
Whisper of the Spirit, 21, 22, 24
Wiesner, David, 36
Wifi, 4
Willems, Mo, 45
Willy's Pictures, 36
The Wonky Donkey app, 45

Worldreader Mobile (WRM) app, 160, 163–164
WowWee Elmoji, 53
Writer's club, 124–127
Writing multimodal texts, 85

XPT software, 106

YouTube video, 35

Zukerburg, Mark, 53

www.ingramcontent.com/pod-product-compliance
Lightning Source LLC
Chambersburg PA
CBHW071205240426
43668CB00032B/2097